Higher Education Accountability

Higher Education Accountability

ROBERT KELCHEN

Johns Hopkins University Press
Baltimore

Johns Hopkins University Press
2715 North Charles Street
Baltimore, Maryland 21218-4363
www.press.jhu.edu

Library of Congress Cataloging-in-Publication Data

Names: Kelchen, Robert, author.
Title: Higher education accountability / Robert Kelchen.
Description: Baltimore : Johns Hopkins University Press, [2018] | Includes bibliographical
    references and index.
Identifiers: LCCN 2017022923 | ISBN 9781421424736 (hardcover : acid-free paper) |
    ISBN 9781421424743 (electronic) | ISBN 1421424738 (hardcover : acid-free paper) |
    ISBN 1421424746 (electronic)
Subjects: LCSH: Educational accountability. | Education, Higher—Standards.
Classification: LCC LB2806.22 .K45 2018 | DDC 379.1/58—dc23
LC record available at https://lccn.loc.gov/2017022923

A catalog record for this book is available from the British Library.

*Special discounts are available for bulk purchases of this book. For more information,
please contact Special Sales at 410-516-6936 or specialsales@press.jhu.edu.*

Johns Hopkins University Press uses environmentally friendly book materials, including
recycled text paper that is composed of at least 30 percent post-consumer waste,
whenever possible.

CONTENTS

ACKNOWLEDGMENTS

When Greg Britton of Johns Hopkins University Press emailed me out of the blue during my first year as an assistant professor asking if I had any ideas for a book, I was quite surprised for two reasons. First, I am a quantitative researcher who normally writes journal articles, so a book felt like something that was completely out of reach. Second, I was less than a year removed from finishing my doctorate at the University of Wisconsin–Madison. Why would anyone be reaching out to someone like me at this point? Nevertheless, I had an enjoyable conversation with Greg, which concluded with me telling him that I didn't have any plans to write a book—but I would let him know if I ever did.

One year later, the idea for this book came to me about five miles into a run. Several of my ongoing research projects were focused on how colleges reacted to policies and practices such as state performance funding systems, financial responsibility scores from the federal government, and college rankings. I then realized that all of these projects covered different aspects of higher education accountability—and that there were not any books that sufficiently covered the current landscape of intertwined accountability policies and practices put in place by a wide range of stakeholders. I talked over the idea with Greg and about the parameters of the book. He seemed excited and the book project was born.

I would particularly like to thank my graduate assistant, Olga Komissarova, for her assistance in preparing portions of the manuscript and for her ability to put up with interacting with me on a regular basis. I appreciate the helpful and candid comments from Martin Finkelstein, Marie Gioiosa, Ethan Hutt, Kevin Majewski, Ben Miller, and Sarah Pingel on different chapters of the book, as well as the useful feedback from several anonymous reviewers. These individuals helped to substantially strengthen the quality of the book. I would also like to thank the large number of people who took time to answer one of my many requests for data sources or existing research on a topic via email or Twitter.

I greatly benefited from my students and faculty colleagues at Seton Hall

University. Portions of these chapters have their roots in lecture notes that I prepared for my graduate-level courses in higher education finance and organization and governance in higher education. Questions and comments from my students over the past four years have helped me clarify my thinking around accountability-related topics and how to explain them to an audience of individuals who may not have had a great deal of experience thinking about these topics. My fellow faculty members, including Rong Chen, Martin Finkelstein, Eunyoung Kim, Carolyn Sattin-Bajaj, Luke Stedrak, Joe Stetar, and Elaine Walker, heard me talk way too much about this project over the last several years and offered consistent encouragement and support.

Like most academics, I am a product of my scholarly background. Two individuals deserve special recognition—Sara Goldrick-Rab of Temple University and Doug Harris of Tulane University, who were my mentors when I was in graduate school. Sara taught me the nuts and bolts of how the student financial aid system works (or in some cases doesn't work). She also encouraged me to take a greater role as a public-facing scholar, which has been incredibly beneficial to my career and helped to make this book a possibility. I learned a great deal from Doug about how accountability works in K–12 education, which got me to thinking about the analogs in higher education. A paper that I began in one of Doug's classes ultimately led to me being asked to take over the *Washington Monthly* college rankings, which has helped give me another view of the landscape of higher education accountability.

On a personal note, I would like to thank my wife, Emily, for her love and consistent support throughout this process. I grew close to her when she was the student representative on our alma mater's board of governors and I was in student government. Our shared experiences provided me with helpful insights on how the political appointment process works on public colleges' governing boards. I would also like to thank the rest of my family for their encouragement and providing support as I kept plugging away at this project.

AACSB	Association to Advance Collegiate Schools of Business
AALE	American Academy for Liberal Education
AAU	Association of American Universities
AAUP	American Association of University Professors
ABA	American Bar Association
ABET	Accrediting Board for Engineering and Technology
ACBSP	Accreditation Council for Business Schools and Programs
ACCJC	Accrediting Commission for Community and Junior Colleges
ACE	American Council on Education
ACICS	Accrediting Council for Independent Colleges and Schools
ACTA	American Council of Trustees and Alumni
AGB	Association of Governing Boards of Universities and Colleges
APLU	Association of Public and Land-Grant Universities
APSCU	Association of Private Sector Colleges and Universities
BEOG	Basic Educational Opportunity Grant
CCSF	City College of San Francisco
CDR	cohort default rate
CHEA	Council for Higher Education Accreditation
COPA	Council on Postsecondary Accreditation
FAFSA	Free Application for Federal Student Aid
FTE	full-time equivalent

GRAD	Granting Resources and Autonomies for Diplomas Act
HBCUs	historically black colleges and universities
HCM	heightened cash monitoring
HEA	Higher Education Act
IPEDS	Integrated Postsecondary Education Data System
JTPA	Job Training Partnership Act
NACIQI	National Advisory Committee on Institutional Quality and Integrity
NAICU	National Association of Independent Colleges and Universities
NASFAA	National Association of Student Financial Aid Administrators
NCAA	National Collegiate Athletic Association
NCES	National Center for Education Statistics
NCLB	No Child Left Behind Act
NC-SARA	National Council for State Authorization Reciprocity Agreements
NLRB	National Labor Relations Board
OECD	Organisation for Economic Co-operation and Development
PBF	performance-based funding
PIRS	Postsecondary Institution Ratings System
RCM	responsibility center management
SACS	Southern Association of Colleges and Schools
SHEEO	State Higher Education Executive Officers Association
STEM	science, technology, engineering, and math
TIAA	Teachers Insurance and Annuity Association of America
TRACS	Transnational Association of Christian Colleges and Schools
U-CAN	University and College Accountability

Higher Education Accountability

The Rationale for Accountability in Higher Education

INCREASING THE COLLEGE ATTAINMENT RATES of American adults has been a key public policy goal over the last several decades, particularly since the Great Recession. In 2008, the influential Bill & Melinda Gates and Lumina Foundations set ambitious goals for college attainment rates, with Gates seeking to double the percentage of low-income young adults earning a degree or certificate by age 26 (Gose, 2008) and Lumina setting a "big goal" of having 60% of adults with a postsecondary credential by 2025 (Hebel, 2009). This led President Barack Obama to set a goal in his first State of the Union address in 2009. He said that by 2020, America would have a higher percentage of its citizens with a college credential than any other country in the world (Hebel & Selingo, 2009).

America has substantially increased its educational attainment rates in recent years but has fallen short of these lofty goals. Just over 45% of American adults now have a degree or credential, up several percentage points in recent years but still falling short about 11 million people of meeting Lumina's 2025 goal (Matthews, 2016). The percentage of young adults between the ages of 25 and 34 with a college credential has increased by 11 percentage points since 1997, but America's rank among the 36 countries providing data to the Organisation for Economic Co-operation and Development (OECD) has fallen from approximately third to tenth during this period (OECD, 2016a).

The modest gains in educational attainment rates come at a time when having a postsecondary credential of some kind is more important than ever before. This is particularly the case as formal apprenticeship programs in vocational fields that lead to solid middle-class jobs without attending college are uncommon in the United States (Weber, 2014). Almost all of the net jobs that have been created since the end of the Great Recession have gone to people with at least some college education, with just 80,000 of the 11.6 million net jobs going to those with a high school diploma or less (Carne-vale, Jayasundera, & Gulish, 2016). The economic and non-economic ben-efits of a college education are large and growing for the average student (e.g., Oreopoulos & Petronijevic, 2013), with particularly large returns for students who are relatively unlikely to attend college (Brand & Xie, 2010).

Although the benefits to a college education are on average substantial, there are widespread concerns about the value of higher education. A nation-wide survey of adults with a bachelor's degree by Gallup and Purdue Uni-versity (2015) found that 50% of all respondents strongly agreed that their education was "worth the cost."[1] Only 38% of students who graduated in the last ten years strongly agreed, while just 18% of the small percentage of students with more than $50,000 in student loan debt strongly agreed. An-other nationwide survey of adults by the Pew Research Center showed that 57% of respondents said that colleges were not a good value for students, even as 86% of respondents who were college graduates said it was a worth-while investment for them (Taylor et al., 2011). In a recent Public Agenda survey of adults, 42% of respondents indicated that a college degree was essential to economic success, down from 55% in 2008 and 2009 (Schleifer & Silliman, 2016).

Higher education is certainly a risky investment that does not always pay off for students and their families. Newly released data from the U.S. De-partment of Education's College Scorecard showed that about 28% of stu-dents who started college in 2002 and 2003 and received federal financial aid earned less than $25,000 per year in 2012 (the typical wage of a young adult without any college experience). Even among students who completed a bachelor's degree, the bottom 10% of earners in any individual major earned less than the top 10% of students with no college experience (Hersh-bein & Kearney, 2014).

One of the reasons that college is an uncertain investment is the risk of dropping out, even though there are economic returns to completing some college without earning a credential (Kane & Rouse, 1995). Although 89% of first-time students at four-year colleges expect to graduate within four years (Eagan et al., 2016), just 58% of first-time students at four-year public colleges and 69% of students at four-year private nonprofit colleges earn a bachelor's degree within six years. For students starting at two-year colleges, completion rates are even lower (Shapiro et al., 2015). Students who drop out of college are far more likely to default on their student loan obligations, even though their debt burdens are relatively small (Dynarski, 2015; Nguyen, 2012).

Rising Accountability Pressures

These concerns about the value of higher education have led to numerous pushes by different stakeholders to hold colleges accountable for their outcomes. Federal and state governments, accrediting agencies, the private sector, and even faculty, staff, and students within a given college are all pushing for colleges to improve their performance without providing additional resources. There are three main reasons that colleges are facing stronger accountability pressures than they were in the past, and these are discussed in the following section.

REASON 1: THE PRICE TAG OF A COLLEGE EDUCATION HAS STEADILY INCREASED

Tuition and fees at both public and private colleges have consistently increased at rates far higher than inflation. As shown in figure I.1, real (inflation-adjusted) tuition and fees rose by about 140% at private nonprofit colleges and community colleges between the 1985–86 and 2015–16 academic years and by 223% at four-year public colleges. During the same period, real household incomes rose by just 5% for the lowest income quintile and 20% for the middle quintile, threatening college affordability for many students from modest economic backgrounds (Ma et al., 2016). Grant aid also in-

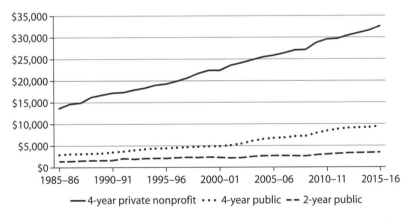

FIGURE I.1. Trends in tuition and fees by sector. *Note*: Amounts are adjusted for inflation. *Source*: Ma et al., 2016.

creased during this period, but not enough to keep up with tuition increases.[2] Between the 1999–2000 and 2011–12 academic years, the average net price of attendance (defined as the total cost of attendance less all grant aid received) increased by between 12% and 23% across all sectors of nonprofit higher education (author's calculations using National Postsecondary Student Aid Study data).

As a result of rising college prices, a higher percentage of students are borrowing more money to pay for college. Twenty-six percent of all students took out a loan to pay for college in the 1995–96 academic year, a number that rose to 42% by the 2011–12 academic year. The increase in borrowing rates was found across all sectors of nonprofit higher education, with the highest borrowing rates at private nonprofit colleges (63%) and the lowest rates at community colleges (18%) (Goldrick-Rab, Kelchen, & Houle, 2014). About 68% of students who earned a bachelor's degree in 2015 graduated with an average of about $30,000 in debt (Cochrane & Cheng, 2016). This is up from about 59% of graduates who borrowed an average of $23,000 (in today's dollars) in 2007, when I graduated college (Reed, 2008).

As both the percentage of borrowers and the amount borrowed per student have increased, total outstanding student loan debt has risen quickly over the past decade. Figure I.2 shows how the amount of student debt nearly tripled between 2005 ($445 billion) and 2016 ($1.26 trillion) after adjusting for inflation. Approximately 40% of this debt is held by graduate and professional students (Delisle, 2014), meaning that about $750 billion of total student loan debt is held by students who pursued an undergraduate education. Rising student loan debt has gotten the attention of policymak-

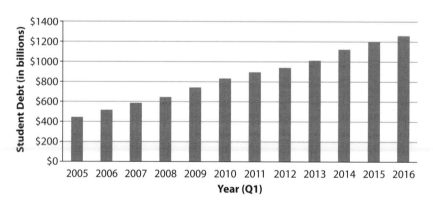

FIGURE I.2. Outstanding student loan debt. *Note*: Amounts are adjusted for inflation. *Source*: Scally & Lee, 2016.

ers and the public alike and is a key reason behind growing accountability pressures.

REASON 2: PUBLIC FUNDING FOR HIGHER EDUCATION
HAS BEEN UNABLE TO KEEP UP WITH RISING PRICES

The United States currently spends a higher percentage of its overall wealth on higher education than any other OECD country, with 2.6% of its gross domestic product going toward public and private funding of colleges and universities (OECD, 2016b). But the percentage of higher education funding coming from public sources has steadily decreased over time as prices have increased faster than governmental funding and enrollment increased. State and local support for public colleges and universities increased by 8% between 1990 and 2015 after adjusting for inflation, but this was far below a 43% increase in full-time equivalent enrollment (Carlson, 2016). Higher education has traditionally served as a "balance wheel" in state budgets as states face pressures to balance their budgets while funding other areas (such as K–12 education and Medicaid) that are unable to generate their own revenue (e.g., Delaney & Doyle, 2011). As a result, the percentage of state budgets going to higher education reached its lowest level in 2015 since at least 1990 (Carlson, 2016).

At the federal level, Pell Grant expenditures for students from modest financial backgrounds rose from $9 billion in inflation-adjusted dollars in 1997 to $17 billion in 2007 and nearly $39 billion in 2010 before falling back to $30 billion by 2014 (U.S. Department of Education, 2016). Yet this sizable increase in Pell Grant funding did little to bring down the price tag for many students, leading President Obama to publicly call out colleges in his 2012 State of the Union address for their inability to keep tuition low (Field, 2012). This served as a precursor to an ambitious, although relatively unsuccessful, accountability effort in Obama's second term as president. Even if federal financial aid does not increase under a Republican presidential administration, politicians will continue to express frustration about colleges increasing their prices.

REASON 3: THERE ARE CONCERNS ABOUT THE QUALITY
OF AMERICAN HIGHER EDUCATION

The American higher education system has long been seen as the envy of the world, and the prominence of its research universities in global college rankings along with the one million international students who choose to study in the United States each year (Redden, 2016) provide support for that assertion. Yet many Americans are skeptical that students are receiving a high-quality education, particularly in light of rising prices and slowly increasing graduation rates. These concerns were magnified after the release of two books that received national attention for questioning colleges' standards. Former Harvard president Derek Bok (2006) wrote *Our Underachieving Colleges*, in which he argued that colleges were doing a poor job of teaching core courses. Then sociologists Richard Arum and Josipa Roksa (2011) found in *Academically Adrift* that 45% of students did not see significant gains in reasoning and writing skills during their first two years of college; however, other research has challenged these authors' findings when considering all four years of a bachelor's degree program (Benjamin, 2013).

There is also a deeper set of concerns about what students are studying while in college that leads various stakeholders to push for control of the curriculum. For example, the American Council of Trustees and Alumni (2013), a group often viewed within the higher education community as being politically conservative, produced a guide for trustees called *Are They Learning?* that encouraged their membership to document student learning on core outcomes such as critical thinking and reasoning. Some faculty members and advocates more aligned with liberals have attempted to require all students to take a diversity course in order to broaden their understanding of the wider world. The University of California, Los Angeles, for example, voted in 2015 to include a diversity requirement after more than a decade of debate (Jaschik, 2015). Other stakeholders are pushing colleges to better prepare students for the workforce. In recent surveys, employers (Sidhu & Calderon, 2014), current college students (Hanover Research, 2016) and the general public (Gallup, 2016) have all expressed concerns about the utility of the college curriculum.

Many people outside of higher education view colleges as inefficient, bloated bureaucracies where faculty and administrators conspire to shift much of the workload to poorly paid adjuncts, teaching assistants, or entry-level staff members. University professors were recently ranked by a career services website as having the least stressful jobs (Kensing, 2013), although faculty members vociferously protested while noting their high workloads and stress levels (Jaschik, 2013). This has led for calls from legislators and advocacy groups to increase teaching loads or reform tenure (e.g., Helfing, 2015; Ludwig, 2011; Stancill, 2015). Policymakers and the public have also expressed concern about the growth in the number of administrators and staff members at colleges (Ginsberg, 2011) as well as the proliferation of high-end amenities such as recreation centers and climbing walls at selective four-year colleges that seek to attract wealthy students (Rubin, 2014; Woodhouse, 2015).

Framework of This Book

As a result of these concerns about the value and quality of higher education, a wide array of stakeholders has placed additional pressure on colleges and universities in an effort to hold them accountable for their outcomes. These accountability policies and practices can take a wide range of forms at different types of colleges. Accountability systems can be informal in nature, such as how students and their families may react to changes in a college's reputation after reading a news article. Formal and increasingly high-stakes systems, such as tying state or federal funding to meeting defined performance metrics, are also becoming increasingly popular. Yet many of these systems are having relatively limited effects on improving student outcomes and are creating incentives for colleges to operate in sometimes undesirable ways.

Most accountability efforts in higher education are viewed in isolation, in spite of colleges having to respond to multiple pressures at once. For example, a public research university may have to balance their responses to accreditors' demands for better student learning outcomes, state performance funding systems tied to the number of degrees awarded, federal requirements to provide information on a wide variety of outcomes, students and faculty pushing for additional transparency regarding budgeting, and alumni pressures to move up in the *U.S. News & World Report* college rankings. Colleges may strategically prioritize responding to certain accountability systems based on the amount of money at stake and whether the system is aligned with their mission and goals. Understanding how colleges must navigate a minefield of accountability pressures with often differing goals helps to explain why some accountability efforts are successful in changing colleges' behavior and why other efforts fail to have the desired effects.

In this book, I endeavor to cover the landscape of key accountability systems in American higher education. After discussing the theoretical underpinnings of accountability and how accountability systems have evolved into the systems that are present today, I detail the state of accountability from each of the key stakeholders before discussing lessons learned from these efforts. A brief outline of each of the chapters is below.

Chapter 1 delves into the theory behind the design of accountability systems in publicly funded organizations such as colleges and universities. Accountability policies generally follow a principal-agent relationship, in which the principal (for example, the federal or state government) tries to generate a set of desired outcomes from the agent (a college) using a set of rewards or sanctions designated in a performance contract. In this chapter, I draw upon several important theories from the field of public administration to explain how public-sector accountability policies are designed and why they may not be as effective as desired, including examples from other public-sector fields such as K–12 education and health care as well as higher education.

Chapter 2 discusses the history of higher education accountability in the United States, which dates back to the origins of the colonial colleges. I discuss the historical development of higher education accountability prior to the passage of the first federal Higher Education Act in 1965. Accountability pressures ebbed and flowed during the preceding centuries, with efforts to closely shape and track colleges' performance being interspersed with periods of relative autonomy. In some cases—such as the federal government's failed efforts to rate colleges in 1911—history has even repeated itself in recent years. Therefore, it is important to understand how the landscape of accountability has developed and changed over time as this has directly influenced how colleges operate today.

Chapter 3 focuses on the federal government's effort to hold colleges accountable using two different types of policies. The first type is a lower-stakes accountability system (such as the College Scorecard) that makes data available on a range of institutional, financial, and outcome metrics. The second set of federal accountability policies directly ties an accredited college's eligibility for student financial aid dollars to meeting a set of minimum quality metrics on areas such as financial stability and student loan default rates. These policies that affect federal financial aid—the lifeblood for much of American higher education—affect a relatively limited section of American higher education at this point, but a number of potential policy changes could make federal accountability policies more salient for a larger number of colleges.

Chapter 4 examines the landscape of accountability at the state level. State governments have traditionally exercised authority over public colleges by controlling appropriations, tuition and fees, or appointing members to governing or coordinating boards. A newer way to hold colleges accountable is through the use of performance-based funding policies that tie a portion of state appropriations to outcomes. Although about three dozen states have now adopted performance funding systems, the research on the effectiveness of performance-based funding policies shows modest effects at best, along with concerns about how colleges are responding to these systems in potentially undesirable ways.

Chapter 5 focuses on accreditation as a key form of accountability. Institutional accreditation began as a way for colleges to demonstrate a level of quality (as judged by a group of their peers) in order to separate themselves from institutions considered inferior. However, the federal government's decision to tie student financial aid eligibility to being accredited by a recognized agency has turned accreditation into a high-stakes proposition. I discuss the two main types of institutional accrediting bodies in existence, regional and national associations, as well as the landscape of program-level accrediting bodies. I also discuss some of the challenges the current accreditation system is facing, as colleges and policymakers alike are calling for changes to the current system.

Chapter 6 examines private-sector accountability policies (both formal and informal) and how they affect colleges' priorities and practices. The most basic form of accountability from the private sector is a college's reputation, as students and donors are less likely to consider a college that they believe to be of inferior quality or that has been the subject of a recent scandal. There are also more formal efforts to hold colleges accountable for their performance, with a large number of college rankings and ratings developing in recent years that affects the behavior of relatively selective colleges. I draw upon my experience as data editor for *Washington Monthly* magazine's college rankings to explain how rankings can push colleges to behave in ways that work both for and against their core missions of access, success, and educational quality.

Chapter 7 focuses on a type of accountability that is not often considered—internal accountability. This includes efforts stakeholders within a college (such as students, faculty, and staff) use to hold their own institution accountable. I discuss the effectiveness of these pressures and examine what can happen when institutional governance becomes dysfunctional due to internal disagreements or competing external pressures. Chapter 8 discusses ten lessons that have been learned from high-stakes accountability policies in higher education as well as other related areas such as K–12 education, health care, and public management. Here, I focus on how the interaction of various accountability pressures can affect the effectiveness of any given system. Finally, I close in chapter 9 by discussing the future of higher education accountability and highlighting five questions that are likely to influence the creation and expansion of accountability systems.

CHAPTER ONE

The Theoretical Underpinnings
of Accountability

COLLEGES AND UNIVERSITIES are facing increased pressures from nearly all stakeholders to operate more efficiently and effectively. But these pressures are far from unique to higher education, with other publicly funded organizations such as K–12 education, health care providers, and government itself having faced similar calls to improve their performance since the 1970s (e.g., Box, 1999; Elmore, Abelman, & Fuhrman, 1996; Moynihan, 2008; National Commission on Excellence in Education, 1983). These pressures in higher education are relatively late in coming but are in many ways inevitable as college prices continue to rise and similar policies having been adopted in K–12 education (e.g., Deming & Figlio, 2016).

As colleges attempt to navigate a potential minefield of organizations trying to influence their actions, colleges' missions or strategic plans can come into conflict with various accountability systems. Consider a college dedicated to serving first-generation and low-income students. It may struggle to balance its mission with an accountability system that rewards colleges for graduation rates, as family income is a significant predictor of student success in college (e.g., Bailey & Dynarski, 2011). Or even if an accountability system is designed to reward colleges for encouraging social mobility, pressures from alumni or college ranking providers may make colleges consider which accountability pressures are the most important and which ones can be ignored.

In this chapter, I discuss the theoretical underpinnings of accountability policies and practices for publicly supported organizations such as colleges and universities. I begin with the general framework of how accountability systems are typically designed in order to encourage entities to prioritize certain outcomes. I then review the literature on public-sector accountability to help tackle five key questions that are likely to influence whether a given policy or practice is effective in inducing a college to change its behavior:

1. Can a college improve its outcomes given its available resources?
2. Can the outcomes of interest be measured effectively and efficiently?
3. Are the expected rewards or sanctions large enough to affect agents' behaviors?
4. Can a college influence the design of an accountability system?
5. Can the accountability system be gamed in an effort to improve outcomes without changing priorities or resource allocations?

How Accountability Policies Are Designed

The typical framework for an accountability model follows a principal-agent design (Spence & Zeckhauser, 1971), in which the principal (for example, the state or federal government) holds the agent (such as a college) accountable for their outcomes. In the classic model, the principal is paid for performing a task on behalf of the agent (Jensen & Meckling, 1976). An example of this would be a state government providing funding for a public college in exchange for the college meeting certain formal or informal performance benchmarks. But principal-agent models can also apply to private foundations or donors, who are increasingly demanding clear outcomes in exchange for their financial support (Benjamin, 2010).

This traditional principal-agent model is also an example of resource dependence theory (e.g., Aldrich & Pfeffer, 1976), in which agents that are dependent on resources from the principal will alter their priorities in order to match the principal's priorities. Yet resource dependence theory can also be applied to examples that are not directly financial in nature. An example of this is the *U.S. News & World Report* college rankings, which have been empirically shown to affect colleges' priorities, as I will discuss in more depth in chapter 6 (e.g., Bastedo & Bowman, 2011; Kim, 2015). Although these rankings do not directly result in additional money for colleges, the prestige resulting from the rankings has been shown to influence the behaviors of prospective students and their families (e.g., Alter & Reback, 2014; Bowman & Bastedo, 2009; Luca & Smith, 2013)—who can then provide financial resources to colleges.

Although the principal can typically set rewards or sanctions for the agent to receive conditional on performance, the agent has one important advantage in this situation. Agents such as colleges have far better information regarding their performance than the principal does—a situation known as asymmetric information (Levinthal, 1988). For example, while colleges are required to report average retention rates to governments and the public, most colleges have student-level information about progress to a degree that is far more detailed than what many principals can access. Additionally, colleges have information on performance before it is released to outside parties, giving them the opportunity to proactively respond in ways that make them look favorable.

The principal will develop a performance agreement to best suit its interests, knowing it has less information than the agent and that the same agreement may apply to multiple agents (Shavell, 1979). Principals can expend additional effort to monitor an agent's performance by requiring additional information disclosures or performing inspections, but these efforts are costly.[1] Monitoring efforts may also be productive only to a given point. Principal-agent models generally assume that tighter monitoring by the principal will improve effort, but crowding-out theory suggests that monitoring will reduce effort by lowering intrinsic motivation (Frey, 2012; Holmstrom, 1979; Laffont & Martimort, 2002). Research by Dickinson and Villeval (2008) has shown that the crowding-out effect outweighs the benefits of monitoring above a certain level, implying that the agent will always have an advantage if the principal optimally monitors performance.

Accountability in publicly funded organizations is often more complex than in privately funded organizations for two main reasons. The first reason is that while private-sector organizations may be accountable to shareholders and customers, colleges are accountable to multiple layers and types of government in addition to customers (students), taxpayers, and internal stakeholders such as faculty and staff (Steinberg, 2010; Van Puyvelde et al., 2012). Even within the government, these stakeholders may be sending mixed messages regarding priorities as legislators, regulatory agencies, and the executive branch pursue their own accountability goals as principals (Moe, 1984). Colleges then have to prioritize which pressures to respond to, requiring them to gather additional information about the external environment by using boundary-spanning personnel such as lobbyists and public relations staffers (e.g., Aldrich & Herker, 1977).

The second reason accountability in nonprofit organizations can be more complicated is the presence of individuals who are committed to the goals of the organization. As nonprofits tend to attract individuals who are more altruistic (Dur & Zoutenbier, 2014; Rose-Ackerman, 1996), these motivated agents (e.g., Dixit, 1999) may require a different type of oversight than at a typical firm with employees who are not as invested in the organization's mission. Organizational theorists such as Davis, Schoorman, and Donaldson

(1997) and Sundaramurthy and Lewis (2003) suggest that traditional principal-agent models (e.g., Jensen & Meckling, 1976) may not be as well suited for nonprofit organizations. Instead, they propose a stewardship model in which principals and agents generally agree on objectives at the time of the employee's hire. This model can break down if the principal's goals change over time, such as when a different political party takes control.

In spite of a range of concerns that could limit the effectiveness of efforts to incentivize greater performance, there is some evidence that performance management systems can improve public-sector agencies' performance. This is based on a recent meta-analysis by Gerrish (2016), who found that performance management systems have had small, but significant, effects on institutional performance. In addition, these observed effects are larger when best practices for performance management are used and more recent studies are included.

CAN A COLLEGE IMPROVE ITS OUTCOMES GIVEN ITS AVAILABLE RESOURCES?

As was discussed in the introduction, one of the primary drivers of increased accountability pressures in higher education is a perception that colleges and universities are wasteful and inefficient. And while per-student educational expenditures have consistently risen faster than inflation since at least 1929 (Archibald & Feldman, 2008a; Desrochers & Hurlburt, 2016), research suggests that a substantial portion of the rising cost of higher education during the twentieth century can be attributed to the labor-intensive nature of providing an education (Archibald & Feldman, 2008a). Economist William Baumol (1967) developed his famous "cost disease" theory around the idea that service-oriented industries with highly educated employees are unable to realize the same efficiency gains as capital-intensive fields such as manufacturing.

A competing theory explaining the increasing cost structure in higher education comes from Howard Bowen (1980), former president of Grinnell College in Iowa. He theorized that because nonprofit colleges seek to raise and spend as much money as possible on activities associated with a college education, the cost of providing an education will continue to increase over time. Research by Martin and Hill (2013, 2014) found that institutional actions were responsible for a larger portion of cost increases than Baumol's cost disease among public and private research universities in the 2000s. Some of these actions include spending on intercollegiate athletics, recreational facilities, and residence halls (e.g., Armstrong & Hamilton, 2013; Cheslock & Knight, 2015) that some consider a less necessary portion of the higher education experience. However, these amenities are disproportionately important in the college search processes of higher-income students with lower standardized test scores who are more likely to pay a college's full sticker price (Jacob, McCall, & Stange, 2013), making these additional expenditures necessary to colleges trying to balance their budgets.

Can colleges improve their performance given their available resources? In order to answer in the affirmative, one of two conditions must be met. The first condition is that colleges must currently be operating inefficiently, which many colleges' leaders would vigorously dispute. There is a body of research suggesting that colleges with similar observed student characteristics and resource levels have significantly different graduation rates and efficiency levels.[2] One group of studies uses regression analyses to estimate predicted graduation rates using institutional-level or student-level characteristics, which are then compared to actual graduation rates to get an estimate of value added (e.g., Bailey & Xu, 2012; Cunha & Miller, 2014; Kelchen & Harris, 2012). A more methodologically advanced technique is data envelopment analysis, which uses linear programming to estimate an efficient frontier. Studies using this technique again find large differences in estimated efficiency levels across institutions after taking observable factors into account (Archibald & Feldman, 2008b; Eckles, 2010; Eff, Klein, & Kyle, 2012), although one study using a similar technique called stochastic frontier analysis has found that most public master's institutions generally operate in an efficient manner (Titus, Vamosiu, & McClure, forthcoming). There is also some evidence from K–12 education that schools were able to respond to the federal No Child Left Behind (NCLB) accountability legislation passed in 2001 by improving below-proficient students' test scores without affecting other students, suggesting the presence of "operational slack" within schools (Springer, 2008, 556).

Colleges do seem to respond to incentives present in accountability systems by reallocating resources to some extent. In work with my Seton Hall University colleague Luke Stedrak, I found that community colleges in states subject to performance-based funding (PBF) systems reallocated slightly more money toward student services than colleges not subject to PBF, while four-year colleges increased their amount of grant aid in a potential effort to improve completion rates (Kelchen & Stedrak, 2016). Additionally, Rabovsky (2012) showed that colleges subject to PBF increased the instructional portion of total expenditures by 0.89 percentage points and decreased the percentage of funds allocated to research by 0.34 percentage points. Yet the overall effects of PBF on degree completion are generally mixed (e.g., Hillman, Tandberg, & Fryar, 2015; Rutherford & Rabovsky, 2014; Tandberg

& Hillman, 2014), suggesting that these small reallocations did not meaningfully improve efficiency.

The second necessary condition for accountability policies to be effective is that a college must have the capacity to expand their services and improve performance.[3] For example, Dougherty and colleagues (2016) interviewed faculty and administrators from 18 public colleges in three states with high-stakes performance-based funding systems. They found that among open-access institutions, a lack of resources or the inability to shape their student bodies in a way that selective institutions do were often cited as reasons why performance-based funding was unlikely to generate expected improvements in college completion rates. Another important issue in Dougherty and colleagues' (2016) book was the issue of institutional capacity—whether a college or university knows how to solve problems that affect its performance. For example, an inadequate institutional research office left some colleges grasping for potential solutions as they were unable to fully pinpoint specific problems.

CAN THE OUTCOMES OF INTEREST BE MEASURED EFFECTIVELY AND EFFICIENTLY?

The second challenge in developing an effective accountability system in higher education is to be able to adequately measure the outcomes of interest to the principal. The most common outcomes in accountability systems reflect quantifiable short-term metrics such as the number of degrees or certificates awarded, completion and retention rates, or initial labor market outcomes.[4] To some extent, the focus on these metrics is entirely rational, as colleges can take steps to improve their performance in a relatively short time period. But even these metrics have delays between recruiting and enrolling students and when outcomes are measured; the six-year window used for federal graduation rate calculations at four-year colleges requires a substantial amount of consistency in policy objectives. But these measures can at best serve as proxies for longer-term outcomes such as job satisfaction, midcareer earnings, and quality of life. For example, a Gallup-Purdue survey of 30,000 bachelor's degree recipients found that specific learning experiences were stronger predictors of the value of an education than their college's *U.S. News* ranking (Gallup, 2015).

When designing an accountability system, the principal must consider both the outcomes it considers important and the outcomes that the agent (college) would consider important. If the desired outcomes are similar, the accountability system can be considered incentive compatible (Myerson, 1979) and the principal does not have to expend as much effort making sure the agent behaves as desired. However, if the principal's and agent's outcomes do not align, then the principal will have to spend more effort monitoring the agent to get an equivalent level of performance (Williamson, 1981).

Many accountability systems evaluate colleges' performance on a number of outcomes, which seems appropriate given the multifaceted goals of most colleges. Measuring too few outcomes can cause what Prendergast (1999) calls dysfunctional behavioral contracts, in which agents focus all of their attention on the outcomes being measured. A related concept is what Van Thiel and Leeuw (2002) call the performance paradox, which reflects the gradual weakening of the relationship between the outcome being measured and true performance in publicly accountable organizations. This distortion of metrics (e.g., Courty & Marschke, 2008) makes measuring true performance difficult.

Conversely, specifying too many goals can result in few or none of them being met. Organizations may have a difficult time reacting to a wide-ranging list of accountability metrics and instead may end up focusing on only a small number of outcomes that their leaders consider the most important (Ethiraj & Levinthal, 2009). A cautionary example comes from South Carolina, which implemented a performance-based funding system for public colleges in 1996 with 37 performance indicators. Although the goal was to tie all funding to performance by 2000, the system instead collapsed under its own complexity and fierce opposition from colleges (Dougherty & Natow, 2015).

ARE THE EXPECTED REWARDS OR SANCTIONS LARGE ENOUGH TO AFFECT AGENTS' BEHAVIORS?

The next key question influencing the potential effectiveness of accountability systems is whether a college or its employees will be induced to change behaviors by a formal or informal accountability system. An institution would theoretically be expected to react to an external accountability system if the expected value of the reward or sanction is sufficiently large, with college leaders and employees alike weighing the size of the incentive and the likelihood of meeting performance goals against the cost of expending additional effort.

Colleges must first view the size of the potential reward or sanction as sufficient to merit taking action. Accountability requirements that the federal government places on colleges have a strong potential to influence institutional behaviors, as the potential penalty for not complying is the loss of all federal financial aid dollars—a sizable part of many institutions' budgets. For example, Florida International University received about $350 million of its $1.3 billion in operating revenue in fiscal year 2014 from federal Pell Grants and student loans, or more than one-fourth of its total budget (data from Federal Student Aid volume reports and institutional budgets). Conversely, nearly all state-level performance funding policies tie only a small percentage of appropriations (which are a declining share of revenues for many public colleges) to outcomes. Florida International University received $25.3 million in performance funding in the same year, or just under 2% of its total budget (Florida Board of Governors, n.d.).

The size of the incentive also must be large enough to outweigh competing incentives from stakeholders both external and internal to the college with different missions and visions. Multiple constituency theory (e.g., Campbell & Lambright, 2016) suggests that organizations will consider various groups' preferences in defining performance, but the organization's own mission also plays an important role in responding to accountability. Consider the case of a public university with a strong organizational mission of serving first-generation students with a lower probability of graduation. This institution would likely need to receive a larger incentive under a performance funding system that rewards graduation rates (which are correlated with selectivity) than another public university that already has committed to increasing selectivity as a part of its strategic plan.

A college or its employees must expect that rewards or sanctions are likely to follow as a result of their actions. This requires that two conditions be met. First, there must be a sufficiently strong relationship between the agent's effort and the outcome being measured. A college may be able to increase the number of graduates by working harder to engage its students, but some students may choose to leave for reasons outside the college's control. This level of risk might influence colleges' responses, as the typical risk-averse agent prefers to insure itself against risk if possible (Benjamin, 2008; Jensen & Meckling, 1976). Additionally, agents tend to be loss-averse, as individuals react far more strongly to a loss of a certain amount of money than an equal-size gain (Tversky & Kahneman, 1991). This means that colleges might put forth extra effort to respond to a potential sanction over a potential reward.

Second, the agent must expect that the principal will follow through on any promised actions under an accountability system. This requires a credible commitment from the principal, potentially by taking binding actions that limit the principal's ability to change the terms of the performance agreement (e.g., Miller, 2000). While private-sector organizations such as accrediting bodies can create truly binding agreements, these arrangements are far more difficult with the state or federal government as a change in political control often results in a change in policy priorities. For example, research by Dougherty, Natow, and Vega (2012) shows that changes in political control (both within and between political parties) were one of the main reasons why some states ended their performance funding systems. If colleges think an accountability system is unlikely to exist in a few years, they may be less likely to change their priorities in response.

While college leaders must be motivated by an accountability system to change their priorities in order for the system to have any chance of generating its desired results, these leaders also have to incentivize lower-level employees to change their behaviors in order for the college as a whole to effectively respond. This difficulty in monitoring the performance of lower-level employees is common in large nonprofit organizations, which can result in organizational slack if employees do not feel incentivized to meet goals they disagree with (Moe, 1984). This is a particularly acute concern in higher education because of the relative autonomy that many faculty and staff enjoy. These street-level bureaucrats (Weatherley & Lipsky, 1977) often have some level of flexibility in implementing policies to meet their own goals as well as the organization's goals. This can result in a group of employees who are altruistic and may not respond to incentives in addition to those who are highly responsive to incentives (e.g., Buurman & Dur, 2012; Prendergast, 2007).

Another challenge faced in getting individuals to respond to an accountability system in higher education is that individuals' contributions to a given outcome may be relatively small. Higher-level administrators in fields such as enrollment management can be assigned credit or blame for their measureable outcomes, and they typically have fixed-term contracts that make holding them accountable fairly easy. But it is far more difficult to hold an individual faculty member (particularly one with tenure) responsible for a student's academic success given that a student might have a certain professor just once or twice in his or her college career. For this reason, incentives based on explicit performance metrics are relatively uncommon among faculty in higher education, although star research faculty can often negotiate pay raises by getting their host institution to match offers from other universities that are primarily based on one's research expertise. This is a common practice at major research universities; for example, the University of Wisconsin–Madison spent $8 million matching outside job offers in the second half of 2015 (Herzog, 2016).

Two potential performance metrics that reflect teaching expertise instead of research expertise are grades earned in a particular course and student evaluations of faculty teaching quality, but these measures have substantial limitations. Rewarding professors based on grades creates a strong incentive for grade inflation, a phenomenon that has existed for decades (Rojstaczer & Healy, 2012). Although a recent meta-analysis has demonstrated a relationship between course evaluation scores and student learning gains (Spooren, Brockx, & Mortelmans, 2013), there is also evidence that course evaluations are higher when students expect to receive higher grades after taking other variables into account (Ewing, 2012).

These difficulties make group-level incentives more feasible than individual-level incentives in much of higher education, but they come with a distinct set of challenges. Basing rewards or sanctions on the performance of a group (such as an academic department) makes identifying the contribution of each individual difficult. Group incentives can cause individuals to become "free riders" (e.g., Holmstrom, 1982; Olson, 1965) by working less and relying on others' contributions since individuals' effort levels cannot be easily identified.

There is a body of research on both group-level and individual-level incentives in K–12 education, which faces some of the same measurement problems that higher education does even with the proliferation of standardized assessments in K–12. Research on the effectiveness of both individual-level and group-level K–12 individual merit pay plans on student outcomes has shown a mix of null and positive findings (e.g., Eberts, Hollenbeck, & Stone, 2002; Neal, 2011; Pham, Nguyen, & Springer, 2017; Springer et al., 2012). However, two other studies show the potential importance of incentive designs in merit pay systems. Ballou and colleagues (2012) show that, in Nashville, an individual-level merit pay system with large incentives was generally ineffective, but this was likely because the performance threshold to receive bonuses was set too high. Goodman and Turner (2013) found that a group-level system in New York City had minimal effects on student outcomes, but there were small improvements when the incentives to "free ride" were reduced.

CAN A COLLEGE INFLUENCE THE DESIGN OF AN ACCOUNTABILITY SYSTEM?

Another aspect of an accountability system to consider is whether the college can influence how the system is designed. Negotiations between principals and agents are standard procedure in the corporate world and are also incorporated into some hiring practices within higher education. But the potential influence of a college when the accountability system is implemented by governmental bodies is less obvious, even though the implications of any negotiations can affect colleges, students, and taxpayers alike. Colleges can attempt to negotiate with governmental bodies regarding accountability systems in two ways: by either directly lobbying elected officials or working through governmental agencies that have some degree of autonomy from the legislative or executive branches.

The premise of direct lobbying is straightforward: a college as a whole or one of its stakeholders (such as students, faculty, or staff) meets with lawmakers or other elected officials in an effort to advance their preferred policy position. Higher education represents a substantial constituency due to the sheer number of postsecondary institutions in the United States, as nearly 7,300 institutions received federal financial aid in 2014.[5] These colleges are dispersed across the country, with each congressional district having at least one college and the median district having 11 degree-granting institutions (Kelly, 2014).[6]

State legislators can be particularly amenable to lobbying because more than three-fourths of legislators who attended college enrolled in their home state, creating strong ties with some of the institutions they oversee (Smallwood & Richards, 2001). This is reflected in a body of research showing the importance of personal connections and lobbying in state appropriations for public colleges and universities. McLendon, Mokher, and Doyle (2009) examined where legislators on appropriations committees attended college and found a relationship between legislators' alma maters (which were disproportionately flagship universities) and state appropriations.

A line of research by David Tandberg has found that an increased number of higher education interest groups is associated with increased effort in higher education funding (Tandberg, 2010a), while a higher concentration of non-education interest groups appeared to crowd out higher education funding (Tandberg, 2010b). McLendon, Hearn, and Mokher (2009) concluded that each additional registered higher education lobbyist was associated with a small, but statistically significant, increase in state funding effort. However, Brackett (2016) did not find a relationship between lobbying expenditures and state appropriations even as college spending on lobbying rose considerably during the 2000s.

Colleges can also seek to enact their policy preferences through lobbying members of the bureaucratic structure set up to oversee higher education, such as employees of the federal or state education departments. This is a particularly common approach for detailed policy issues regarding accountability, as the legislative and executive branches often delegate authority to career employees and political appointments within the department regarding complicated issues (e.g., Gailmard & Patty, 2007). However, this delegation of power to experts creates an additional opportunity for colleges to influence the design and implementation of accountability policies.

The existence of these bureaucratic agencies creates an opportunity for regulatory capture (Dal Bo, 2006; Laffont & Tirole, 1991; Stigler, 1971), in which the groups being regulated seek to influence the rulemaking process in order to benefit their best interests. The American higher education system includes a number of large interest groups, including the influential American Council on Education and Washington Higher Education Secretariat—two groups that represent nearly all public and private nonprofit colleges in the country. Additionally, more targeted groups such as the National Association for College Admission Counseling and the National Association of Student Financial Aid Administrators, both with thousands of members, work to influence policy implementation within their more narrow fields of interest.[7]

The influence of colleges and their professional associations on policy-making was brilliantly shown in Natow's (2015) analysis of negotiated rulemaking panels at the U.S. Department of Education. Under negotiated rulemaking, the Department of Education brings together a panel of stakeholders, including students, White House representatives, and representatives from affected colleges, before releasing new regulations. Her work found that both broader and special-interest higher education organizations had substantial voices in the rulemaking process, in part due to these interest groups frequently having employees who had worked at the Department of Education. For example, the chairman of the for-profit Apollo Education Group was a deputy secretary at the Department of Education during President Barack Obama's first term (Cohen & Bray, 2016), while the chief compliance officer at the for-profit Bridgepoint Education took a leave of absence to take a high-level position under President Donald Trump's Department of Education (Kreighbaum, 2017).

A concrete example of the influence higher education associations have on the enforcement of accountability systems is the Department of Education's 2014 decision to change how student loan default rates were calculated just a few days before releasing the rates to the public. By excluding approximately 400 students with loans from multiple agencies, an unspecified number of colleges that would have been over the 30% default rate threshold to face sanctions ended up just under the threshold (Baker, 2014; McCann & Miller, 2014). This change meant that no community colleges or historically black colleges—both politically powerful organizations—faced potential sanctions under this accountability system (Stratford, 2014).

CAN THE ACCOUNTABILITY SYSTEM BE GAMED IN AN EFFORT TO IMPROVE OUTCOMES WITHOUT CHANGING PRIORITIES OR RESOURCE ALLOCATIONS?

When colleges or other publicly funded organizations face pressures to improve their performance, they can respond in a number of different ways in an effort to generate the desired result. They can direct additional resources toward improving performance, provide additional training for employees, or reach out to stakeholders to get constructive criticism in an effort to change practices and policies. These are the types of responses that principals expect from agents in an accountability system, and there is some evidence that organizations do change their behavior in desirable ways. For example, K–12 schools subject to high-stakes accountability systems in the 1990s and 2000s did respond by improving the alignment between teachers' instructional practices and test content (Polikoff, 2012) or increasing instructional resources (Chiang, 2009; Rouse, Hannaway, Goldhaber, & Figlio, 2013).

However, not all organizations respond in intended ways to meet the specified performance metrics. In this section, I highlight five different types of efforts to game the accountability system by doing little to change actual practices while changing performance on the observed outcomes. These efforts range from more subtle efforts to manipulate outcomes by changing who organizations are serving to outright cheating, which can land administrators in jail.

The first type of unintended response is *cream skimming*, in which organizations try to only serve individuals with the highest probability of success. In one sense, selective colleges and universities frequently engage in this practice as admissions policies are typically designed to select students with high standardized test scores—which is strongly correlated with graduation rates.[8] Some accountability systems (such as the *U.S. News* college rankings) explicitly reward colleges for enrolling students with top test scores and high school GPAs, but other systems (such as state performance funding systems) instead reward completions.

There are examples of cream skimming in response to accountability policies throughout higher education, as well as in similar fields such as public administration. For example, Umbricht, Fernandez, and Ortagus (2017) show that Indiana public colleges and universities responded to performance funding incentives by becoming more selective, which matches interview findings from college officials in the state (Dougherty et al., 2016). Principals could attempt to reduce cream skimming by giving more weight to groups that are harder to serve, such as first-generation or low-income students, but the presence of asymmetric information favoring the agent still allows for the possibility of selecting cases within the subgroup. An example of this type of cream skimming within subgroups comes from the Job Training Partnership Act (JTPA), which provided funding for job training programs in the 1990s conditional on the programs meeting certain performance criteria (Courty, Kim, & Marschke, 2011).

The second response is *parking*, or not serving individuals with a low probability of success. To some extent, it is the exact opposite of cream skimming—and the admissions process can eliminate most prospective students whose success is far from guaranteed. But even among students who a college accepts, there can still be incentives to immediately park students. A good example of parking in higher education occurred at Mount St. Mary's University in Maryland, where now-former president Simon Newman developed a plan to encourage first-year students with a low probability of graduation (based on a student survey of which respondents were not made aware of its purpose) to leave college in the first month of the semester and receive a full refund. This plan to "drown the bunnies" would remove students before they would be included in the graduation and retention rate cohorts, thus making outcomes appear better (Mangan, 2016).

There is ample evidence of parking in other publicly supported sectors. For example, Koning and Heinrich (2013) examined Dutch job placement assistance data from 2002 to 2005 and found evidence that agencies were not serving clients who were less likely to get jobs. Within K–12 education, several studies have found that some schools tried to game accountability systems by excluding low-performing students from the pool of tested students (Chakrabarti, 2013; Cullen & Reback, 2006; Figlio, 2006; Jennings & Beveridge, 2009; Lemke, Hoerander, & McMahon, 2006). Parking in K–12 education even made an appearance in the animated television show *King of the Hill* in 2008. In one episode, Tom Landry Middle School attempts to game the accountability system by designating several average students as having special needs so they did not have to take the test. In this fictional example, the principal was fired and became a door-to-door steak salesman (Croston, Hall, & Garcia, 2008).

The third type of unintended response is to focus on those cases *on the bubble*, representing individuals who are on the margin of being counted as successful outcomes or failures. This is an understandable response, as organizations with limited resources often want to focus on getting as many individuals as possible to reach the passing threshold. However, this can also mean that cases further away from the margin (either likely successes or likely failures) do not get attention. There is research evidence in K–12 education that schools shifted time and resources toward students closer to the proficiency threshold (Booher-Jennings, 2005; Krieg, 2008; Lauen & Gaddis, 2016; Neal & Schanzenbach, 2010; Reback, 2008) and away from nontested subjects into the tested subjects of math and reading (Dee, Jacob, & Schwartz, 2013; McMurrer, 2007). However, there is little work examining this phenomenon in higher education.

The fourth unintended response is *selective reporting*, in which organizations take advantage of any flexibility they have in reporting results to improve their outcomes. For example, colleges can take advantage of the federal definition of the graduation rate cohort (first-time, full-time students beginning in the fall semester) by enrolling the highest-achieving students on a full-time basis in the fall semester and offering access to other students as spring enrollees or part-time students. For example, the University of Maryland enrolled 21% of its students in the spring semester, and these students had significantly lower SAT scores than fall enrollees (Anderson, 2014). Two studies by Courty and Marschke (1997, 2004) find evidence of job training providers selectively reporting outcomes by waiting to report failed job searches until a period in which they were comfortably above the passing threshold to receive additional funds.

The final unintended response is *cheating*, in which organizations simply make up results or change true results in order to meet performance thresholds. Research by Jacob and Levitt (2003) concludes that about 5% of Chicago elementary school teachers and administrators cheated on standardized tests based on large changes in test scores or unusual response patterns within classrooms. This is supported by a number of cheating scandals in K–12 education across the country, typically where pay is tied to performance (Gabriel, 2010). Evidence from the New York State high school exit exam suggests that about 40% of students who are on the margin of passing had their scores increased by school officials prior to policy changes designed to reduce schools' ability to manipulate their students' scores (Dee et al., 2016). In higher education, there is also some evidence of cheating. For example, five colleges admitted to reporting false data about their outcomes or selectivity metrics to *U.S. News & World Report* in the 2012–13 academic year in an effort to climb in the rankings (Jaschik, 2013).

Conclusion

Public policymakers, accreditors, private organizations, and the public generally expect that colleges will respond to their accountability pressures by changing their behaviors and priorities in desired ways. However, a sizable body of literature on responses to public-sector and nonprofit accountability pressures suggests that organizations such as colleges will respond in both intended and unintended ways. In the remainder of this book, I will refer back to the five key questions about accountability policies from this chapter in an effort to dissect why accountability policies either had their desired effect or failed to induce colleges to change their behaviors. These questions are also helpful to keep in mind when analyzing any new accountability policies or practices within higher education.

CHAPTER TWO

The Historical Development of Higher Education Accountability

FRUSTRATED WITH THE STATE of higher education in the United States, the federal government works to develop a way to rate colleges and universities based on their perceived academic quality. When colleges hear about the plan, they lobby the White House to stop ratings from ever being released to the public due to concerns about the federal role in higher education, the accuracy of the lists, and the impossibility of lumping together all of the functions that colleges serve into just one number. The lobbying effort is successful, and the draft set of college ratings is never released to the public.

In what years did the attempt to rate colleges take place? If you said between 2013 and 2015, you are partially correct. The Barack Obama administration's Postsecondary Institution Ratings System, which I discuss in more detail in the next chapter, followed this exact course of events. But what is less known is that an effort in 1911 and 1912 to rate colleges also traveled along the same trajectory. Accountability efforts in higher education often repeat past attempts, so it is crucial to understand how accountability policies and practices have developed through the history of American higher education.

Most discussions of accountability in American higher education are relentlessly focused on the implications of current accountability structures and what policies could be coming in the future. However, colleges and universities have faced multiple types of accountability pressures from various stakeholders ever since their inception. In some cases, the types of accountability that colleges faced more than a century ago were far stronger than the pressures faced by today's colleges, while in other cases past proposals and policies look quite similar to recent events (as noted in the above example). In this chapter, I detail the historical development of accountability systems prior to 1965—the passage of the first Higher Education Act and a turning point regarding the federal role in higher education accountability.

This chapter is divided into four sections. In the first section, I discuss the development of the first colonial colleges prior to the American Revolution and how the political battles around these institutions helped to shape a distinctly American system of governance and accountability. In the second section, I detail the developing higher education system in the United States prior to the Civil War, with a particular focus on the development of the first public colleges as well as reasons why a federal higher education system did not develop. The third section includes a discussion of the rapid growth of higher education following the Civil War, including the growth of an increasingly diverse higher education sector and fights over autonomy and academic freedom. In the final section, I detail the focus on standardization and quantification in the late 1800s and first half of the 1900s and how that led into the development of modern accountability systems.

The Colonial Colleges

American higher education slowly began to develop during the 1600s and 1700s, as religious denominations and some colonies sought to create colleges in order to educate the next generation of clergy without having to send these individuals to Europe. Harvard was the first colonial college chartered in 1636, followed by eight other colleges prior to the signing of the Declaration of Independence in 1776—all of the Ivy League institutions (except Cornell), the College of William and Mary, and Rutgers (then known as Queen's College [Thelin, 2011]). These colleges were typically organized by the colony's prevailing religious denomination (such as Baptists in Rhode Island and Anglicans in New York), and the colony would then grant the college an exclusive charter to operate in the colony and grant degrees (Trow, 2003).

As colonies had the exclusive right to charter colleges, there were often political fights about whether a new college should be approved and what the denominational affiliation should be. This was particularly important as colleges often restricted attendance to members of the sponsoring denomination, in spite of sometimes receiving state funds (Thelin, 2011). Four of the ten attempts to charter colleges in the three decades prior to the American Revolution were unsuccessful, mainly due to religious conflict or not being tied to a particular denomination (McCaul, 1960).

An example of two successful charter petitions comes from New Jersey, the only colony with multiple colleges before 1776. The College of New

Jersey (now Princeton) was chartered in 1748 after years of dispute between Presbyterians (who sponsored the college) and Anglicans.[1] The college was only chartered after it agreed to start in West Jersey instead of East Jersey and did not pursue funding from the colonial legislature (Robson, 1985). Queen's College (now Rutgers University) was chartered in 1766 by the colonial legislature and was affiliated with the Dutch Reformed Church (Herbst, 1982).

Although these colleges are now among the wealthiest institutions in the world, they had few resources during this time period and were highly dependent on unstable funding streams from a range of sources. Religious denominations were expected to help support their colleges and did so on a voluntary basis, often with the assistance of congregations in England that wished to see American colleges educate native students (Herbst, 1982; McAnear, 1952). Funding from the colonies was limited at best, as only Harvard, William and Mary, and Yale were able to get consistent state funding in the mid-1700s, while Penn, King's College (now Columbia), and Dartmouth only got small amounts. Towns desiring colleges would often donate money to attract a college and help construct buildings, but consistent local funding after opening was rare (McAnear, 1952).

Support from private individuals within the college's colony played a crucial role in these institutions' survival, and these fundraising campaigns were often conducted in interesting ways. For example, Harvard raised funds locally in the late 1640s and early 1650s by asking every family in the area to contribute one-quarter bushel of corn each year ("colledge corne") to help fund operations (Curti & Nash, 1965). In the mid-1700s, the best sources of soliciting private support were through selling subscriptions (promises to donate in the future over a period of time) or through lotteries sanctioned by the colonies. Although collecting on subscription pledges was often difficult, the 18 completed lotteries in the colonies represented one-fourth of Americans' contributions to higher education during this period (McAnear, 1952).

The first American colleges were organized in a similar manner as English colleges and universities, with faculty largely self-governing the institutions. However, this model was quickly challenged as the colleges' funders wanted a larger say in governance. External governing boards, modeled after existing boards at colleges in Scotland, gained power over faculty self-governance in the late 1600s and early 1700s. The authority of these boards, whose members were generally a mix of public officials and individuals affiliated with the college's preferred religious denomination(s), was confirmed through disputes at Harvard in the 1720s and William and Mary in the

1750s (Herbst, 1982). These boards of trustees, through their power to hire and fire faculty and presidents, became a powerful mechanism for holding colleges accountable for their own actions. These boards also provided an early example of colleges having to manage relationships with stakeholders who sometimes had diverging opinions and goals.

Early Colleges in the United States

As the fledgling United States of America began to develop during the first several decades of its existence, the nascent American higher education system also expanded. States slowly began to allow multiple colleges within their boundaries by ending exclusivity provisions in colleges' charters, with Harvard losing its monopoly status in Massachusetts to Williams in 1793 and Yale having to coexist with Trinity College in Connecticut beginning in 1823 (Herbst, 1982). Religiously affiliated colleges in most states slowly lost state appropriations during the early 1800s, which hurt colleges' finances but allowed them to focus their attention on their religious denominations instead of also attempting to respond to the whims of state legislators. For example, Harvard last received appropriations from Massachusetts in 1823 in spite of attempts to regain state funding in 1848 and 1849 on the grounds that they were performing public service (Hofstadter & Smith, 1961). Amherst College's 1825 charter explicitly stated that no state support was included (Trow, 2003). However, some northeastern states were still providing appropriations to some private colleges as late as the 1920s (Rudolph, 1990).

Public colleges and universities slowly began to develop in the late 1700s and early 1800s. Georgia was the first state to establish a state university in 1785, with North Carolina, Vermont, and Tennessee following by 1800 (Tewksbury, 1932).[2] These institutions did have separation between church and state and some measure of external control, but not to the same extent as modern institutions. Although the University of North Carolina had a politically appointed board of trustees in the early 1800s, the board was dominated by Presbyterians for decades (Tewksbury, 1932). The University of Georgia was created with a self-perpetuating board of trustees, in which current members select new members, and the legislature did not end this practice and take over trustee selection until 1876 (Brubacher & Rudy, 1958).

The vast majority of colleges that existed in the early 1800s were still private and affiliated with a local branch of a particular Protestant denomination. These ties may have helped get support for colleges to open, but they also limited colleges' appeal to an increasingly pluralistic society. It also made colleges heavily reliant on local congregations' continued voluntary support, as regular appropriations from a denomination were unusual during this period (Curti & Nash, 1965) and modern fundraising campaigns at private colleges did not come into existence until Harvard's ten-year capital campaign in the 1920s (Kimball, 2014). Religiously affiliated colleges were often used to advance a denomination's interests on the frontier, and some closed once denominations decided to support advancing their sect on the new frontier instead of focusing on settled areas. This led to approximately 81% of colleges failing prior to the Civil War (Tewksbury, 1932). A number of Catholic colleges also opened in this period, led by Georgetown in 1788, but their centralized control by the broader church helped reduce the risk of closure due to changing priorities even if they were susceptible to closing due to a lack of enrollment (Geiger, 2000).

THE *DARTMOUTH* CASE AND INSTITUTIONAL AUTONOMY

A key moment that helped to guarantee colleges' autonomy from state governments occurred in 1819, when the U.S. Supreme Court ruled in favor of Dartmouth College in the *Trustees of Dartmouth College v. Woodward* case. Prior to this ruling, there was a lack of clarity as to whether state-chartered colleges were private corporations or whether states could change charters at will or assert their control in other ways (Duryea, 2000). Dartmouth, a private college, was chartered by the state of New Hampshire and at the time had the exclusive right to grant degrees in the state. However, New Hampshire's governor, William Plumer, wanted Dartmouth to focus more on the practical arts than the liberal arts and wanted to change the self-perpetuating board of trustees in order to gain more control over the institution by appointing members. The New Hampshire legislature passed a bill, which was then signed by Governor Plumer, changing Dartmouth's charter to create a separate board of overseers with veto power over the trustees and that had public officials serving as ex officio members (Herbst, 1982).[3]

Dartmouth sued the state, alleging that their actions to unilaterally revise the charter were unconstitutional. The Supreme Court, led by Chief Justice John Marshall, agreed, stating that the charter was guaranteed as a legal contract and that colleges either had to agree to changes in the charter or the corporation had to commit wrongdoing (Herbst, 1982). This decision is often interpreted as helping to draw a distinction between public and private colleges, although scholars have noted that the true meaning of the case is that colleges' governing boards enjoy relative autonomy from their states (e.g., Thelin, 2011; Whitehead & Herbst, 1986). In any case, the amount of state oversight that private colleges were subject to declined considerably following the *Dartmouth* ruling.

The *Dartmouth* case did provide states with an incentive to charter new public colleges and universities with restrictions that gave states more power over their institutions. Combined with federal funding for education from land sales via the Northwest Ordinance, more states began to found public universities. By the start of the Civil War, 21 of the approximately 182 colleges in existence at the time were public universities (Tewksbury, 1932). The strongest universities at the time were generally found in the midwestern states, where private colleges were not as well established and higher education was seen as more of a public pursuit.

An example of the new wave of public universities was the University of Michigan. It was initially started by the territorial government in 1817 as the *Catholepistemiad* before taking its current name upon statehood in 1837 (Brubacher & Rudy, 1958). The state legislature gave the university unusual powers, including the sole right to grant degrees in the state for nearly two decades. They also allowed for the governing board to be elected by the public beginning in 1850, a tradition that continues to this day (McLendon, 2003). Private colleges in Michigan were not allowed to incorporate until 1855, and even then were not allowed to use the term "university" in their name. However, the university did not get regular state appropriations until 1867 (Brubacher & Rudy, 1958), meaning that the public got to have a voice in the university's operations without providing consistent funding. This concern of accountability without funding is salient today as state governments implement higher-stakes accountability systems (see chapter 4 for more details) while providing a smaller portion of total operating budgets (e.g., Emrey-Arras, 2014; Schmidtlein & Berdahl, 2005).

THE FAILED IDEA OF A NATIONAL UNIVERSITY
During this time period, the federal government played a relatively small role in higher education outside of providing funding to states from land sales. Yet the idea of a national university was discussed at length during the 1700s and 1800s and continues to be proposed in more recent times (e.g., DeParle, 2009; Wesley, 1936). Benjamin Rush, a physician, founder of Dickinson College, and signer of the Declaration of Independence, proposed in 1787 that the federal government create a national university focused on graduate education in practical fields like medicine and agriculture. James Madison brought up the idea at the constitutional convention in 1789, but it was voted down due to concerns about states' rights and the Tenth Amendment (Madsen, 1966). President George Washington also appealed for a national university in the late 1790s and left money in his will for it if Congress would also support it, yet the idea failed in Congress by a single vote

in 1797 (Madsen, 1966). But although the first six presidents all supported the idea, the closest thing to a national university was the creation of the military academy at West Point in 1802 (Brubacher & Rudy, 1958).

The Era of Expansion

The late 1800s and early 1900s marked an era of rapid expansion in American higher education. In the fall of 1869, 62,839 students were enrolled at 563 American colleges and universities. By 1899, 355,430 students were attending 951 institutions, and enrollment reached 1.1 million students at 1,409 colleges in 1929 (Snyder, 1993). Although the 1929 enrollment figure represented just 7.2% of young adults between the ages of 18 and 24, higher education was beginning to reach a larger percentage of students. Much of this expansion was due to the growth of normal schools devoted to teacher education, which are now comprehensive regional public universities (Fraser, 2007; Fryar, 2015; Ogren, 2005), junior colleges, and the first group of modern research universities. This expansion brought new stakeholders into the mix and thus affected the landscape of accountability.

FEDERAL SUPPORT FOR HIGHER EDUCATION

The development of land-grant universities helped to cultivate many of today's flagship public universities, cementing their status at the top of the public higher education hierarchy. Prior to the Civil War, there was a modest land-grant program, with 17 of the newer states receiving land grants of between 46,080 acres and 100,000 acres to help support higher education (Tewksbury, 1932; Thelin, 2011). However, these were one-time grants that did not come with recurring federal support, limiting their effectiveness. The original states also wanted to participate in the program but were unsuccessful in obtaining land grants prior to the Civil War (e.g., Key, 1996).

Vermont representative Justin Morrill proposed a federal land-grant program in 1858 that would establish agricultural colleges. This program, which was framed as a way to make American agriculture more productive, would give 30,000 acres of land to each state for each member of Congress it had at the time. The original proposal was vetoed by President James Buchanan in 1859 over concerns about the bill depriving the federal government of revenue as well as questions about its constitutionality, and Congress was unable to override the veto. But the bill passed in 1862 as southern representatives were not in Congress and President Abraham Lincoln supported it (Key, 1996).

The 1862 Morrill Act did help a number of states create or expand their public research universities, but not all states used the proceeds for this purpose. New Hampshire and Connecticut gave their funds to existing private colleges Dartmouth and Yale, while Massachusetts funded the creation of the private Massachusetts Institute of Technology using Morrill Act funds (Thelin, 2011). California initially targeted its funds to the new University of California, which was intended to be a polytechnic university but initially operated similar to a liberal arts college (Douglass, 2000). New York gave its funds to the newly founded Cornell University, which now has both public and private components (Becker, 1943). The federal government's next source of funding for higher education, the 1887 Hatch Act, which established agricultural experiment stations, came with reporting requirements so the federal government could verify whether states were spending the money as required (Brubacher & Rudy, 1958).

The passage of the second Morrill Act in 1890 designated additional land-grant colleges in the South, with restrictions in place limiting the fields eligible for federal funding to practical studies in response to lessons learned from the first Morrill Act of 1862. Although the original version of the legislation would have required that universities be integrated to get federal funding, the final version gave funds to both white-only state universities and 17 colleges for African Americans, including some of the best-known historically black colleges (Lucas, 2006; Thelin, 2011). A small but growing number of African American students attended both the black land-grant colleges and dozens of new private colleges that were financially supported by religiously affiliated organizations (Curti & Nash, 1965).

STATE AND LOCAL FUNDING

Another sector of higher education that began to develop in the early 1900s was the junior college, which is now typically known as the community college. This idea gained the support of the presidents of several elite colleges in the late 1800s, led by William Rainey Harper, president of the new University of Chicago. These leaders pushed for the first two years of college to be taught at a separate institution, leaving the junior and senior years for universities (Brubacher & Rudy, 1958). By the fall of 1929, there were 37 public and 19 private junior colleges, typically funded and governed by their local communities; the majority of the public junior colleges at this time were located in California (Douglass, 2000; Snyder, 1993). Ten years later, the number of junior colleges had grown to 150 (108 public and 42 private) (Snyder, 1993).

During the late 1800s and early 1900s, the governing structures within public higher education started to become more centralized as states began to consolidate control of normal schools from local communities. Some states that moved early toward centralized structures gave their state's governing board for higher education a great deal of autonomy. For example, the University of California was given special status as a public trust with appointed trustees in 1879 that effectively made it a fourth and coequal branch of the state's government (Douglass, 2000). Other states moved to one board of trustees per system or per state in the early 1900s, with many institutions losing their own governing boards and thus some of their previous autonomy (Kelly & McNeely, 1933). By the early 1940s, 15 states had statewide governing boards and three others had statewide coordinating boards of higher education (McGuinness, 2016). As a more centralized governance structure began to develop, additional public colleges could also count on consistent appropriations (McLendon, 2003; Thelin, 2015), thus guaranteeing a more consistent source of revenue but also coming with the price of increased oversight.

BATTLES OVER INSTITUTIONAL ACCOUNTABILITY AND ACADEMIC FREEDOM

The late 1800s and early 1900s were a period during which Americans' expectations of all levels of government changed substantially. Public frustration with corruption, nepotism, and political favoritism, highlighted by state and local political machines such as the Tammany Hall system in New York (Hirsch, 1945; Riordon, 1948), led to a series of government reforms during the Progressive Era. These reforms included civil service protections and merit selection and promotion in an effort to reduce political patronage and improve transparency (Tolbert & Zucker, 1983), rules that generally remain in place today. Another effort to hold publicly supported institutions accountable for their actions was through the adoption of state open records laws. Utah adopted the first state open records law in 1898, followed by Florida in 1905. A wave of actions in the 1950s led to 20 states having these laws by 1959 (Braman & Cleveland, 1984). Today, these laws—combined with the federal government's Freedom of Information Act that was passed in 1967—provide journalists and members of the public with opportunities to scrutinize many colleges' actions.

The movements of political progressivism and populism in the late 1800s were strongest in the midwestern states, where there was already a history of supporting public colleges that focused on trying to solve practical problems (Wheeler, 2011). The populist movement continued this trend by generally supporting consistent appropriations for public colleges and universities at a time when most other states did not regularly fund their colleges

(Gelber, 2011). Populists also went beyond the traditional focus on agriculture to support the social sciences, with politicians turning to sociologists and economists to help address issues facing the state (Thelen, 1972). The additional support for public colleges came with additional scrutiny of faculty members and administrators. Populists paid very close attention to colleges' finances to make sure funds were being used as efficiently and in a manner they agreed with. Even relatively small expenses could raise the ire of politicians, as evidenced by the 1887 firing of University of Missouri president Samuel Laws after he had the university pay $1,100 for a taxidermied elephant to go in a proposed natural history museum (Gelber, 2011).

Politicians often struggled with faculty members speaking their minds on controversial issues and attempted to censor academics in a number of states (Gelber, 2011). Perhaps the most famous example of this came in 1894, when the Wisconsin state superintendent of public instruction forced the University of Wisconsin's board of regents to investigate economics professor Richard Ely, who was a strong supporter of organized labor. The board of regents unanimously ruled in favor of Ely's academic freedom and the importance of "sifting and winnowing" to discover truth (Herfurth, 1949). The university then moved on to develop strong connections with the legislature during the Progressive Era (Brubacher & Rudy, 1958). This led to the development of the Wisconsin Idea, in which the boundaries of the university are the boundaries of the state; this close coexistence between university and state also helped the university get significant and steady appropriations (Veysey, 1965).

Faculty and administrators at private colleges faced a similar set of issues, but in these cases donors or trustees were seeking to hold employees accountable for their speech. A good example of this is Edward Ross, a Stanford sociologist who advertised political views contrary to what Jane Lathrop Stanford (founder Leland's wife and the only trustee at the time) believed in, even though the university had previously banned political speech. Stanford's president, David Starr Jordan, tried to placate both Mrs. Stanford and the faculty but was eventually unable to keep the peace, and Ross was forced to resign in 1900. This led to other faculty resigning and a scathing report from the American Economic Association about how Stanford violated faculty members' academic freedom (Veysey, 1965). This situation was only resolved when Mrs. Stanford resigned as a trustee in 1903.

Faculty members gained additional power in the early 1900s as faculty and professional associations began to push for tenure and academic freedom protections that were not present at many colleges during the 1800s (Ludlum, 1950). In 1915, the newly founded American Association of University Professors (AAUP) released a set of guidelines on academic freedom and tenure (to which Richard Ely was a contributor), including the expectation that faculty would automatically gain tenure after ten years of employment and that any doctrinal tests at religious colleges would be clearly specified (Seligman et al., 1915). The AAUP released updated statements of principles in 1925 and 1940, which reduced the maximum length of probationary employment to seven years (AAUP, 1940).

Standardization and Quantification

The rapid expansion of the American higher education system in the late 1800s and early 1900s raised concerns about the quality of the education being provided at many institutions. These concerns are best illustrated by two examples. Issac Sharpless, the president of Haverford College in Pennsylvania, noted a common concern about the low standards of some colleges and universities: "There are universities with twenty students of low college grade and a considerable preparatory department. Others are simply fraudulent institutions formed for the purpose of selling degrees, and with their announcements filled with false or exaggerated statements of their physical and intellectual equipment" (Sharpless, 1915, 65). There were few quality control provisions during this period to ensure that colleges that granted a certain degree had high standards. For example, in the spring of 1899, Gale College of Galesville, Wisconsin, granted 15 PhDs, in spite of the rigor of the academic instruction being more similar to a high school than a graduate institution (Bicha, 1990; Hollis, 1945). In the same year, the University of Wisconsin, one of the most prestigious universities in the country at the time, granted just five doctorates (Hawkins, 1992). These concerns about quality led to a movement to both standardize and quantify American higher education between 1890 and 1950, and this movement was integral in shaping the development of some of the accountability frameworks that exist to this day.

THE BUREAU OF EDUCATION AND ITS FAILED
COLLEGE RATINGS

The federal government's role in holding colleges accountable for their performance slowly increased in the years following the Civil War. The first U.S. Department of Education was established on March 2, 1867, after several unsuccessful efforts in the 1840s and 1850s to start a national agency (Lykes, 1975). Due to skepticism about the federal role of education, it was not a cabinet-level agency and had a commissioner in charge instead of a secretary (Act to Establish a Department of Education, 1867). The agency, which was known as the Bureau of Education, and the Office of Education in the following century, was established with the goal of generating statistical reports about the state of American education (Snyder, 1993).

Some of these statistical reports went beyond providing mere facts and figures and became informal accountability systems, although little is known about why the federal government began to make this transition. The first example of this came in 1887, when the U.S. Bureau of Education listed women's colleges in two divisions based on characteristics of the colleges associated with quality. Just seven colleges were in Division A in that first year, while 200 were in Division B (U.S. Bureau of Education, 1888; Webster, 1986). This classification system continued through 1911, when although very few colleges were in Division A, the distinction between the two groups had faded somewhat (U.S. Bureau of Education, 1912; Webster, 1984). But the small number of colleges in Division A and the exclusion of coeducational or all-male colleges led to these ratings getting relatively little attention (Webster, 1986).

While the last set of women's college ratings was being published, the Bureau of Education was working on a broader set of ratings that would group colleges based on how much additional preparation their students would need before enrolling in top graduate programs. The ratings, compiled by former University of Arizona president and new bureau specialist Charles Babcock (1911), placed 344 of the 602 existing four-year colleges and universities into five divisions ranging from no additional preparation to at least two years of additional preparation to be ready for a top master's program. A draft of the ratings was inadvertently released to the media, which led colleges to even more vigorously dispute their classification. This led President William Howard Taft to sign an executive order banning the document's distribution in February 1913 (Lykes, 1975). President Woodrow Wilson (former president of Princeton) declined to reverse the executive order when he took office later that year (Webster, 1984), and the next direct federal effort to rate colleges (described in more detail in the next chapter) did not occur for 100 years.

VOLUNTARY ACCREDITATION

The quality of institutions calling themselves "colleges" or "universities" varied tremendously in the late 1800s, with a mix of highly regarded educational institutions, struggling smaller schools with lax admission standards, and outright diploma mills all having similar names. This frustrated colleges that considered themselves to be of high quality, and they took action to create a signal of their quality to both students and other colleges—the accreditation system (Harcleroad, 1980).

Although the State of New York had done annual visits to all colleges since 1787 to determine whether institutions met basic quality standards (Selden, 1960), the modern higher education accreditation system can in large part be attributed to an effort begun by the University of Michigan in 1871 to inspect and accredit the state's high schools. Any graduate from an accredited high school was automatically granted entry into the university, giving colleges a lever to improve high schools' performance. By the late 1890s, nearly 200 colleges were accrediting high schools (VanOverbeke, 2008).

At this time, colleges were also beginning to seek their own accreditation as a signal of quality. The first accrediting body to cross state lines was the New England Association of Schools and Colleges, which was founded in 1885 to evaluate both K–12 schools and colleges in the northeast. By 1924, each region of the country had its own accrediting body for higher education, with some accreditors focusing solely on higher education and others covering K–12 education (Sanders, 1969).[4] These accreditors were typically founded by more elite institutions; for example, the North Central Association (now known as the Higher Learning Commission) was initiated by Chicago, Michigan, Northwestern, and Wisconsin (Davis, 1945).

By 1913, the North Central Association had released its first list of fully accredited institutions, with the other accrediting bodies following over the next several decades (Harcleroad, 1980). The criteria for accreditation were highly quantitative during the early 1900s, with factors such as the size of the library and the percentage of faculty members with PhDs included in this period (Wiley & Zald, 1968). At this time, some disciplines such as law, medicine, and dentistry also began developing their own standards for accreditation amid concerns that disciplines with accreditation would get more resources than ones without accreditation. These factors led some colleges to push back against the existing criteria—or even the need for accreditation at all.

A vocal critic was Samuel Capen, a former lead official in the Office of Education who was then president of the University at Buffalo. He found accreditation unnecessary for most colleges and proposed replacing accreditors with an investigating body, saying, "it takes no very ponderous armament to deal with an occasional picaroon (scoundrel)" (Capen, 1931, 550). Capen doubled down on his criticism of exacting quantitative standards in a 1939 speech titled "Seven Devils in Exchange for One" (Capen, 1939). By that point, some of the regional accreditors had moved to more flexible standards that better reflected the diversity of institutions accredited (Wiley & Zald, 1968). By the 1950s, accreditors moved to ten-year review cycles for evaluating colleges in good standing (Pfnister, 1971), which generally continues today.

States had the constitutional authority to oversee private higher education during this period, but most states chose not to regulate private non-profit or for-profit colleges. By 1934, only 20 states had any standards in place for colleges operating within their boundaries, with New York and Pennsylvania having the most stringent standards regarding financial resources, degree length, and faculty qualifications. Institutions that were unable to meet these standards could not call themselves a college or university (Brubacher & Rudy, 1958). Even by 1954, at least 17 states did not have the ability to shut down phony diploma mills (Selden, 1960), even as this dubious group of for-profit enterprises grew rapidly in the early 1900s (Angulo, 2016). An example of one of these diploma mills is Potomac University, which granted thousands of bachelor's, master's, and doctoral degrees out of the District of Columbia from 1904 through 1930 without any academic standards (Lykes, 1975).

In addition to the accrediting bodies that still exist to this day, the Association of American Universities (AAU), a group of major research universities founded in 1900, also functioned as an accrediting agency in the first half of the twentieth century. But unlike the regional or state accreditors, the AAU sought to limit their seal of approval to only the best colleges. Their effort began in the early 1900s in response to a request from the University of Berlin to develop a list of colleges with bachelor's degrees similar in quality to those from German institutions for the purpose of graduate study. Rather than quickly expand their membership, the AAU created the first list of high-quality institutions in 1914 (Speicher, n.d.). Colleges on the list were considered high quality, while other bachelor's degrees from the United States were not accepted (Zook & Haggerty, 1936). The AAU continued publishing this list through 1948, at which time more than 300 non-AAU members were on the list (Sanders, 1969).

PRIVATE-SECTOR STANDARDIZATION EFFORTS

In addition to colleges' efforts to regulate themselves through the accreditation process, private-sector organizations and individuals sought to improve the quality of education by creating new ratings and rankings. The most influential entity during the early 1900s was the Carnegie Foundation for the Advancement of Teaching, which was founded in 1905 with a $10 million gift from industrialist Andrew Carnegie (Lagemann, 1983). The first priority of the foundation was to establish a pension system for college professors, and the foundation's board took it upon themselves to define what a college was.

They set two main requirements for colleges to be eligible for the pension fund, limiting the initial pool to 52 of the over 600 colleges in existence at the time. First, colleges had to have a rigorous set of courses leading to a bachelor's degree, with certain requirements on academic preparation and the number of faculty. In order to have a reasonably consistent measure of the rigor of a program, the Carnegie Foundation looked toward accreditors of high schools and their adoption of course units based on the amount of time spent on a particular subject. This requirement led to the creation of the Carnegie unit for measuring academic progress—the modern credit hour (e.g., Hutt, 2016; Shedd, 2003). The credit hour still plays a crucial role in higher education accountability, particularly in how federal financial aid is allocated to students attending eligible colleges (Laitinen, 2012).

The second requirement from the Carnegie Foundation was that only private nonprofit colleges that were not controlled by religious denominations were eligible (Lagemann, 1983). Public colleges were excluded due to the assumption of state support, while denominational colleges were excluded because it was expected that denominations should support their own colleges and due to the low salaries at denominational colleges (Pritchett, 1908). The incentive of faculty pensions induced some Protestant colleges, such as Bowdoin, Drake, Rochester, Syracuse, Vanderbilt, and Wesleyan, to leave their denominations to participate in the pension plan (Brubacher & Rudy, 1958; Rudolph, 1990), while some others (such as Randolph-Macon) had to walk a fine line between appealing to a denomination and being independent (Hohner, 1987). By 1915, a total of 73 colleges (mostly private nonprofits) were in the Carnegie plan (Pritchett, 1915), which was renamed the Teachers Insurance and Annuity Association of America (TIAA) in 1917 (Lagemann, 1983).

The Carnegie Foundation played a large role in the effort to standardize professional education with the goal of improving quality. In addition to creating the modern credit hour, the foundation supported an endeavor by Abraham Flexner to evaluate the facilities and academic standards of medical schools, as the existing medical associations had delayed enforcing higher standards due to concerns about how it would affect their member institutions (Lagemann, 1983). The resulting Flexner Report recommended closing or merging 120 of the existing 155 medical schools in the United States over quality concerns (Flexner, 1910), and the number of medical schools dropped to just 80 by 1927 (Floden, 1980). However, this did result in reduced access to medical care in rural areas, as well as the closure of six of the eight African American medical schools (Beck, 2004). In addition to medical education, Flexner also critiqued the quality and necessity of vocationally oriented graduate programs such as home economics and education, in part by listing dissertation titles. This effort was not as successful as his attempt to reform medical education (Hofstadter & Smith, 1961).

A number of other individuals created rankings and ratings of their own during the first half of the twentieth century. Psychologist James McKeen Cattell created two college rankings called *American Men of Science* in the early 1900s. In the 1906 version (Cattell, 1906), he listed the top 1,000 scientists associated with a college or university based on where they went to graduate school. In the 1910 version (Cattell, 1910), he ranked colleges based on where the top 1,000 scientists currently worked. This was followed by a number of disciplinary rankings and ratings in graduate education released prior to 1960, mostly based on reputational surveys (e.g., Foster, 1936; Hughes, 1925, 1934, 1946; Keniston, 1959).

Colleges also began to standardize the admissions process during the late 1800s and early 1900s due to concerns about the quality of high schools and large amounts of variation in students' academic preparation for college. The move to accredit high schools beginning in the 1880s helped to provide some minimum standards, but this was generally viewed as being insufficient. Two attempts in the 1890s to provide additional information about academic preparation and set standards, one by the National Education Association and another by Harvard president Charles Eliot, failed. The next attempt from 12 eastern colleges to create a standardized admission test under the auspices of the College Board was successful in 1900, although the organization grew slowly in its first several decades (Lawrence et al., 2003; Riccards, 2010; Valentine, 1987). The College Board then created the SAT in 1926, while archrival ACT did not create its entrance exam until 1959. The tests of general educational development (GED) were created during World War II following a meeting of college presidents and quickly began to serve as a common measure of high school equivalency for all students, even though they were not created for that purpose (Hutt, 2014).

The Transition to Modern Federal Accountability Policies

Prior to the Great Depression (and in part due to the spectacular failure of the 1911–12 college ratings initiative), the ongoing federal role in higher education was generally limited to funding certain programs in the sciences and making statistical information about colleges and universities available to the public. But as both higher education and the federal government grew in power following the end of World War I, the stage was set for growing federal involvement in the activities of individual colleges. The Great Depression, which reduced colleges' revenues by as much as 40%, provided the impetus for federal action (Loss, 2012).

The first federal effort in funding students came in 1934, with the creation of the ambitiously named Federal Student Aid Program through the Federal Emergency Relief Administration and the National Youth Administration (Kelly & McNeely, 1935). This was a work-study program that gave students at public and private nonprofit colleges up to $20 per month for part-time work on campus, an amount that was sufficient to pay for tuition as well as cover some living expenses (Bower, 2004). Nearly 80% of colleges participated in this program, which funded $93 million in aid for 620,000 students during the Great Depression (Brubacher & Rudy, 1958; Greenleaf, 1935). The program ended in 1943 amid opposition from Republican legislators and the National Education Association (which opposed portions of the National Youth Administration unrelated to college students) and ambivalence from many colleges (Bower, 2004).

The next federal student aid program was the Servicemen's Readjustment Act (GI Bill), which was signed into law in 1944 and provided among its benefits tuition remission and a living allowance for qualified veterans of World War II (Servicemen's Readjustment Act, 1944). The bill was enacted not due to concerns about low levels of college education in America but, rather, due to concerns about the millions of returning veterans overwhelming the labor force and causing mass unemployment and social unrest (Olson, 1973). The program turned out to be far more popular than expected among soldiers, with 2.2 million of the approximately 15 million veterans using GI Bill benefits at a price tag of $5.5 billion, far higher than earlier predictions of between 500,000 and one million students (McGrath, 1945; Olson, 1973). By 1947, fully half of the nation's college students were veterans (Altschuler & Blumin, 2009), as the GI Bill significantly increased the educational attainment of young adults who were eligible to receive benefits (Bound & Turner, 2002).

One key component in the GI Bill was that students could take the funds to any approved college of their choice, which forced the federal government to consider which postsecondary institutions were worthy of receiving federal funds. The federal government initially relied on states to submit lists of qualified institutions (Servicemen's Readjustment Act, 1944), but there were concerns about low-quality proprietary colleges popping up to harvest GI Bill funds while charging high prices. This led to a series of hearings in the U.S. House of Representatives in which some of the most egregious institutions faced questioning over their policies and practices (Investigation of GI Schools, 1951).

As Korean War veterans began to come home, Congress began debating an updated version of the GI Bill that would address concerns about students being able to use their federal aid dollars at unscrupulous institutions. The question was then how to develop a list of approved institutions, and there were two main possible ways to do so. The federal government could have developed directly a list of approved institutions, or it could delegate that authority to already existing accrediting agencies. In the passage of the Veterans Readjustment Assistance Act in 1952, lawmakers generally chose the latter approach (Conway, 1979; Finkin, 1973). The commissioner of education was required to publish a list of nationally recognized accrediting agencies at both the institution and program level, along with helping states set up their own approval processes. The accrediting standards and list of approved accreditors largely came from the National Commission on Accrediting, a newly established organization representing accreditors (Proffitt, 1979). This setup, which largely continues to this day, preserved some of the autonomy of colleges from the federal government while providing a mechanism for quality control.

There were additional proposals following World War II to create permanent peacetime financial aid programs. The most ambitious proposal came from President Harry Truman's Commission on Higher Education, which was formed to examine the future of higher education following the war. The commission called for the number of students at nonprofit colleges and universities to double to 4.6 million by 1960 (a goal that was met by 1964) and recommended tuition-free public education through the fourteenth grade and financial assistance for needy students (President's Commission on Higher Education, 1947). Although the committee's report was not adopted at the time, the language used in the report regarding financial assistance was echoed in the first Higher Education Act in 1965 (Gilbert & Heller, 2013).

The intensification of the Cold War following World War II led to stronger ties between the federal government and research universities, as evidenced by the first sustained federal efforts to fund research at universities in the name of national defense (Bush, 1945). The federal government established two new financial aid programs with the passage of the National Defense Education Act in 1958. This act, a response to the Soviet Union launching the satellite *Sputnik* into space in 1957, was designed to improve America's scientific capacity by creating a new fellowship program for graduate students in strategic fields and the National Defense Student Loan program (now known as the Perkins Loan program) for financially needy students (National Defense Education Act, 1958). Funds for this program were given directly to the approximately 65% of colleges that chose to participate, and colleges had to provide a 10% match of funds (Flemming, 1960).

But a provision in the act that required all individuals who received federal support to swear they would not overthrow the federal government led 31 colleges to opt out of the program and over 100 more to pass resolutions of disapproval over concerns about academic freedom (AAUP, 1962). Although the Secretary of Health, Education, and Welfare had pushed for the oath's removal in the late 1950s, it was not removed until 1962 (AAUP, 1962; Flemming, 1960). This represented one of the first battles between the federal government and colleges regarding the requirements placed on federal financial aid dollars.

Conclusion

American higher education has changed tremendously since the founding of the early colonial colleges, both in terms of the complexity and diversity of colleges and universities and regarding colleges' interactions with an ever-changing mix of stakeholders trying to hold them accountable for their actions. Throughout the last several centuries, colleges have generally attempted to be as autonomous as possible, while funders of different types have tried to impose accountability systems in order to make sure their resources are used in an efficient and effective manner relative to their priorities. The power of stakeholders changed considerably during this period, with religious denominations controlling a smaller proportion of institutions and state and federal governments gaining power alongside voluntary organizations such as accrediting bodies. In the remainder of this book, I will discuss these key stakeholders and how their role in the accountability framework has continued to change over the last several decades.

CHAPTER THREE

Federal Accountability Policies

A TURNING POINT in the federal government's role in American higher education came in 1972 as Congress was debating the second reauthorization of the Higher Education Act (HEA). The initial passage of the HEA in 1965 resulted in the creation of the first federal grant program based on financial need (now known as the Supplemental Educational Opportunity Grant) and the creation of the Federal Work-Study program, in addition to a Guaranteed Student Loan program for students from lower-income families (Gladieux, 1996). Both of these programs, along with the National Defense Student Loan program began in 1958 (now known as Perkins Loans) were administered through participating colleges, which then allocated funds to students within a set of federal guidelines. Meanwhile, the guaranteed student loans were given directly to students, who could take them to nearly any accredited college of their choice.

Both chambers of Congress and President Richard Nixon wanted to expand grant aid to students from lower-income families, but there was disagreement in how to do so. President Nixon wanted to replace the existing campus-based programs with a new Basic Educational Opportunity Grant (BEOG) (Gladieux, 1996). Legislation passed by the House of Representatives provided more money to the existing campus-based programs, while Senate legislation created the BEOG and maintained the existing programs. The Senate bill was adopted by the joint conference committee, in large part due to the efforts of Senator Claiborne Pell (D-RI); the new BEOG was eventually renamed the Pell Grant after him (Gladieux & Wolanin, 1976).

Today, all but $2.7 billion of the estimated $140 billion in federal financial aid awarded under Title IV of the HEA (grants, loans, and work-study programs) is awarded to students attending approved colleges instead of being awarded directly to colleges (Baum et al., 2016).[1] This distinction is important for accountability purposes, as the voucher-like nature of student financial aid dollars requires a different set of policies to hold institutions accountable for their performance than under a financing system in which funds are given directly to colleges (Goldrick-Rab, Schudde, & Stampen, 2014). The majority of state dollars for public higher education are appropriated to colleges, and I will discuss how that affects the development of accountability systems (as well as the interaction between federal and state accountability policies) in chapter 4.

In order for students at a college to be able to receive federal Title IV dollars, the college must sign a program participation agreement with the U.S. Department of Education that specifies a number of requirements that must be satisfied (Office of Federal Student Aid, 2014). These agreements are complex, requiring institutional leaders to certify that they will comply with antidiscrimination, liability, and student privacy regulations in addition to two main sets of federal accountability provisions specified in the HEA or other federal regulations.

The first set of accountability systems I discuss in this chapter focuses on consumer information, requiring colleges to report and disclose data on a range of outcomes with the hope that the information will help students make better choices. The second set of systems consists of high-stakes policies that tie institutional Title IV eligibility to meeting a set of minimal financial and performance metrics. I conclude this chapter with a discussion of the factors influencing the development and implementation of federal accountability policies, highlighted by a case study of the Obama administration's short-lived effort to tie federal Title IV dollars to a set of performance metrics through a college ratings system that resulted in the revised College Scorecard tool.

Low-Stakes Accountability (Consumer Information)

The first set of federal accountability policies is designed to make information about a range of institutional characteristics and outcomes available to students and their families. The federal government requires colleges to meet data reporting and disclosure requirements as a condition of receiving federal financial aid dollars. The U.S. Department of Education then uses some of those data elements to create consumer-oriented websites designed to reach students as they consider colleges. However, some have criticized the consumer information portion of federal accountability as being ineffective and burdensome. In this section, I detail the range of consumer information policies and evaluate whether they have been effective in meeting their goals of getting useful information to students and affecting their college choice processes.

DATA REPORTING AND DISCLOSURE REQUIREMENTS

Since the 1992 reauthorization of the HEA, colleges are required to compile and submit data to the U.S. Department of Education's National Center for Education Statistics (NCES) on a range of metrics in order to remain eligible for federal Title IV dollars (Ginder, Kelly-Reid, & Mann, 2014). Colleges must complete 12 different surveys each year on topics as diverse as academic libraries, enrollment, human resources, and student financial aid, including a new survey in 2015–16 for student outcome measures that goes beyond the traditional measure of graduation rates for first-time, full-time students (NCES, 2015a).[2] All of these data are then compiled by NCES and released to the public through the Integrated Postsecondary Education Data System (IPEDS) Data Center with a delay of approximately one to two years; however, no formal audits or checks of the reported data are made before being posted online.

The sheer magnitude of data collected through IPEDS makes it a valuable resource to researchers and analysts, but at a substantial compliance cost to colleges. The official federal burden estimate from the Office of Management and Budget is that colleges are expected to spend 1,037,130 hours collecting and reporting IPEDS data in the 2015–16 academic year, at a cost of over $40 million per year across the approximately 7,500 institutions receiving federal financial aid (NCES, 2013). While the average compliance cost to a college is estimated at approximately $5,000, a U.S. Government Accountability Office (2010) report concluded that NCES likely underestimates compliance costs by a significant amount.

In addition to the data that must be submitted for IPEDS, Congress and the Department of Education require that colleges also disclose approximately 40 other items on a range of factors, including fire safety information, Pell Grant graduation rates, voter registration forms, and employment placement. Some of these items (such as textbook information) are required to be posted on a college's website, while other disclosure items (such as articulation agreements) must be made available upon request (Fuller & Salerno, 2009). However, a significant percentage of colleges have failed to either post these items on their website or to disclose them to the public upon request (Carey & Kelly, 2011).

Probably the most prominent piece of information that colleges must post on their websites is a net price calculator, through which students and their families can enter key financial elements of the Free Application for Federal Student Aid (FAFSA) to get an estimate of their likely financial aid package before applying to a given college.[3] Colleges were mandated to post net price calculators by late 2011 as a part of the 2008 reauthorization of the HEA (Carey & Kelly, 2011). Colleges were given flexibility in how to construct net price calculators, with some colleges using a simple form with a small number of questions developed by the federal government and others using more detailed forms from third-party vendors (Fallon, 2011).

Research has shown that getting accurate information about the net price of college to students can influence how students perceive their college options and actually choose colleges (Hoxby & Turner, 2013). The good news is that net price calculators appear to be reaching a portion of prospective students. A series of surveys of students who took the SAT showed the percentage of respondents who reported using a net price calculator on a college's website increased from 24% in 2011 to 44% in 2012 (Art & Science Group, 2013). However, this percentage fell to 36% by 2015 in a survey of ACT takers with similar demographics, suggesting that net price calculators may have not become more popular in the years following mandatory adoption by colleges (Art & Science Group, 2015).

These net price calculators suffer from three main flaws that have likely reduced their effectiveness as an accountability tool. First, although colleges are required to post net price calculators on their websites, an analysis of a sample of colleges revealed that a number of colleges have their calculators located in obscure or unintuitive portions of their websites—limiting usage (Cheng, 2012). Second, the information on the net price calculators is up to five years old at some colleges, which results in underestimates of net prices as tuition has increased significantly during that period (Anthony, Page, & Seldin, 2015). Finally, the differences in formats and questions across net price calculators make comparing net prices across colleges difficult, particularly as some colleges have blocked access to third-party websites designed to pull net price data from multiple institutions at the same time (Field, 2013).

CONSUMER INFORMATION ON FEDERAL WEBSITES

In addition to requiring colleges to place information about selected measures on their institutional websites, the federal government also uses the data reported by colleges receiving Title IV dollars to create three different consumer-facing websites designed to get information to students and their families. The first website, College Navigator, was initially released in 2000 as College Opportunities On-Line after being mandated by the 1998 reauthorization of the HEA (Carnevale, 2000). College Navigator is maintained by NCES as a portal through which the public can easily see key information on the price of college, student loan default rates, completion rates, intercollegiate athletics, and a number of other factors (National Center for Education Statistics, 2015b). Students can also simultaneously compare multiple colleges using this website, with the goal that the information might influence students' college choices. However, a critique of College Navigator is that it overwhelms students and families with information instead of focusing on the most important elements (Castleman, 2015).

The second consumer accountability measure from the federal government is the College Affordability and Transparency List, whose creation was mandated by Congress in the 2008 reauthorization of the HEA. Although initial proposals in the U.S. House of Representatives would have required colleges with above-average tuition to form cost-reduction committees, the proposal included in the HEA contained a website identifying the top 10% and bottom 5% of colleges on tuition and fees and net price (Field & Newman, 2014). This website also contains lists of colleges with the largest annual percentage increases on these two measures (U.S. Department of Education, n.d.). Colleges with the highest increases in tuition and net price are required to submit an explanation to the Department of Education explaining those increases, which are typically attributed to rising costs of providing an education and reduced per-student state appropriations (U.S. Department of Education, 2014b).

These tuition "shame lists" do call attention to colleges with unusually high prices, but their utility is limited in several key ways. First, with six lists for each of nine institutional sectors (ranging from public less-than-two-year colleges to for-profit four-year colleges), students can peruse 54 lists if they so choose—enough to thoroughly confuse them. Second, the lists for public colleges are dominated by a small number of states with lower levels of per-student state appropriations. Seventeen of the 34 public four-year institutions on the high tuition list in 2015 are in Pennsylvania. As former Department of Education staffer Ben Miller (2013) quipped about a prior version of the list: "If you live in Pennsylvania, the lists tell you that you're basically screwed. If you don't live in Pennsylvania, the only thing the lists tell you is that you probably shouldn't move to Pennsylvania." Third, the percentage increase in tuition measure often includes colleges with high percentage increases, but smaller increases in dollar terms than other colleges. For example, New Mexico Highlands University was included on the tuition watch list in 2015 for a 21.8% increase in tuition during the previous two years—from $3,284 to $4,000 per year. This $716 increase is dwarfed by the $2,331 increase ($13,132 to $15,463) at the College of William and

Mary, but the 17.8% increase was small enough to not make the top 10% of increases.

The final—and most prominent—consumer-facing website is the College Scorecard, which was first announced by President Barack Obama in a 2012 speech at the University of Michigan as a part of a larger package of proposals on college affordability and accountability (White House, 2012). The website was significantly updated in 2015 as a result of the abandoned effort to rate colleges (which I will discuss later in this chapter). The updated Scorecard includes newly released data on debt burdens, student loan repayment rates, and earnings of former students who took out federal financial aid. The earnings data cover about 70% of all students attending Title IV institutions (Council of Economic Advisers, 2015), and there is some preliminary evidence that prospective students are already using the data in making their college choice decisions (Hurwitz & Smith, 2016).

The Scorecard consists of two portions, a public-facing website and a massive underlying dataset that can be used by researchers or other organizations interested in disseminating data to students and their families. The public-facing portion was intentionally kept simple, with just a small number of metrics included. The net price, graduation rate, debt, earnings, and student loan payment metrics are shown in low, medium, and high categories in an effort to give students context regarding a college's performance. Some have criticized the Scorecard for not taking institutional resources and student characteristics into account, making the performance of minority-serving institutions with few resources look poor compared to better-resourced colleges (Collins, Jenkins, & Strzelecka, 2014).

These federal accountability efforts focused on consumer information are often criticized for not being able to give students more detailed information on what they should expect from a given college (Hershbein & Hollenbeck, 2014). Students can access information on the net price of attendance by family income level and graduation rates by race/ethnicity and gender (if they are first-time, full-time students), but a Latina with a 3.8 high school GPA, a 26 on the ACT, and a family income of $50,000 is unable to get information from the federal government or prospective colleges about how students like her perform at a given institution.

The main reason the federal government has not been able to provide more individualized information is due to a provision enacted in the 2008 HEA reauthorization that banned the creation of a federal student unit record dataset due to data privacy concerns. This prevents the federal government from having information on the outcomes of individual students, instead forcing them to rely on aggregate outcomes for larger groups of students at a particular college (such as Pell Grant recipients). Legislation has been introduced over the course of several years to overturn this ban, but opposition from some congressional Republicans and the National Association of Independent Colleges and Universities (NAICU)—the lobbying organization for private nonprofit colleges—has contributed to the continuation of the ban (McCann & Laitinen, 2014). It is possible under the unit record ban to provide data at the program level, but this has yet to happen due to concerns about institutional burden.

Higher-Stakes Accountability Policies

In addition to requiring that colleges report or disclose information on a range of performance metrics in order to receive federal financial aid dollars, the federal government also ties a college's eligibility to receive student financial aid dollars to meeting a set of minimum quality and stability metrics.[4] These metrics include cohort default rates, financial responsibility scores, heightened cash monitoring, gainful employment, and the 90/10 rule. In this section, I detail each of these metrics, how many colleges are affected, and how colleges have responded to facing accountability pressures—both in intended and unintended ways.

COHORT DEFAULT RATES

As student loan volume increased during the 1980s, policymakers grew concerned about the percentage of students who were unable to repay their federally guaranteed loans. The U.S. General Accounting Office (1989) found that over 600 colleges had at least 40% of their students who left college with federal loans in 1983 default on their loans by 1987. This led the Department of Education to start regularly tracking and publishing estimates of the cohort default rate (CDR)—the percentage of students with federal loans who defaulted within a given period of time after leaving college. Education Secretary Lauro Cavazos also issued regulations in 1989 that would cut off colleges with two-year CDRs above 60% from receiving federal student loan dollars while requiring improvements from colleges with default rates over 20% (DeLoughry, 1990a).

Congress then took additional action in 1990 that was designed to bring down CDRs, which were 17.6% within two years for the 1987 repayment cohort. The Omnibus Budget Reconciliation Act (1990) barred colleges from receiving federal student loans for the next three years if their two-year CDR was at or above 30% in three consecutive years unless the secretary of education granted a waiver. Congress tightened the default rate requirement in the 1992 reauthorization of the HEA by lowering the maximum allowable default rate from 30% to 25%. In addition, colleges were not allowed to receive any federal Title IV dollars (grants or loans) if the default rate was above 40% in any given year (Higher Education Amendments, 1992).

Due to some of the lowest-performing institutions losing access to federal student loans, improved economic conditions, and increased efforts from colleges to implement default management plans, the overall student loan default rate decreased each year from a peak of 22.4% for students entering repayment in 1990 to 5.6% for students entering repayment in 1999 (table 3.1). But the default rates by type of college (first available in 1994) varied considerably during the 1990s and early 2000s, with for-profit colleges consistently having the highest default rates and private nonprofit colleges having the lowest default rates. Two-year default rates then remained around 5% through 2006 before rising to 8.8% for the 2009 cohort of students, who left college during the Great Recession.

During the 2000s, numerous concerns were raised about the quality of the two-year cohort default rate measure, particularly after 1998 amendments to the HEA changed the definition of default from being 180 days delinquent to being 270 days delinquent (Office of Inspector General, 2003). Because the CDR was based on students who entered repayment in one fiscal year and tracked through the end of the second year (for example, students entering repayment in fiscal year 2007 were tracked through the end of fiscal year 2008), some students who entered repayment at the very end of the first fiscal year would barely have time to default by the end of the second fiscal year. For-profit colleges were accused of encouraging students to go into forbearance, postponing payments until after the accountability window had passed, even though that practice resulted in mounting debt burdens for students. These concerns led policymakers to change the default rate window from two years to three years, first using the metric for accountability purposes in 2014 using data from the 2009–11 cohorts (Blumenstyk, 2010). If 30% of borrowers defaulted within three years from three successive cohorts, the college was subject to the loss of all federal Title IV dollars, while a 40% default rate in any given cohort resulted in the loss of federal student loan eligibility.

Both two-year and three-year default rates are available for students entering repayment in 2009, providing insights into the importance of tracking students through the third year. As table 3.1 shows, default rates increased from 8.8% within two years to 13.4% within three years—reflecting a 50% increase in the number of defaults during the third year of measurement. In spite of expectations that for-profit colleges would be disproportionately

TABLE 3.1   Cohort default rates by sector and year (in percentages)

Year entering repayment	Overall	2-year public	4-year public	Private nonprofit	For-profit
1987	17.6				
1988	17.2				
1989	21.4				
1990	22.4				
1991	17.8				
1992	15.0				
1993	11.6				
1994	10.7	13.8	6.8	6.9	21.1
1995	10.4	14.2	7.1	7.4	19.9
1996	9.6	13.3	7.0	7.0	18.2
1997	8.8	12.7	6.9	6.1	15.4
1998	6.9	10.7	5.7	4.7	11.4
1999	5.6	8.8	4.6	3.8	9.3
2000	5.9	9.3	4.8	4.0	9.4
2001	5.4	8.7	4.4	3.5	9.0
2002	5.2	8.5	4.0	3.2	8.7
2003	4.5	7.6	3.3	2.8	7.3
2004	5.1	8.1	3.5	3.0	8.6
2005	4.6	7.9	3.0	2.4	8.2
2006	5.2	8.5	3.4	2.5	9.7
2007	6.7	9.9	4.3	3.7	11.0
2008	7.0	10.1	4.4	4.0	11.6
2009 (2-year)	8.8	11.9	5.2	4.6	15.0
2009 (3-year)	13.4	18.3	7.9	7.5	22.7
2010	14.7	20.9	9.3	8.2	21.8
2011	13.7	20.5	8.9	7.2	19.1
2012	11.8	19.0	7.6	6.8	15.8
2013	11.3	18.4	7.3	7.0	15.0

SOURCE: Office of Federal Student Aid, U.S. Department of Education.

Notes: Two-year default rates were used prior to the 2009 cohort for accountability purposes, while three-year rates were first used in 2009. Public two-year colleges include colleges offering credentials of less than two years in length. Data by institutional sector are unavailable prior to 1994.

affected by the shift to a three-year default rate, the number of defaults in each sector increased by about the same percentage. Additionally, the three-year CDRs at for-profit colleges fell from 22.7% for the 2009 cohort to 19.1% for the 2011 cohort, while default rates at community colleges rose from 18.3% to 20.5%. Three-year default rates further declined for the 2012 and 2013 cohorts, reaching 11.3% in 2013.

Only a small percentage of colleges have default rates high enough to trigger potential sanctions. In the 2013 cohort, 63 of the 4,759 colleges that participated in the federal student loan program had default rates at or above 30%. Just eight colleges had default rates over 30% in three consecutive years, which would potentially subject them to the loss of all Title IV aid (Office of Federal Student Aid, 2016a). Yet history suggests that most of these colleges will keep access to federal financial aid dollars upon appealing to the Department of Education for relief. A Congressional Research Service analysis of default data concluded that only 11 colleges have lost access to all Title IV aid dollars due to high CDRs between 1999 and 2015, even though several colleges each year have registered default rates high enough to lose access to federal financial aid dollars (U.S. Senate Committee on Health, Education, Labor, & Pensions, 2015). Some analysts have also questioned whether the Department of Education has the political will to sanction nonprofit or minority-serving institutions with high default rates. This position is supported by a 2014 change to the default rate calculation metric that removed certain defaulted borrowers with loans from multiple servicing agencies from the calculations, thus slightly lowering default rates (Field, 2014a). This change was announced two days before default rate data were released and may have contributed to all community colleges and minority-serving institutions passing this metric (Stratford, 2014a).

A substantial body of research has examined the extent to which institution-level and student-level factors are associated with cohort default rates. Much of this research concludes that colleges serving higher percentages of students from less-competitive high schools, first-generation and low-income students, and minority students are more likely to have higher default rates than colleges serving a higher percentage of affluent white students (Gross et al., 2009; Hillman, 2014; Jackson & Reynolds, 2013; Kelchen & Li, 2017), and similar trends exist when examining colleges with default rates over the threshold for triggering sanctions (Hillman, 2015).

The College Scorecard includes a new metric to examine former students' outcomes—a repayment rate that reflects whether students were able to pay down at least $1 in principal one, three, five, or seven years after entering repayment. This metric immediately gained attention as it showed that hundreds of colleges receiving federal financial aid dollars had less than half of students paying down any principal within seven years of entering repayment—a far higher number of institutions than the number facing sanctions over default rates. But even this number turned out to be incorrect, as the Department of Education quietly revealed on the last Friday of the Obama administration (Mahaffie, 2017). It turns out that the Department of Education's contractor made a coding error that resulted in repayment rates being overstated by between 10 and 20 percentage points, pushing repayment rates below 50% at the three-year and five-year marks (author's calculations using College Scorecard data). The number of colleges with seven-year repayment rates below 50% rose from 477 to 1,029 after the coding error was fixed, placing the federal student loan system under heightened scrutiny (Fuller, 2017).

In an article written with Amy Li at the University of Northern Colorado, I examined the extent to which CDRs and the revised loan repayment rates generated similar results. (The announcement of the coding error sent us scrambling to update the essay to meet a publication deadline, but thankfully the general pattern of results didn't change.) We found that for the same time period and cohort of students, default rates one year after entering repayment averaged 7% between 2006 and 2009 while the percentage of students unable to repay any principal averaged 44% during that period (Kelchen & Li, 2017). Additionally, attending a for-profit college was a much stronger predictor of not paying down any principal than it was of defaulting. This suggests that for-profit colleges are either encouraging students to enroll in income-driven repayment programs (generally a good outcome for students) or using default management tactics to push back defaults but increase loan balances (a bad outcome).

Colleges with high default rates have made strategic decisions about how to best respond to the threat of sanctions. Some colleges may find opting out of offering their students loans to be in the institution's best interest in order to preserve grant aid eligibility. Opting out is particularly common among community colleges, where a smaller percentage of students take out loans, and less-expensive for-profit colleges (Hillman & Jaquette, 2014). This is true even though colleges with low borrowing rates can qualify for a waiver of sanctions based on the number of defaulters and borrowers relative to total enrollment (Office of Federal Student Aid, n.d.-b). Nationally, approximately one million students attended community colleges that did not offer their students federal loans, representing nearly 10% of community college students. These colleges had higher percentages of minority students than colleges offering their students federal loans (Cochrane & Szabo-Kubitz, 2016). This practice is a particular concern because research by Wiederspan (2016) shows that Pell-eligible students who attend community colleges that participate in student loan programs have better academic outcomes than similar students at colleges that opted out.

Under current federal laws, colleges are unable to restrict what some financial aid professionals consider to be "overborrowing"—students taking out more loans than they deem necessary to pay for college. Colleges fear that without the ability to restrict borrowing below the current federal limits (up to $5,500 in student loans for first-year dependent students, with higher levels for independent and upper-division students), students will exhaust their lifetime federal loan limits before completing college and be more likely to default due to higher debt burdens. Both the professional association representing financial aid administrators and Senator Lamar Alexander (R-TN), the chairman of the U.S. Senate Health, Education, Labor, and Pensions Committee, have called for colleges to have some flexibility in reducing students' borrowing in individual cases (Alexander, 2015; Draeger, McCarthy, & McClean, 2013). This is in spite of empirical research suggesting that a significant percentage of students are unwilling to borrow for college, putting their ability to complete college in jeopardy (Cunningham & Santiago, 2008; Goldrick-Rab & Kelchen, 2015).

The only way colleges can limit the amount of money students can borrow is by reducing the total cost of attendance, which includes allowances for room and board, books, and miscellaneous expenses such as transportation, laundry supplies, and entertainment in addition to tuition and fees. Because students cannot receive a greater financial aid award than their cost of attendance, a lower cost of attendance reduces borrowing amounts. Colleges have discretion in determining all of these allowances, and research I have conducted with Sara Goldrick-Rab at Temple University and Braden Hosch at Stony Brook University showed large variations in estimated living expense allowances across colleges in the same county (Kelchen, Goldrick-Rab, & Hosch, 2017). This also means that net prices can vary in ways that may not reflect actual student expenses. I then dug deeper into whether colleges with default rates close to the threshold for facing sanctions reduced living allowances, and whether for-profit and nonprofit colleges responded in different ways. I did not find much evidence that colleges were trying to change their tuition prices or living allowances to reduce student borrowing (Kelchen, 2017a). More research is needed to examine how colleges respond to accountability pressures regarding cohort default rates.

FINANCIAL RESPONSIBILITY SCORES

The goal of financial responsibility scores as a federal accountability policy is to protect federal student financial aid dollars by ensuring colleges have sufficient financial resources to operate. This policy was first recommended by a 1989 investigation by the Office of the Inspector General that found that 53 colleges receiving Title IV funds closed for financial reasons in the late 1980s, leaving students and taxpayers on the hook; financial responsibility scores were implemented in the 1992 HEA reauthorization (DeLoughry,

1990b). Currently, all private nonprofit and for-profit colleges must submit audited financial statements each year and either pass a financial responsibility test or be subjected to additional oversight. Public colleges are exempt from this requirement, as the federal government assumes that state or local operating support guarantees financial responsibility. Colleges must also have sufficient cash on hand to service debt and meet other financial obligations in order for a financial responsibility score to be calculated (Office of Federal Student Aid, 2014).

Financial responsibility scores are calculated using three measures, which vary slightly between private nonprofit and for-profit colleges to reflect their different goals. The primary reserve ratio (40% of the score for private nonprofit colleges, 30% for for-profit colleges) reflects the amount of liquid assets a college can access if additional capital is needed. The equity ratio (40% of the score for both sectors) reflects a college's ability to borrow additional funds, and the net income ratio (20% of the score for private nonprofit colleges, 30% for for-profit colleges) represents a college's excess revenue or profitability (Office of Federal Student Aid, 2014).

Colleges can receive scores from –1 to 3, which are rounded to the nearest one-tenth of a point before being released. Colleges that score at or above 1.5 are considered financially responsible and face no additional sanctions. A score between 1.0 and 1.4 results in a college being placed under additional oversight from the Department of Education's Office of Federal Student Aid; if the score is not raised within three years, the college will not be considered to have passed the test. Finally, colleges scoring 0.9 or below are not considered financially responsible. These colleges must post a letter of credit equal to at least 10% of their Title IV funds and be subject to heightened cash monitoring oversight from the Office of Federal Student Aid in order to receive federal financial aid dollars (Office of Federal Student Aid, 2014).

Table 3.2 shows the distribution of financial responsibility scores by type of college since the 2006–07 academic year, the first year in which the Department of Education released the scores to the public in response to a Freedom of Information Act request from the *Chronicle of Higher Education* (Blumenstyk, 2009). The effect of the Great Recession on nonprofit colleges' financial responsibility scores is immediately evident, as the number of colleges with failing scores rose from 88 to 185 between the 2007–08 and 2008–09 academic years, while the number of colleges in the additional oversight zone rose from 63 to 116. By 2010–11, the number of nonprofit colleges facing sanctions declined back to prerecession levels. The for-profit

TABLE 3.2 Distribution of financial responsibility scores by institutional sector and year

Academic year	Private nonprofit			For-profit		
	Pass	Additional oversight	Fail	Pass	Additional oversight	Fail
2006–07	1,554	50	64	1,150	80	170
2007–08	1,517	63	88	1,135	101	166
2008–09	1,418	116	185	1,277	76	207
2009–10	1,495	94	123	1,423	62	146
2010–11	1,556	76	84	1,456	76	141
2011–12	1,500	66	80	1,454	79	122
2012–13	1,518	57	75	1,487	69	113
2013–14	1,533	50	73	1,489	84	126
2014–15	1,519	59	67	1,457	79	116
Ever in oversight zone		376			518	
Ever failed		328			617	
Number of colleges		1,832			2,117	

SOURCE: Office of Federal Student Aid, U.S. Department of Education.

Notes: Public colleges and universities do not receive financial responsibility scores. Private nonprofit and for-profit colleges do not receive scores if they do not meet basic financial stability criteria. Institutions based outside the 50 United States and Washington, DC, are excluded from the analyses. A small number of colleges appear in both the "ever in oversight zone" and "ever failed" categories.

sector did not see a dramatic rise in the number of colleges receiving low scores. In 2014–15, 116 for-profit colleges received failing scores, lower than the number in 2006 when there were 300 fewer colleges in the marketplace.

These financial responsibility scores have been challenged by a number of affected colleges and universities. The NAICU (2012), the professional association representing private nonprofit colleges, released a report claiming that the definitions used to calculate scores had not been updated in response to changes in Financial Accounting Standards Board guidelines and that errors were made in the calculation process. Colleges have also had difficulty appealing financial responsibility scores that they viewed as being inaccurate. For example, Bethel University in Minnesota received a financial responsibility score of 0.4 in fiscal year 2012, while the college claims its score should be 2.4—well above the score of 1.5 needed to fully pass the

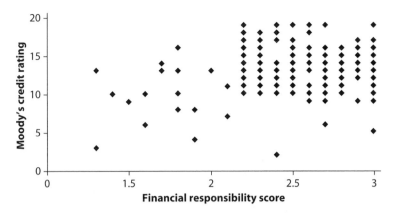

FIGURE 3.1. Moody's rating versus financial responsibility score, FY 2011. *Note*: Ratings in this figure go from Caa (0–most risk to bondholders) to Aaa (19–least risk), with all ratings of Ba1 (9) or below being considered subprime. *Sources*: Cooney, 2012; Office of Federal Student Aid, n.d.-a.

test (Blumenstyk, 2013). Bethel's auditors claimed that the Department of Education made four errors in calculating their score, but the score has yet to be revised (Friedrich, 2013).

Policymakers and the public have also raised concerns about the usefulness of this accountability metric. One reason is because a low financial responsibility score does not guarantee that a college will close, or vice versa. Of the ten private nonprofit colleges that closed in 2014 or 2015 and had financial responsibility scores, four of them had consistently received passing scores in the previous several years.[5] Another concern with the metric is that it is at best weakly correlated with private-sector measures of creditworthiness. In figure 3.1, I show the Moody's credit ratings and financial responsibility scores of the 270 private nonprofit colleges rated by Moody's in 2011. Although colleges with stronger financial profiles are more likely to seek external financing (and get a credit rating), the correlation of just 0.038 suggests a weak alignment of metrics.

After discovering no empirical research exploring how colleges respond to the accountability pressures placed upon them by financial responsibility scores, I began a project examining whether colleges changed their revenue or expenditure patterns in response to being subject to additional federal oversight. By comparing colleges with scores just above and below the cutoffs for sanctions, I did not find a meaningful pattern of responses in response to receiving a low financial responsibility score (Kelchen, 2016).

HEIGHTENED CASH MONITORING

Another way the Department of Education holds colleges accountable is through the use of heightened cash monitoring (HCM), which delays student aid disbursements to a college if it has accreditation, financial, program review, or administrative capacity concerns. Colleges facing the lower level of heightened cash monitoring, HCM-1, have to submit regular disbursement records to the Office of Federal Student Aid in order to receive funds instead of automatically getting the funds upon enrollment. Colleges facing the more severe HCM-2 requirements can only be reimbursed after the fact for any financial aid dollars the students received (Office of Federal Student Aid, 2014). The Department of Education also puts 21-day holds on disbursement on some colleges facing HCM; this delay in reimbursement is blamed for the 2014 collapse of Corinthian Colleges, formerly one of the largest chains of for-profit colleges, as Corinthian did not have enough cash to meet its obligations after the delay was enacted (Blumenstyk, 2014).

Although colleges have been subject to heightened cash monitoring requirements for decades, the list of colleges facing HCM was not made available to the public until a 2015 feature article in *Inside Higher Ed* highlighted the Department of Education's denial of a Freedom of Information Act request for the data (Stratford, 2015a).[6] The data, which were released less than a week later, showed that 474 colleges—primarily very small colleges with little name recognition beyond their local community—were subject to HCM-1 requirements and an additional 69 were subject to HCM-2 as of March 1, 2015. This list has been updated every three months since then, with a total of 745 U.S.-based institutions having been on the list at least once by September 1, 2016, and 139 of those having HCM-2 status at least once. Table 3.3 shows details of the 481 U.S.-based institutions subject to HCM as of September 1, 2016.

A majority of the colleges subject to HCM-1 and HCM-2 are for-profit, with proprietary institutions numbering 237 of the 414 colleges facing HCM-1 and 45 of the 67 colleges facing HCM-2. The most common reason colleges were placed under HCM-1 was for having a low financial responsibility score (293 of 414), which helps explain why so few public colleges are on the list. An additional 98 colleges were facing HCM due to a failure to submit financial information or audits. Most of the 67 colleges facing HCM-2 were listed as having administrative capacity issues, accreditation concerns, or problems with Department of Education program reviews.

To this point in the chapter, I have discussed three different high-stakes accountability policies (cohort default rates, financial responsibility scores,

TABLE 3.3   Institutions facing Heightened Cash Monitoring as of
September 1, 2016

Characteristic/reason	HCM-1	HCM-2	Total
Institutional sector			
Public	68	7	75
Private nonprofit	109	15	124
For-profit	237	45	282
Reason for facing HCM			
Financial responsibility score	293	5	298
Financial data late/missing	92	6	98
Administrative capacity	17	18	35
Accreditation	1	17	18
Program review findings	0	14	14
Other	11	7	18
Number of institutions	414	67	481

SOURCE: Office of Federal Student Aid, U.S. Department of Education.
   Notes: Institutions based outside the 50 United States and Washington, DC, are
excluded from the analyses. "Other" reasons include concerns over common ownership,
cohort default rates, audit concerns, and issues with a change in ownership.

and heightened cash monitoring) that affect most colleges receiving federal
financial aid. But do these three metrics show the same colleges performing
poorly across the board, or do they capture different elements of colleges'
performance? I explored this question in a data piece in the *Chronicle of
Higher Education*, focusing on the 1,150 private nonprofit and for-profit
colleges that faced heightened cash monitoring in early 2015, had a financial responsibility score in the oversight zone in the last three years, or had
a cohort default rate over 30% in the last three years. I found that only 26
institutions faced potential sanctions under all three metrics, suggesting that
the metrics do in fact capture different elements of colleges' performances
(Kelchen, 2015). This also highlights the fact that relatively few colleges have
truly awful performances across a wide range of metrics, which can create
challenges for implementing accountability systems designed to identify the
lowest-performing institutions.

THE 90/10 RULE

Due to concerns that for-profit colleges were making large profits for themselves from tuition revenue financed by federal Title IV dollars, Congress
included a provision limiting the percentage of total revenue that proprietary institutions could receive in the 1992 reauthorization of the HEA.
This provision limited for-profit colleges to getting 85% of their revenue

TABLE 3.4 Distribution of for-profit colleges' reliance on federal financial aid dollars by year

Year	Percentage of total revenue from Title IV funds (number of colleges)						Number of colleges
	0–70	70–75	75–80	80–85	85–90	90–100	
2007–08	1,041	167	205	229	188	1	1,831
2008–09	830	215	238	272	236	7	1,798
2009–10	706	206	297	373	292	10	1,884
2010–11	781	226	280	346	329	14	1,976
2011–12	730	214	272	351	404	28	1,999
2012–13	712	225	269	287	368	27	1,888
2013–14	765	220	271	286	332	14	1,888
2014–15	830	222	236	277	256	17	1,838

SOURCE: Office of Federal Student Aid, U.S. Department of Education.

Note: Institutions based outside the 50 United States and Washington, DC. Colleges with two consecutive ratios over 90% are subject to the loss of Title IV aid eligibility for the following two years.

from federal sources (veterans' benefits excluded) and first took effect in 1995 (Zook & Burd, 1994). Although a U.S. General Accounting Office (1997) report found that colleges getting higher percentages of their revenues from federal financial aid dollars had higher student loan default rates, Congress loosened the rule in the 1998 HEA reauthorization to allow for 90% of funds to come from federal sources (also known as the 90/10 rule) (Skinner, 2007). The penalty for violating the 90/10 rule in two consecutive years is the loss of Title IV aid eligibility for the following two years (Office of Federal Student Aid, 2014).

Table 3.4 shows a breakdown of the percentage of for-profit colleges' revenue coming from federal financial aid between the 2007–08 and 2013–14 academic years. In 2007–08, 1,041 of the 1,831 for-profit colleges (57%) accepting federal financial aid dollars got less than 70% of their total revenue from federal funds (excluding veterans' benefits), a percentage that fell to 37% just two years later and stayed near that level through 2012–13 before rising back to 45% in 2014–15. At the same time, the number of colleges receiving between 85% and 90% of their revenue from student financial aid dollars increased from 188 to 404 by the 2011–12 academic year before dipping to 256 in 2014–15. Although 39 colleges had between 89% and 90% of their revenue coming from Title IV aid in 2014–15, only 17 colleges violated the 90/10 rule. Yet only two of these colleges (with combined total revenue of under $1.5 million) were above 90% two consecutive years and lost Title IV eligibility (Office of Federal Student Aid, 2016b). This suggests that colleges are managing their revenue sources very carefully in order to stay below 90% of revenue coming from the federal government and losing aid eligibility.

I then examined the 11 largest for-profit colleges as of the 2013–14 academic year, all of which received over $600 million in Title IV revenue in a single year. Most of these colleges received between 70% and 85% of their revenue from federal financial aid, with DeVry University and the American Public University System being the only two colleges below 70% (Kelchen, 2017b). Notably, DeVry has voluntarily limited its federal funds (including veterans' benefits) for all of its affiliated institutions to 85% of total revenue (Smith, 2016).[7]

For-profit colleges can pursue several options in order to reduce their reliance on Title IV aid. Traditionally, employer subsidies have represented a substantial portion of revenue at some for-profit colleges, as employers have found it worthwhile to subsidize their employees' educational expenses as a job benefit. However, the percentage of all grant aid given out by employers has held steady over the last two decades even as for-profit enrollment has increased until recently (Baum et al., 2016). Veterans' benefits also represent an important revenue source for some for-profit colleges, with some institutions tailoring programs to current and former members of the military. The U.S. Department of Education released a dataset in the final weeks of the Obama administration that showed that about 200 colleges got at least 90% of their revenue from federal sources in the 2013–14 academic year, when veterans' benefits are included in the calculation (U.S. Department of Education, 2016). Of the 11 largest for-profits in 2013–14, five got at least 10% in total revenue from veterans' benefits (Kelchen, 2017b).

Another way for-profit colleges can guarantee that sufficient funds come from sources other than federal financial aid is to increase tuition. This may sound like a counterintuitive idea, but if tuition is high enough, many students cannot receive enough federal aid to pay tuition. For example, a first-year student who is unable to qualify for a PLUS loan due to having poor credit can receive a maximum of $9,500 in federal loans. If tuition is set at $19,000 per year, even receiving the maximum Pell Grant ($5,815 in 2016–17) would still result in a student paying more than 10% of total tuition from private loans or personal savings. Research has shown that for-profit colleges that receive federal Title IV aid have far higher tuition prices than colleges that do not participate in federal financial aid programs (Cellini & Goldin, 2014), and the former president of the now-defunct Corinthian Colleges chain even stated in a letter to the *Chronicle of Higher Education* that they raised tuition significantly in order to stay below the 90% threshold (Massimino, 2011).

GAINFUL EMPLOYMENT

The final high-stakes federal accountability policy is the Department of Education's newly enacted set of gainful employment regulations, which were designed to eliminate access to federal financial aid for vocationally oriented programs (defined as all programs at for-profit colleges and nondegree programs at public and private nonprofit colleges) with poor labor market outcomes. Prior to 2009, vocational programs were required to prepare students for gainful employment in their field of study, but the term was not defined and no sanctions were in place (Gonzalez, 2010). The U.S. Department of Education released a first set of gainful employment regulations in 2010 that required individual programs to meet one of two requirements over a period of several years in order to remain eligible for Title IV aid: either at least 35% of former students must have been current on their student loan obligations or graduates' average debt burdens must have been less than 12% of annual total income or 30% of annual discretionary income (any income over 150% of the federal poverty line) (Office of Postsecondary Education, 2010). These rules were challenged by the Association of Private Sector Colleges and Universities (APSCU), the largest association representing for-profit colleges, and a judge threw out the regulations in 2012 because the loan repayment metric was arbitrarily defined (Huckabee, 2012).[8]

The Department of Education began a second effort to promulgate gainful employment regulations in 2013, culminating with the release of a new set of regulations in late 2014 (Office of Postsecondary Education, 2014). APSCU (2014) sued to block implementation of the new version of the regulations, which they called "arbitrary and capricious." A federal court sided with the Department of Education in June 2015 (Thomason, 2015), which allowed the regulations to go into effect and the first data release to take place in January 2017.

A program designated as vocationally oriented passes the gainful employment metric if the estimated annual loan payment of program completers is less than 8% of total income or 20% of discretionary income. A program is placed in a warning zone if the debt-to-income ratio is between 8% and 12% or the debt-to-discretionary income ratio is between 20% and 30%, while colleges with both a debt-to-income ratio above 12% and debt-to-discretionary income ratio above 30% fail. A program will become ineligible for Title IV funds for three years if it fails the test in two out of three

TABLE 3.5   Distribution of 2017 gainful employment scores by sector and level

Sector	Pass	Zone	Fail	Total
Public, less than four-year	2,183	8	0	2,191
Public, four-year or more	301	1	0	302
Private nonprofit, less than four-year	194	46	6	246
Private nonprofit, four-year or more	147	19	10	176
Private for-profit, less than four-year	2,284	698	299	3,281
Private for-profit, four-year or more	1,159	466	488	2,113
Total	6,268	1,238	803	8,309

SOURCE: Office of Federal Student Aid, U.S. Department of Education.

Notes: Institutions based outside the 50 United States and Washington, DC, are excluded from the analyses. These scores are at the program level, not the institution level.

years or if it either fails or is in the warning zone for four consecutive years (Lederman, 2015).

Table 3.5 summarizes the outcomes of the initial gainful employment data release from January 2017. Overall, 6,268 of the 8,309 programs (75%) in the 50 states and Washington, DC, that were covered by the regulations passed, while 1,238 programs (15%) were in the warning zone and 803 programs (10%) failed. But there were large differences in passing rates by institutional sector. For example, none of the 2,493 certificate programs at public colleges failed gainful employment and just nine programs were in the warning zone. Few programs at private nonprofit colleges failed, with just 16 of 422 programs failing and an additional 65 programs ending up in the warning zone. A few prestigious colleges had programs fail gainful employment, including graduate certificate programs in the fine arts at Harvard, Johns Hopkins, and the University of Southern California. Harvard's theater certificate program suspended admission within two weeks of the scores becoming public, which will effectively end the program going forward (Gay, 2017).

Nearly all programs that failed the gainful employment metrics were private for-profit colleges, where only 64% of programs passed. The highest percentage of failures were in associate and bachelor's degree programs, while the failure rate among short-term undergraduate certificates (where students took on limited amounts of debt) was about 3%. Even before the initial data were released to the public, for-profit colleges began to react to the impending regulations by ending programs with a high likelihood of failure. Brookstone College of Business, a small for-profit college in North Carolina with its largest program likely ending up in the warning zone, announced its closure in 2015 and cited compliance costs resulting from gainful employment as a contributing factor (Dunn, 2015). The University of Phoenix is in the process of ending most of its associate degree programs, many of which would likely have run afoul of the gainful employment rules (Scott, 2015).

While consumer groups have hailed the gainful employment regulations as a first step toward improving the quality of vocationally oriented programs, the regulations have been criticized by different groups of stakeholders. One key limitation is that, by only focusing on the debt-to-income ratios of graduates, colleges with low completion rates may still be able to pass. Miller (2014) has shown that programs with more student loan defaults than graduates can pass the debt-to-income metrics even though they would fail a default rate-based metric. Additionally, the for-profit sector has contended that far more programs at nonprofit colleges, such as law schools and MBA programs, should be subject to gainful employment regulations (Office of Postsecondary Education, 2014). Leichter (2015) estimates that about 50 public and private nonprofit law schools would be likely to fail a gainful employment metric if they were subjected to it. Finally, a what-if analysis by Cooper and Delisle (2017) shows how part of the difference in pass rates between certificate programs at community colleges and for-profit colleges is due to the presence of state subsidies—a distinction that may not be relevant for students as they choose colleges, but could be important for policymakers considering the value of programs to society as a whole.

As of this writing, the future of gainful employment regulations remains murky. The regulations are currently scheduled to be phased in through the 2021–22 academic year, but the Department of Education under the Trump administration has shown an interest in revising or limiting gainful employment regulations. In early 2017, they announced a three-month delay in the further implementation of the regulations in order to study whether changes were desired (Office of Federal Student Aid, 2017). The Department of Education then used its statutory authority in June 2017 to reopen the negotiated rulemaking process in order to allow the regulations to be changed (Kreighbaum, 2017). But given the length of time negotiated rulemaking takes to complete, revisions to gainful employment regulations are unlikely to take effect until July 2019 at the earliest.

A Case Study: The Postsecondary Institution Ratings System

The federal government has a number of high-stakes accountability policies in higher education, but, as shown above, a relatively small number of colleges are truly at risk of losing any federal funds. This is a substantially different landscape than in K–12 education, where the passage of the No Child Left Behind Act in 2001 meant that a far higher percentage of schools potentially faced the loss of either institutional autonomy or federal funds if they failed to meet academic performance standards. For example, about one in four elementary schools failed to make adequate yearly progress in 2003 (Reback, Rockoff, & Schwartz, 2014)—the precursor to potentially losing Title I funds. Yet the efforts of President George W. Bush's education secretary, Margaret Spellings, in the mid-2000s to hold colleges accountable for their student learning outcomes (Secretary of Education's Commission on the Future of Higher Education, 2006) were quickly abandoned amid intense criticism from the higher education community.

The next ambitious effort to hold colleges accountable for their performance was through the Obama administration's effort to develop a federal college ratings system. The concept of the Postsecondary Institution Ratings System (PIRS) was first announced by President Obama in an August 2013 speech as an effort to improve the quality and reduce the price of higher education (Obama, 2013). Although the goal was to release draft ratings by fall 2015 and tie the ratings to at least some federal financial aid by 2018, the Department of Education announced in June 2015 the ratings portion of PIRS was being dropped and efforts being refocused on creating additional consumer information tools—which later became a substantially improved version of the College Scorecard (Fain, 2015). In this section, I draw upon my experience working with college rankings and involvement advising the Department of Education as they worked to develop PIRS to provide a postmortem of the failed ratings endeavor.

The goals of PIRS were quite simple: colleges would be rated on metrics of access, affordability, and student outcomes. Yet the Department of Education had to carefully consider the range of potential options for each metric, the quality of the underlying data, the relevance of each metric to students and the federal government, how to best compare colleges to one another, and the political ramifications of each of these decisions. The Department of Education hosted a series of public forums across the country, received written comments from hundreds of individuals and associations, and hosted a technical symposium in February 2014 where nearly two dozen experts (myself included) presented their ideas of what a college ratings system should look like. The technical symposium highlighted the difficulties in coming to a consensus on ratings, with the largest divide coming between those who wanted PIRS to focus on consumer information and those who wanted it to focus on institutional accountability (Field, 2014b).

While the NCES was working on the difficult task of developing a ratings system that would withstand a great deal of scrutiny, much of the higher education lobby was frantically working in public and in private to oppose the concept of PIRS. The leader of the opposition was the powerful American Council on Education (ACE), the main professional and lobbying association for public and private nonprofit colleges and an organization recognized by Department of Education insiders as extremely influential in the development of federal policies (Natow, 2015). A January 2014 letter from ACE emphasized its opposition to a federal rating system due to concerns about the appropriate role of the federal government and concerns about the accuracy of any ratings system that would be created (Broad, 2014). Additionally, a 2013 Gallup–*Inside Higher Ed* survey found that 65% of college presidents opposed tying ratings to aid, while just 16% supported the idea (Jaschik, 2013).

The Department of Education's initial goal was to have a draft set of college ratings released to the public in spring 2014, a timeline that was pushed back in May 2014 to the fall of that year (Nelson, 2014). While the timeline was delayed due to difficulties coming to a consensus regarding what PIRS should look like, a *New York Times* report (Shear, 2014) noted a speech by Deputy Undersecretary Jamienne Studley to college presidents in which she said rating colleges is like "rating a blender . . . this is not so hard to get your mind around." This public relations blunder only served to rally colleges against ratings, and they worked to lobby against the creation of ratings. David Warren, the president of NAICU, worked to rally his membership. "Tell your story to your member of Congress, why this is an ill-conceived notion . . . no congressman wants an ugly rating for an institution in his district" (Marcus, 2014). These efforts led to bipartisan legislation in Congress (which was never passed) to block the Department of Education from implementing ratings (Stratford, 2014b).

Instead of releasing a draft set of ratings in the fall of 2014, the Department of Education released a broad framework in late December in order to meet their deadline and receive additional public comments. The framework included a list of possible metrics and ways to group colleges, and also noted the potential development of a new website to house the ratings (U.S. Department of Education, 2014a). By not including a set of draft ratings, the Department of Education's goal of producing ratings by fall 2015 was put in doubt. The timeline was even further jeopardized in March 2015, when the Department of Education announced the creation of two ratings systems—one for consumer information and one for accountability (Field, 2015). At that point in time, the writing was on the wall to drop the high-stakes rating system and instead focus on consumer information; the official announcement three months later that the ratings were being removed from PIRS was more of a formality.

Although the higher education community had largely moved on from the ratings endeavor in the summer of 2015, the White House and Department of Education were still hard at work trying to create a new consumer information tool—which was released in the form of an updated College Scorecard in September 2015. Before releasing the revised College Scorecard to the public, they had given 11 organizations advanced access to the data through an application programming interface so these groups could develop their own consumer tools using the data that could launch simultaneously (Gelobter, 2015). The website quickly got 3.7 million page views in the first four days of its relaunch (*Washington Post* Editorial Board, 2015), nearly six times as many views as it had received in the prior year (Ciaramella, 2015).

The future of the College Scorecard remains uncertain at this point, as the system could take one of three divergent tracks. One possibility is that future versions of the Scorecard include earnings and student loan data for individual programs, as the federal government has already begun collecting the data (Kelly-Reid, 2016). Second, the dataset could be regularly updated as is, but without the addition of any new elements such as mentioned above. Finally, the delicate negotiations across different federal agencies required to create the dataset may not be a priority for the Trump administration, resulting in the dataset no longer being updated.

A key lesson learned from PIRS is that implementing high-stakes federal accountability policies in higher education is an extremely difficult endeavor and has probably become even more difficult after the federal role in K–12 education accountability was curtailed through the passage of the Every Student Succeeds Act to replace No Child Left Behind in 2015. Implementing gainful employment regulations, which primarily affect for-profit colleges, was extremely difficult for the Obama administration due to opposition from congressional Republicans as well as many Democrats who are members of the influential Congressional Black Caucus (Grasgreen, 2014).

The prospect of college ratings that affected all of higher education only upped the political stakes. Every congressional district had at least one degree-granting institution and the median district received $167 million in Title IV aid to undergraduate students in the 2011–12 academic year (Kelly, 2014). The sheer amount of money involved when all colleges face high-stakes accountability places a great amount of pressure on Congress to preserve the status quo. Even though no money is tied to the College Scorecard, many college leaders remain skeptical of the tool due to concerns about whether the outcomes included accurately reflect their institutions. A 2017 survey of college presidents found that 71% opposed maintaining the Scorecard going forward (Jaschik & Lederman, 2017).

Conclusion

Although high-stakes accountability policies will be difficult to implement, policymakers will continue to discuss new ways to hold colleges accountable for their outcomes as long as tuition prices continue to increase. A potential accountability option gaining traction among policymakers is the concept of risk sharing, or holding colleges financially accountable for a portion of students' defaulted loan dollars in order to encourage colleges to improve student outcomes. The idea has bipartisan support, although Republicans and Democrats disagree on whether many community colleges should be exempted from the proposal due to lower borrowing rates (Stratford, 2015b). One thing is for certain, however—once an accountability proposal is officially proposed, stakeholders will get involved in the policymaking process as much as possible in order to make sure the legislation reflects their best interests.

CHAPTER FOUR

State Accountability Policies

A s detailed in the previous chapter, the federal government's efforts to hold colleges accountable for their actions and performance have received a great deal of attention in recent decades. This attention is for good reason, as the federal government provided an estimated $75.6 billion in grant aid, contracts, and appropriations in 2013.[1] Yet states provided an additional $72.7 billion in higher education funding, including appropriations going directly to colleges and grant aid going to students (Pew Charitable Trusts, 2015). About seven in ten American college students attend public institutions (Ginder, Kelly-Reid, & Mann, 2015), and states have the ability to regulate private nonprofit and for-profit colleges, so state policymakers and agencies play a large role in the overall landscape of higher education accountability. And as the price of higher education has continued to rise while states face budgetary pressures, the relative autonomy that public colleges have enjoyed is often eroding (e.g., Zumeta, 2001). This has led to states increasing the range of actions they take to encourage colleges to increase affordability and improve completion rates. Unlike the federal accountability policies discussed in the previous chapter, state accountability policies place a portion of a college's funding at stake for a large percentage of public colleges and universities.

A feature of American federalism is that states have a significant amount of latitude to set their own policies and regulations in many areas, and higher education is no exception. States have taken many different paths regarding how they hold colleges accountable for their performance. Even though the diversity of state accountability policies is somewhat less than in 1990 (Cheslock & Hughes, 2011), the variety of strategies allows for the opportunity to examine whether certain policies seem to be more effective than others in encouraging colleges to become more efficient and improve their outcomes. In this chapter, I begin by overviewing the traditional ways that states have held public colleges accountable for their performance before I discuss newer methods that states are using to incentivize certain outcomes and whether these methods are obtaining their desired results. Finally, I will discuss how states regulate private and out-of-state colleges in addition to their typical role of overseeing public colleges.

Traditional Methods of Accountability

States have traditionally used three different methods to hold public colleges accountable for their performance, and these methods are still in use today. First, nearly all states can control how centralized the higher education governance structure is and how much autonomy individual colleges or systems have to determine their own policies. Second, the formal process of passing legislation and granting appropriations to public colleges provides policymakers with opportunities to influence colleges' actions. Finally, informal actions by state policymakers (such affect how colleges behave.

HIGHER EDUCATION GOVERNANCE STRUCTURES

Prior to the rapid expansion of public higher education early in the twentieth century, most public colleges had fairly decentralized systems of higher education. The general trend for most of the last century was to centralize governance at the system or state level, with the number of states with a statewide governing or coordinating board rising from 18 in 1940 to 46 in 1972 (McGuinness, 2016). This move toward centralization was an effort by states to have closer oversight over their colleges, but it also brought complaints from colleges whose autonomy was being reduced (e.g., Eisenhower, 1959; Moos & Rourke, 1959).

Colleges' pushback against centralized state governance became much stronger in the 1980s and 1990s, particularly as per-student higher education funding (in inflation-adjusted dollars) began to decline in many states (SHEEO [State Higher Education Executive Officers Association], 2016). Between 1991 and 2001, 20 states restructured their higher education governance structures in ways that generally allowed college to have more autonomy (McLendon, 2003a), although a few states (such as Montana and Louisiana) moved in the other direction (McLendon, Deaton, & Hearn, 2007). Below, I discuss two representative examples of states that have adopted decentralized governance structures that limit one way in which states can hold colleges accountable for their actions.

California, which was known for a centralized structure following the passage of the state's 1960 master plan, moved toward decentralization in the decades that followed. The California Postsecondary Education Commission was created to help resolve disputes and coordinate strategic planning among the California Community Colleges, the California State University system, and the University of California system. Yet the commission gradually lost its authority over the three systems in the following decades, with its only remaining function by the 2000s being its responsibility for collecting data about California higher education (Finney et al., 2014). The commission was disbanded in 2011 after the state's governor vetoed its funding, calling it "ineffective" (Murphy, 2011).

New Jersey has also moved from a centralized to a decentralized structure in recent decades. In the 1980s, New Jersey had a strong state board of higher education that made one of the first statewide efforts to assess student learning outcomes. Colleges lobbied the state legislature and governor for a less-powerful higher education commission, which they received in 1994 (McGuinness, 1995).[2] This commission was replaced with a secretary of higher education in 2011 (State of New Jersey, 2011) after a 2010 report written by the governor's higher education task force recommended further increasing autonomy and giving colleges full authority to control tuition and fees (New Jersey Higher Education Task Force, 2010).

As of 2015, 31 states had some kind of centralized agency with the ability to coordinate the entire state's higher education system. Twenty-one of these states, including Illinois, Maryland, Tennessee, and Texas, have coordinating boards that work across multiple institutions or systems and have oversight over the entire state. Ten states, including Montana and Kansas, have one statewide system for all of public higher education, meaning that one body can control all state-supported colleges and universities. Eighteen states, including California, Florida, and Wisconsin, have a mix of system-level and institutional governing boards with no state-level governing or coordinating agency, while Michigan is the only state where public colleges each have their own governing board (McGuinness, 2016).

Statewide governing and coordinating boards serve as important mediating agencies between colleges and their states, helping to reduce the effectiveness of colleges' lobbying efforts by placing an intermediary between colleges and legislators (Tandberg, 2013). These boards may also temper colleges' requests for additional appropriations (Knott & Payne, 2004; Ness & Tandberg, 2013) and funding for capital projects such as constructing new buildings (Ness & Tandberg, 2013; Tandberg & Ness, 2011).[3] Tandberg (2010a) showed that centralized governance was associated with less state higher education funding per $1,000 in personal income of state residents (a metric for the priority states place on higher education), while Tandberg (2010b) did not find a relationship between centralized governance structures and the share of state budgets going toward higher education. However, Lowry (2001b) concluded that more centralized structures were associated with higher levels of appropriations, potentially reflecting the value of colleges being able to present a united front to the legislature.

Centralized governance agencies can also hold individual colleges accountable to a state's overall goals instead of their own by encouraging colleges to cooperate with one another rather than compete by creating their own individual programs. For example, South Carolina has a clear system in place to identify and eliminate duplicative programs that have low enrollment (Morrison, 2010). Empirical research across public colleges has found that more centralized governance structures are associated with less program duplication within public colleges, resulting in the potential for cost savings for students and taxpayers alike (Calhoun & Kamerschen, 2010). This is echoed in findings by Lowry (2001a), who showed that per-student instructional expenditures declined as governing structures became more centralized.

A state's higher education governance structure may also affect the prices that students pay, which is a key goal of many states' accountability efforts. Centralized structures are generally associated with lower tuition and fee prices after controlling for other factors (e.g., Kim & Ko, 2015; Knott & Payne, 2004; Lowry, 2001a), although Doyle (2012) did not find a relationship between governance structures and either tuition or financial aid. In a recent study of factors affecting student fees at four-year public colleges, I found that giving a state-level board instead of the college the ability to set fees was associated with lower fee levels (Kelchen, 2016). This suggests that centralized governance structures can play a role in making college more affordable for students, although this could certainly result in a trade-off with quality.

STATE LEGISLATIVE AND EXECUTIVE ACTIONS

The second main way in which states can hold colleges accountable for their actions is through legislative and executive activities. In addition to determining higher education governance structures (as discussed in the previous section), states control the annual appropriations process and can also control the level of autonomy given to individual colleges in areas such as setting tuition and fee prices. Given the interdependency of tuition and appropriations (e.g., Koshal & Koshal, 2000), states' actions regarding higher education directly affect both colleges and students alike.

Some states limit the amount that an individual college or a system of higher education can increase tuition or fees in an effort to curb the rising price of college, even if a contributing factor to tuition increases in some states is appropriations that fall short of both enrollment and inflation growth. A survey of state higher education executive officers in the 2012–13 academic year found that 15 of 34 states responding had placed formal limits on how much tuition could increase over the last three years, while eight states had caps or curbs on fees (Carlson, 2013). Since the late 1990s, the number of states with tuition and/or fee caps has fluctuated somewhat, but there is no clear upward trend in the number of states implementing these restrictions (author's calculations using SHEEO surveys).

States attempt to limit tuition and/or fee increases with the explicit goal of improving college affordability and inducing colleges to become more efficient. For example, the Missouri legislature passed a law in 2007 that limited in-state tuition increases to the Consumer Price Index and penalized colleges that went above the cap without prior approval, with the bill's sponsor citing affordability and accountability as the reasons for the bill (Cook, 2007). Colleges did comply with the tuition cap, but they responded by increasing supplemental fees by 112% per full-time equivalent student between 2009 and 2015 (Office of Missouri State Auditor, 2016). This matches empirical research on the effectiveness of tuition and fee curbs and caps, which has generally found that these programs are ineffective in lowering prices or simply encourage colleges to increase tuition when fees are capped (Kelchen, 2016; Kim & Ko, 2015).

One challenge in examining the effectiveness of tuition and fee caps or curbs is that the maximum allowable increases vary considerably across states. In 2012–13, four of the 15 states with tuition caps froze tuition at last year's levels, while other states tied limits to inflation, state funding, or seemingly arbitrary numbers (Carlson, 2013). Michigan, for example, allowed colleges to raise tuition and fees by no more than a certain amount (ranging from 3.2% to 7.1% between 2011–12 and 2015–16) without losing state appropriations. During this time, three colleges chose to raise tuition far above the allowed amount, forgoing some appropriations. For example, in the 2015–16 academic year, Eastern Michigan University and Oakland University increased tuition and fees by 7.9% and 8.5%, respectively, gaining ten times as much in new tuition revenue as they lost in state funding (Bowerman, 2015).

Louisiana provides another interesting example of the relationship between state control of college prices and what students actually pay. The state's Granting Resources and Autonomies for Diplomas (GRAD) Act took effect in 2010 and resulted in a six-year performance agreement between Louisiana's board of regents and individual colleges in the state's higher education system. If colleges met all of the annual performance metrics, they were able to raise their tuition by up to 10% per year until they reached their peer group average (Louisiana Board of Regents, n.d.); this temporarily replaced a law that required a two-thirds majority of the legislature voting to raise tuition by any amount. This act expired at the end of 2016 and a statewide vote to allow colleges to raise tuition without getting state approval failed, meaning that legislators must again approve tuition increases (Allen, 2016).

Three states (Illinois, Oklahoma, and Texas) require public colleges to offer tuition guarantees, in which first-year students will pay the same price for each of the next four years as long as they maintain continuous enrollment. These programs are designed to make the price of higher education more predictable for students and their families, but they have not been effective in making college more affordable for state residents. Similar to the research mentioned above, the Illinois plan was associated with increases in student fees—which were not capped by the program (Delaney & Kearney, 2016). However, the plan was also associated with higher tuition levels as colleges hedged against uncertainty by setting very high guaranteed rates (Delaney & Kearney, 2015b) and lower appropriations as colleges had a predictable funding source from tuition (Delaney & Kearney, 2015a).[4]

Finally, a few states have moved toward tuition deregulation in recent years, which allows colleges to set their own prices for in-state students instead of systems or the state. An example of this is Texas, which delegated tuition setting to individual colleges' boards in 2003 with the caveat that 20% of funds raised had to go to financial aid. Texas colleges raised their prices faster than in other states and used differential tuition across majors as a revenue-generating strategy. However, since students in the higher-priced programs did receive additional need-based aid to help compensate for the higher price, lower-income students shifted toward these programs (Andrews & Stange, 2016; Kim & Stange, 2016). Flores and Shepherd (2014) also examined Texas's tuition deregulation and found an increase in Pell Grant recipients' enrollment after deregulation amid declining enrollments for Hispanic students relative to neighboring states.

The partisan makeup of a state's governor and legislature has repeatedly been shown to affect both the accountability frameworks that colleges face.[5]

First, when partisan control of the legislature or governor's office changes, changes to state governing boards or systems are far more likely than when the same party keeps control (McLendon, Deaton, & Hearn, 2007). Second, Republican-controlled legislatures are more likely to adopt policy changes than Democratic ones (McLendon, Heller, & Young, 2005). The balance of power at the state level has swung toward Republicans over the last several decades; Republicans controlled both chambers of the legislature in 30 states in 2016 compared to the Democratic Party's 12—with seven states split between the parties—while Republicans controlled just six states in 1990 compared to the 29 held by Democrats at that time (National Conference of State Legislatures, 2016). This factor has likely contributed to some of the changes in higher education accountability in recent years.

A sizable body of research has examined whether partisan political control affects state support for higher education, sometimes finding counterintuitive results. The common perception is that a Democratic legislature would yield an increase in higher education funding relative to a Republican legislature, and some studies indeed come to this conclusion (Dar & Lee, 2014; McLendon, Hearn, & Mokher, 2009; Tandberg, 2010a). However, other studies have found no significant relationship between partisan control and state funding (Knott & Payne, 2004; Tandberg & Ness, 2011), and others have determined that either additional Republicans in the legislature or a Republican governor is associated with more funding (Ness & Tandberg, 2013; Tandberg, 2010b; Weerts & Ronca, 2012). Finally, Li (2017a) shows that united Republican and united Democratic state governments were both twice as likely to make large cuts to higher education funding than divided governments. The inconsistent findings in the literature can likely be attributed to differences in the types of colleges and years of data included in the studies, as well as control variables used to help isolate the relationship between partisan control and funding effort.

Colleges work to actively shape the accountability landscape by lobbying legislators and their state's governor to adopt their preferred policy priorities (or at the very least, not adopt priorities that they strongly dislike). This is an area in which little research has been conducted, in part due to a lack of a centralized data source on lobbying efforts. Using data from 15 states with publicly available data on lobbying expenditures, Brackett (2016) found no relationship between a college's lobbying expenditures and state appropriations. A more effective way to increase state funding appears to be having more alumni in the legislature; Chatterji, Kim, and McDevitt (2016) show that a higher share of legislators who attended a public college was associated with additional state appropriations.

The final way in which state policymakers have traditionally imposed their preferences upon public colleges is through the use of informal signals. Instead of using legislation to shape colleges' actions, legislators and governors can promise rewards or sanctions if a college acts (or does not act) in a certain way. These informal methods of influencing colleges are difficult to track systemically but are important accountability mechanisms that are not always considered in empirical research.

An example of an informal signal is the role that many states play in how colleges set tuition prices. The 2012–13 survey of state higher education executive officers by Carlson (2013) found that although only a small number of states gave full legal authority to set tuition to the governor or legislature, politicians had an informal role in the tuition-setting process in about half of the 34 states that responded. Key legislators or the governor can threaten to cut a college's appropriations if they increase tuition more than a certain amount (similar to the formal mechanism in place in Michigan), or they can promise funding increases if a college freezes tuition. This gives state policymakers the ability to influence colleges' actions in ways that are difficult to systemically track.

The power of threats was recently exhibited in Pennsylvania, where new governor Tom Wolf was willing to increase state funding for the Pennsylvania State System of Higher Education (the state's four-year public colleges excluding Pennsylvania State University, the University of Pittsburgh, and Temple University) by $45.3 million or 11% for the 2015–16 academic year if the system's board agreed to freeze in-state tuition. Governor Wolf was successful in getting the board to pass a resolution guaranteeing the freeze, but the sharply divided board passed it by a slim 9–8 margin (Esack, 2015). However, the board eventually increased tuition by 3.5% for the 2015–16 academic year after Pennsylvania's governor and legislature were unable to reach a budget agreement by the start of the academic year (Palochko, 2015).

Newer Methods of Accountability

Enrollment at public colleges and universities continued to grow over the last several decades while state budgets were increasingly stressed by paying for K–12 education, health care, and the correctional system. This led states to focus more on the value of each dollar they gave to public colleges and universities, with nearly all states adopting one or more of three newer methods of holding colleges accountable for their performance. These three accountability systems (performance reporting systems that required colleges to provide information on their outcomes, performance budgeting systems that allowed states to consider outcomes when allocating resources, and performance funding systems that directly tied funding to outcomes) are all outgrowths of the new public management wave of the 1980s and 1990s that sought to increase transparency and tie funding to results (e.g., Moynihan, 2006).[6] However, it is not always clear that these efforts have been successful in improving either the efficiency of the higher education system or student outcomes.

A PRIMER ON STATE HIGHER EDUCATION FUNDING

Before I discuss the three types of accountability, it is important to explain how state higher education budgets are typically put together and how they could affect the stakeholders to whom a college is accountable. States that wish to make higher education more affordable for their students must first decide whether to give funds directly to students through grant aid programs or to colleges through general or capital appropriations. As discussed in the previous chapter, the federal government allocates the majority of its support for higher education directly to students through programs such as the Pell Grant. States, conversely, have traditionally directed most of their funds to colleges through the form of appropriations. In 2015, the median state awarded about 9% of its total higher education funds directly to students in the form of grant aid. This percentage varied from 40% in South Carolina to none in New Hampshire (National Association of State Student Grant and Aid Programs, 2015).

If a state wishes to give grant aid directly to students, it must then decide whether to allocate grant aid based on financial need, academic merit, or a combination of the two. Merit aid programs, which are the dominant form of financial aid in many southern states, were initially created to help keep high-achieving students in state for college amid concerns about "brain drain" (e.g., Heller, 2002). These programs have generally been effective in keeping more students in state (Toutkoushian & Hillman, 2012; Zhang & Ness, 2010), although there is no evidence that merit aid has increased states' overall educational attainment levels (Sjoquist & Winters, 2015).[7] Need-based aid programs are designed to make education more affordable for families from modest financial backgrounds, and some research suggests that need-based aid is more effective than appropriations in raising educational attainment (Toutkoushian & Shafiq, 2010).

While most states primarily fund higher education by giving money directly to colleges in the form of appropriations, Colorado took a different approach to funding undergraduate education for in-state students when it moved to a voucher-based model in 2004 with the creation of the Colorado Opportunity Fund. All qualified in-state students received a fixed amount of money per credit hour ($80 in 2004 and $75 in 2016), which was then applied as a discount to their tuition (College Opportunity Fund, n.d.; Western Interstate Commission for Higher Education, 2009).[8] The effects of the voucher program appear to be mixed, as minority student enrollment fell after the program began relative to other states while community colleges were induced to operate more efficiently (Hillman, Tandberg, & Gross, 2014a).

The other 49 states that provide traditional appropriations for undergraduate education fall into four groups based on their appropriations (high and low) and grant aid (high and low) strategies. Toutkoushian and Shafiq (2010) examined states using 2005–06 funding strategies and determined that the majority of states fell into a high-appropriations, low-aid category, with most funding going directly to colleges instead of to students. Figure 4.1 below shows data from the 2013–14 academic year on state appropriations per full-time equivalent student (SHEEO, 2015) and state grant aid per full-time equivalent (FTE) undergraduate student (National Association of State Student Grant and Aid Programs, 2015).

The dark horizontal and vertical lines in the middle of the figure reflect average levels of per-FTE state appropriations ($7,049) and grant aid ($589),

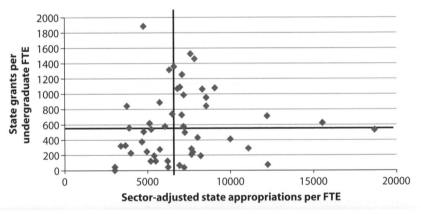

FIGURE 4.1. States' grant aid and appropriation strategies, 2013–2014. *Note*: The horizontal and vertical lines reflect the typical state's per-FTE spending on appropriations and student financial aid. *Sources*: National Association of State Student Grant and Aid Programs, 2015; State Higher Education Executive Officers Association, 2015.

and a number of states are closely clustered around the intersection of these lines. Oklahoma, with per-FTE appropriations of $7,172 and grant aid of $576, is the most average state in this regard. Eight states are clearly in the top right quadrant for having high levels of both appropriations and aid, including Arkansas, Illinois, New Mexico, and New York. Seven states, such as Pennsylvania and South Carolina, are in the top left quadrant, reflecting low appropriations but high grant aid. Eight states, including Connecticut, Hawaii, and North Dakota, are clearly in the bottom right quadrant for having high levels of appropriations but little grant aid. Finally, the largest quadrant is the bottom left—reflecting states such as Arizona, New Hampshire, and Michigan that offer relatively little grant aid alongside low appropriations.

State political and governance factors affect how colleges receive state funding. Lowry (2016) found that states with more professional legislatures or coordinating boards spend more on need-based aid relative to appropriations than states with decentralized structures, potentially representing a willingness of centralized organizations to delegate power to students instead of to individual colleges. McLendon, Tandberg, and Hillman (2014) showed a link between a Republican legislature and governor and lower appropriations and slightly higher need-based aid, and they did not find evidence that grant aid and appropriations crowd each other out. They concluded that increases in merit-based aid tended to crowd out need-based aid (and vice versa), but Doyle (2010) did not find a significant relationship.

Since the 1950s, states have generally appropriated funds to colleges using some kind of formula (Moss & Gaither, 1976). These funding formulas have typically been based on a combination of student enrollment, mission, and historical allocations as well as comparisons to similar states or colleges in other states (Layzell & Lyddon, 1990; McKeown, 1993; McKeown, 1996). Once these formulas are implemented, states often provide across-the-board percentage increases or decreases in following years. This means large funding inequities across similar institutions can develop due to changes in enrollment or the types of students served. An example of this is in Wisconsin, where the state provided its research university at Madison with $12,140 per FTE and its other research university at Milwaukee with just $5,157 per FTE (Goldrick-Rab & Kolbe, 2015). This funding mechanism also does not explicitly reward performance, providing little leverage for states to incentivize colleges to change their actions. For these reasons, the number of states using a funding formula fell from 25 states in the 1970s (Moss & Gaither, 1976) to 17 in 2012 (SRI International, 2012) as states have moved to implement higher-stakes accountability systems tied to outcomes.

PERFORMANCE REPORTING

The origins of performance reporting date back to state open records laws that gained popularity between the 1950s and the 1970s, with all states adopting some variation of the law by 1976 after the Watergate scandal (Braman & Cleveland, 1984; McLendon & Hearn, 2006a). These laws were designed to make the vast majority of meetings (except when sensitive personnel issues were being discussed) open to the public and to make previously collected information about public organizations' performance available upon request. A small number of public universities, such as Pennsylvania State University and the University of Delaware, are considered partially or fully exempt under state open records laws (Belson, 2011; Fisher, 2016), but most public institutions must comply with requests from the public under the law.

A common usage of state open records laws is by newspapers, which compile and publish the salaries of public college employees with a focus on institutional leaders and athletic coaches. Colleges raise concerns about these salary databases, noting that it can make it easy for other colleges to recruit away faculty or administrators with more lucrative contracts (University of Wisconsin–Madison, 2008). Institutional leaders are also concerned that making all details public can jeopardize searches for college presidents and subject colleges to time-consuming requests from a disgruntled member of the public (McLendon & Hearn, 2006b). Many flagship public colleges rely heavily on foundations for fundraising support and to supplement certain employees' compensation, as these foundations are technically separate from the institution and thus are not always subject to the same open records laws (Capeloto, 2015).

More formal performance reporting systems require colleges to publish detailed information about their outcomes and finances without tying any state funds to the results. This is a step beyond open records laws, which limit information to what an institution has already created. This method of accountability began in the early 1990s (Ruppert, 1995) and gained popularity in the late 1990s and 2000s as a way to make colleges more transparent without states having to provide any additional funds. Between 2000 and 2003, the number of states with performance reporting systems jumped from 30 to 46 (Burke & Minassians, 2003) as these were often viewed as a "no-cost" accountability system (Burke & Minassians, 2002, 1).

Although performance reporting systems have been overshadowed by higher-stakes accountability systems in the last decade, a number of states require their colleges to post performance metrics on their websites. An example of this is in Wisconsin, where the state's governor required the University of Wisconsin system in 1993 to form a task force to create an accountability report—one of the first such efforts in the nation (Boatright, 1995). The system is now required under legislation passed in 2011 to report a specified set of performance metrics in areas such as access, economic development, and faculty retention to the legislature each year in a single document (University of Wisconsin System, 2014).

Another form of performance reporting is through the use of state-level student unit record datasets, which contain information on students attending public colleges in 47 states, with only Delaware, Iowa, and Michigan not having unit record datasets for at least some of their colleges and universities. Twenty-six states have datasets that cover a student's entire trajectory from preschool through the labor market, including higher education (Armstrong & Whitfield, 2016), spurred on by federal funding to help create these new data systems (National Center for Education Statistics, n.d.).[9] Some states, such as Virginia, have created public-facing dashboards that allow the public to quickly access institutional-level data on outcomes such as graduation rates, student debt, and wages of graduates that are far more detailed than are available from federal sources (State Council of Higher Education for Virginia, n.d.). However, there is no existing research examining whether policymakers or students use state-level dashboards when making decisions or whether these dashboards improve institutional performance.

PERFORMANCE BUDGETING

The second modern form of state higher education accountability is performance budgeting, in which states can consider a college's outcomes in determining appropriations to individual institutions but are not required to actually tie funding to these outcomes. Performance budgeting reached its heyday in 2000, when 28 states reported having this type of accountability system. By 2003, the number of states with performance budgeting had fallen to 21 (Burke & Minassians, 2003) as states began tying funds to outcomes rather than using the performance information on an informal basis. Early research on the effectiveness of accountability systems (e.g., Payne & Roberts, 2010; Shin & Milton, 2004) combined performance budgeting and funding systems, making it difficult to identify the effectiveness of performance budgeting. In any case, performance budgeting is rarely discussed today as performance funding has become the most common accountability system.

PERFORMANCE FUNDING

The third form of accountability is performance funding, in which states directly tie at least a portion of a college's appropriations to outcomes. The rationale behind this system is both straightforward and intuitive—instead of states relying heavily on enrollment-based formulas or historical allocations, colleges can get additional funds if they improve their students' outcomes. The inherent assumption present is that colleges are operating inefficiently, and that placing colleges under additional accountability pressures will induce them to improve student outcomes. However, in the nearly four-decade history of performance funding, the positive effects have been relatively modest and have been accompanied by some unintended consequences. This suggests that either colleges are already operating efficiently or that the amount of funds at stake is insufficient to change institutional priorities.

States adopted performance funding systems in three distinct waves, with a number of states later abandoning plans and sometimes implementing performance funding again in following years. Figure 4.2 shows the number of states with performance funding systems in place for each year between 1990 and 2015, based on published work by Burke and Minassians (2003), Dougherty and Natow (2015), and the National Conference of State Legislatures (2015) as well as checks of states' websites to confirm whether performance funding systems were in place when discrepancies arose across data sources.[10]

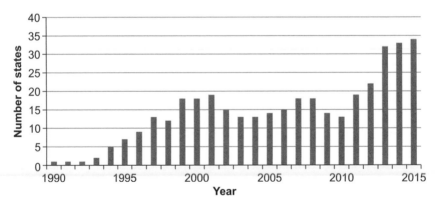

FIGURE 4.2. Number of states with performance-based funding by year. *Sources:* Burke & Minassians, 2003; Dougherty & Natow, 2015; National Conference of State Legislatures, 2015; author's research.

Tennessee was the first state to adopt performance funding in 1979, using five equally weighted metrics (program accreditation, graduates' performance on general education, performance on major field tests, stakeholders' evaluations of colleges, and peer evaluations of academic programs) to distribute up to 2% in additional funds to colleges (Banta et al., 1996). By 1993, funding was up to a potential bonus of 5.45% and covered ten fields, including persistence and completion for the first time. Beginning in 1993, other states began adopting performance funding systems, growing from five states in 1995 to ten states in 1997 and 19 states in 2001 (Burke & Minassians, 2003).

The first wave of performance funding systems often looked much like Tennessee's system, with a small amount of bonus funds tied to meeting an often-sizable number of performance metrics. These systems were implemented with the support of state higher education agencies, Republican legislators, and business leaders (Dougherty et al., 2014). McLendon, Hearn, and Deaton (2006) looked at the factors affecting the spread of the first wave of performance funding and found that additional Republican legislators and the lack of a consolidated governing board were associated with a higher likelihood of adopting performance funding.

Although Tennessee has maintained performance funding in some form since 1979, other states decided to drop their early performance funding systems. Eleven states abandoned their systems between 1996 and 2003, with three main reasons often cited (Dougherty, Natow, & Vega, 2012). First, because these funds were add-ons instead of in the base budget, some states abandoned their systems because of tight budgets following the early 2000s recession. Second, political support from policymakers eventually waned and colleges were often in opposition to these plans. Third, some of the systems were overly complicated. An example of this is South Carolina, which developed a system with 37 indicators in 1996, with the goal of tying all state funding to these outcomes by 1999–2000. The highest percentage of funding ever tied to performance was 38% in 1999, which was then cut to 3% through 2001–02 and then abandoned (Dougherty & Natow, 2015).

The decline of performance funding in the late 1990s and early 2000s led some to see the newest accountability system as a passing trend. For example, Schmidtlein (1999, 172) said the following about performance funding: "Like other fads that have afflicted higher education it seems likely to end up in the 'trash heap' of history." Although his words appeared prescient for a while (particularly as the number of states with performance funding fell to 13 by 2003), a second and smaller wave of performance funding systems began operating in 2006 and 2007. By 2008 (just before the Great Recession), 18 states had these systems. The new systems created in the 2000s had a smaller number of metrics than in the first wave, while the institution-specific nature of the systems better reflected differences in colleges' missions and goals (Dougherty & Natow, 2015). Yet this second wave was quite small, as the Great Recession forced states to retrench their budgets. By 2010, the number of states with performance funding was back down to 13—the same level as in 2004.

In 2011, a third wave of performance funding systems began to be implemented across the country (Jones, 2013). Unlike the first two waves, the newest systems tie a larger percentage of funding to performance metrics and use base funds instead of bonus funds. At least 34 states had adopted performance funding for at least some sectors of public higher education by 2015, with ten new states adopting this accountability system in 2013 alone.

This wave of performance funding adoptions is being actively promoted by governors, as was the case for the first two waves (Dougherty & Natow, 2015). But a new player in the third wave is the foundation world, with the influential Gates and Lumina Foundations and advocacy/consulting organizations such as HCM Strategists working to spread performance funding to more states (Dougherty et al., 2014).[11] Both the Gates and Lumina Foundations have portions on their websites advocating for what they call "outcomes-based funding" and emphasizing the benefits of allocating funds in this manner (Bill and Melinda Gates Foundation, 2015; Lumina Foundation, n.d.).

HCM Strategists, which has received funding from both Gates and Lumina, has produced a series of reports entitled "Driving Better Outcomes," in which they classify outcomes-based funding systems into four groups based on how much money is tied to outcomes, whether it is base funding, and whether different goals are set for different colleges. To be in the most advanced type (Type IV), 25% of funds statewide must be tied to outcomes for at least two consecutive years. Only Ohio and Tennessee met this definition as of January 2016 (Snyder & Fox, 2016). But in addition to these helpful additions to the body of knowledge on performance funding, they have also questioned empirical research disputing the effectiveness of performance funding through the use of op-eds titled "Don't Dismiss Performance Funding" (Shulock & Snyder, 2013) and "Jumping to Conclusions" (Snyder, 2016).

The theory of action behind performance funding systems is that the financial incentives will encourage colleges to focus more on practices and policies that will help more students complete college. A growing body of evidence suggests that colleges are changing to desired behaviors in response to performance funding systems. Several studies have found that performance funding systems have positively affected the ways that colleges budget, advise students, analyze data, and do strategic planning, factors that should be related to improved student success or increased efficiency (Dougherty et al., 2016b; Dougherty & Reddy, 2011; Li & Zumeta, 2016; Rabovsky, 2012). In some states, the message of how colleges respond to performance funding is reaching individual faculty (Zumeta & Li, 2016), although faculty resistance in some states is strong due to concerns about a loss of autonomy and disagreement with state priorities (Dougherty et al., 2016a).

Although performance funding is changing colleges' actions in some states, these systems are having limited effects on student outcomes at this point. The earliest quantitative work examining the effectiveness of performance funding systems typically used graduation rates at four-year colleges as outcomes. Studies using both single-state and national datasets generally showed a null or small negative relationship between performance funding and graduation rates (Fryar, 2011; Rabovsky, 2012; Rutherford & Rabovsky, 2014; Sanford & Hunter, 2011; Shin, 2010), although Rutherford and Rabovsky's (2014) results suggest that the new wave of performance funding programs may slightly improve graduation rates.

The newest wave of studies on performance funding have used the number of credentials awarded as the outcome of interest to reflect state policymakers' goals of increasing the number of graduates and to guard against colleges admitting fewer students in an effort to boost graduation rates. State-level and nationwide studies again generally find null effects on degree production in both the two-year and four-year sectors (Hillman, Tandberg, & Gross, 2014b; Li, 2016; Rabovsky, 2012; Tandberg & Hillman, 2014; Tandberg, Hillman, & Barakat, 2014). However, Tandberg and Hillman (2014) did find some small positive effects of performance funding after programs had been in effect for seven or more years, suggesting that colleges may need a long time to respond to the system's incentives.

An important concern regarding performance funding is the presence of unintended consequences. Several studies have uncovered evidence that colleges may be trying to meet the performance funding system's goals by attempting to game the system rather than changing their day-to-day operations. Hillman, Tandberg, and Fryar (2015) examined Washington state's high-stakes performance funding system for community colleges and discovered a jump in the number of short-term certificates relative to long-term certificates and a decrease in the number of long-term certificates. As colleges received credit for any certificate awarded, shifting students to shorter-term certificates that tend not to be as valuable in the labor market was a rational choice for colleges.

Two studies that interviewed public college administrators and leaders provide insights into how some colleges are becoming more selective in response to performance funding systems. Dougherty et al. (2016a) interviewed public college officials in Indiana, Ohio, and Tennessee—three states with performance funding systems that give bonuses for serving high-risk students and are widely considered to be models for the rest of the country—while Minckler (2016) interviewed higher education leaders in Ohio. Both studies found that colleges were changing their admissions policies and standards as well as financial aid practices in an effort to become selective, even as the performance funding systems were explicitly designed to guard against that happening. These studies are reinforced by new empirical work on Indiana public colleges showing that Indiana's model performance funding program resulted in an increase in selectivity without increasing the number of bachelor's degrees awarded relative to other states (Umbricht, Fernandez, & Ortagus, 2017).

Finally, I teamed up with my Seton Hall colleague Luke Stedrak to examine whether two-year and four-year public colleges subject to performance funding policies change their revenue or expenditure patterns relative to colleges not facing performance funding. We did not see any evidence that colleges reallocated funds toward instruction, student services, or other areas that could be directly associated with student success. Rather, we found that both two-year and four-year colleges subject to performance funding received less Pell revenue per student, which is a likely indicator that colleges are recruiting and enrolling fewer low-income students if they are subject to meeting performance metrics (Kelchen & Stedrak, 2016). This hypothesis is supported by our finding that four-year colleges increased unfunded grant aid in a likely effort to recruit higher-achieving students.

Given the body of evidence suggesting that some colleges are trying to game the performance funding metrics, it is surprising that the observed effects of performance funding on degree completions are not larger. It is worth noting, however, the amount of funds currently at stake in most systems is still fairly small. Only 11 states currently tie at least 10% of all state appropriations to performance metrics,[12] but it is too early to fully evaluate the effectiveness of these systems on the number of degrees awarded due to the number of years between when colleges begin to recruit students and when they actually graduate. Other states, such as Illinois and New York, technically have performance funding systems but tie less than 1% of total appropriations to outcomes (National Conference of State Legislatures, 2015). This is likely insufficient to change behaviors. Research on Michigan's low-stakes system, which is in part based on restraining tuition increases, suggests that administrators did not change their actions in response to the implementation of performance funding (Opoczynski, 2016).

Eighteen states currently give additional financial bonuses to public colleges that successfully serve at-risk students in an effort to encourage social mobility while discouraging efforts to meet performance goals by becoming more selective (National Conference of State Legislatures, 2015; state higher education websites). Yet these bonuses may not be well publicized or sufficient to cover the additional cost of educating students who require services such as remediation. Texas, for example, provides bonuses for completing developmental coursework in addition to completion bonuses to help reduce incentives to become more selective in admitting or enrolling students. But these bonuses are relatively modest ($185 for each student who completed the developmental math sequence and half that for each student who completed writing or reading in the 2014–15 academic year), and colleges that enroll larger percentages of white and higher-income students receive larger performance bonuses (McKinney & Hagedorn, 2017). Indiana tied 0.9% of total state appropriations (or 15% of funds tied to performance-based funding) in fiscal year 2015 to at-risk completion measures, including $1,500 for a certificate, $3,000 for an associate degree, and $6,000 for a bachelor's degree. While not trivial, these bonuses are far smaller than the $23,000 bonus for completing a bachelor's degree in four years or a $20,000 bonus for a bachelor's degree in a field considered "high-impact" (Indiana Commission for Higher Education, n.d.).

To follow up my previous study of performance-based funding policies, I examined whether PBF policies with bonuses for serving at-risk or underserved students were effective in increasing the number of low-income, Pell recipient, underrepresented minority, or adult students enrolled. In general, PBF policies as a whole did not increase at-risk student enrollment, but I found some evidence that policies that have underrepresented student bonuses may increase low-income and adult student enrollment relative to PBF policies without these bonuses (Kelchen, 2017). Essentially, PBF policies without at-risk components may reduce at-risk student enrollment levels, while adding at-risk components help to mitigate somewhat colleges' incentives to serve students with a higher probability of completion.

College leaders also appear to be skeptical of the idea of performance funding, or at least that performance funding will be implemented fairly or truly reflect their performance. A common concern is that performance funding will be used for political reasons, or even potentially to reduce or end funding for public higher education (Dougherty & Natow, 2015; Rabovsky, 2014). There are also philosophical objections among some college leaders to the idea that colleges should be funded based on outcome measures viewed as simplistic (e.g., Li, 2017b). Finally, colleges' capacity to make the changes needed to meet performance goals may be limited; this is a particular concern for colleges serving large numbers of low-income and minority students that may not have the capacity to develop new data systems or improve student services (Dougherty & Natow, 2015; Hillman, 2016; Jones, 2014).

STATE ACCOUNTABILITY FOR PRIVATE COLLEGES

States focus most of their accountability efforts on the public colleges that they financially support, but they also play an important role in regulating other colleges that serve their residents. All states authorize private non-profit and for-profit colleges to operate in their states, as well as out-of-state public and private colleges that wish to enroll students via distance education. These setups differ quite a bit across states. For example, some states have separate boards for out-of-state public colleges and for-profit colleges that have a physical presence in the state (SHEEO, n.d.).

In order for a private or out-of-state college to operate in a state, the college must show that it can meet minimum quality standards. This typically includes measures of faculty qualifications (often via providing copies of curriculum vitae), acceptable student/faculty ratios, and proof that facilities necessary for the programs of study are adequate. Finally, colleges must typically provide information about their consumer protection standards to make sure students have recourse against any fraudulent actions (Kelly, James, & Columbus, 2015). Most states then require colleges to renew their authorization to operate every year or two as an additional quality control measure, although about one-third of state authorization agencies do not require colleges to report outcome data on a regular basis (Columbus, 2016).

States have historically been rather aggressive in regulating colleges from other states that wish to come into their state, placing far more requirements on out-of-state colleges than colleges located in their own state that wish to operate in other states (Lane, Kinser, & Knox, 2013). Additionally, the typical amount of time to approve a new institution was about six months, with five states telling colleges to expect at least one year for approval (Kelly et al., 2015). But states are generally less aggressive in setting clear outcomes requirements for colleges. Florida is the only state that sets an explicit performance threshold, requiring colleges to have retention rates over 50% and job placement rates over 60% (Columbus, 2016).

This approval process was initially designed for colleges that wished to open a physical campus in a given state, not colleges with online programs that enrolled students from across the country. The U.S. Department of Education had proposed rules in 2010 that would require colleges to get approval from all states in which they enroll students in order for those students to receive federal financial aid. Although a federal court threw out these rules and they were never enforced (Poulin & Boeke, n.d.), a new group was formed to help streamline standards for operating across state lines.

The National Council for State Authorization Reciprocity Agreements (NC-SARA) began operating in 2014 with support from the Lumina Foundation to set consistent standards for offering distance education across state lines. Colleges only need approval from their home state, simplifying the approval process. As of June 2016, 40 of the 47 eligible states are NC-SARA members, meaning that they only need approval from their home state to operate in other participating states (NC-SARA, 2016).[13]

State attorneys general also play an important role in holding private colleges (particularly for-profit colleges) accountable for their performance via consumer protection laws. In recent years, attorneys general (particularly those affiliated with the Democratic Party) have been active in trying to shut down for-profits they view as having misled students. Between 2004 and 2014, the National Consumer Law Center (2014) documented 45 cases in which attorneys general had sued for-profit colleges over a range of issues. All of these lawsuits were either successful or still pending. Twelve Democratic state attorneys general also jointly wrote a letter to the U.S. Department of Education in 2016 urging the federal National Advisory Committee on Institutional Quality and Integrity (NACIQI) to deny the Accrediting Council for Independent Colleges and Schools (ACICS) recognition for federal financial aid purposes (Waldman, 2016)—an effort that helped encourage NACIQI to deny ACICS recognition.[14]

Highlighting the interconnected nature of state and federal accountability policies, a key component of the U.S. Department of Education's proposed "borrower defense to repayment" regulations is that any college that faces a sizable lawsuit from a state attorney general's office would be required to file a letter of credit with the federal government before being eligible to continue receiving federal financial aid dollars (U.S. Department of Education, 2016). States that become more aggressive in suing colleges over concerns of fraud or misrepresentation could therefore trigger federal sanctions, showing that colleges must consider how actions by one of the agencies holding them accountable may end up affecting how another agency responds.

Conclusion

State governments typically provide the most consistent and salient accountability pressures for public colleges, and also play an important oversight role over private colleges (particularly in the for-profit sector) in a number of states. Yet states' roles in holding colleges accountable have typically been overshadowed in national public policy discussions by other stakeholders such as the federal government and accreditors. This is beginning to change, as national advocacy organizations are paying more attention to how states are overseeing their colleges and universities—in part due to a federal higher education accountability system that has been fairly stable in recent years.

Yet relatively little is known about the effectiveness of various state accountability policies and practices in improving institutional outcomes. The growth of detailed student-level data systems in states such as Florida, Texas, and Virginia makes it possible to examine in more detail whether changes in state-level governance practices or funding structures affect targeted groups of students. Although the highest-profile state accountability system (performance funding) has shown very modest effects on the number of students who complete college, the wide variation in how states structure their higher education oversight and funding systems creates a multitude of opportunities for researchers and policymakers to discover which policies work and which ones do not. The results coming out of the laboratories of democracy are then likely to influence other parts of the accountability landscape.

CHAPTER FIVE

Accreditation and Accountability

UNLIKE THE TWO TYPES of accountability discussed in the preceding chapters (federal and state), the accreditation system in American higher education does not have its origins with a governmental body that sought to implement its public policy priorities. Rather, accreditation began in the late nineteenth and early twentieth centuries as a series of voluntary associations in which teams from peer institutions would visit a college to see if it met minimum quality standards; this was of particular importance during an era in which the academic preparation of incoming students and colleges' available resources varied dramatically. Accreditation prior to World War II generally remained optional for colleges, although receiving accreditation increasingly became a signal of prestige that enhanced the value of a credential from that institution (Harcleroad, 1980).[1] Some types of accreditation, particularly for individual programs within a college, still primarily function as a signal of prestige.

Although institutional accreditation remains optional in theory, it has become essential for colleges' survival. One reason is the signal of minimum quality: credits earned at unaccredited institutions are rarely accepted by other colleges and graduates in certain programs may not be able to gain professional certifications if they did not attend an accredited program. The second reason, however, has nothing to do with the actions of accreditors. The 1952 passage of the federal Veterans Readjustment Assistance Act limited federal financial aid funds to colleges that were accredited by an agency that was recognized by the federal government (Conway, 1979), meaning that colleges had to be accredited by an acceptable agency to receive the lifeblood of federal funds. Accreditation agencies now find themselves as one of the three components of the "regulatory triad," alongside the U.S. Department of Education and state higher education authorization agencies, which seek to guarantee minimum quality standards for colleges (Crow, 2009). This is often an uneasy relationship because accreditors represent accountability through peer review and governmental agencies represent a form of accountability that is often more adversarial in nature.

Accreditation in the United States is relatively decentralized compared to the systems in other countries. While the federal governments in some countries (such as in northern Europe and Japan) directly accredit or license colleges, the American accreditation system relies heavily on a peer review system in which teams from other institutions will judge whether a given college meets quality standards (Mori, 2009; Shah, Nair, & Wilson, 2011). The federal government's involvement has traditionally been limited to making sure that the accrediting bodies themselves are of sufficient quality. Part of the hands-off nature may be due to the sheer size of the American higher education system; 9,728 postsecondary institutions (not all of which receive federal financial aid) and nearly 42,000 academic programs or internships were accredited as of April 2017 (Office of Postsecondary Education, 2017).

In recent years, the federal government has pursued a more active role in the quality assurance process and has questioned the efficacy of the current accreditation system. This was spurred in part by a *Wall Street Journal* feature that noted how 11 four-year colleges with graduation rates below 10% maintained accreditation (Fuller & Belkin, 2015a) and a U.S. Government Accountability Office (2014) report that showed accreditors disproportionately sanctioned colleges for financial issues over academic issues. The pressures for accreditors to focus more on minimum compliance standards than helping colleges above the performance threshold improve their quality (Eaton, 2015) were heightened by the U.S. Department of Education's 2016 decision to derecognize the Accrediting Council for Independent Colleges and Schools (ACICS), one of the largest accreditors of for-profit colleges, thus taking away their colleges' ability to receive federal financial aid (Thomason, 2016). Elizabeth Sibolski, the president of the Middle States accrediting agency, summed up the tensions faced by accreditors nicely: "What's an accrediting agency supposed to do?" (Sibolski, 2012, 22).

In this chapter, I begin by discussing the basics of the accreditation system in American higher education, including how the accreditation process typically works and the two main types of accreditation. I then examine the quality control process for accreditation and how that plays a key role in the accountability landscape, focusing on the interaction between accrediting agencies and the U.S. Department of Education. Finally, I examine some of the potential pressures accreditors face to heighten their standards—and the backlash that sometimes occurs when they do exactly that.

How Accreditation Works

The modern framework for accreditation began to take place during the 1950s, when accreditors developed a system with fixed review cycles to evaluate colleges and universities (Pfnister, 1971). Colleges or programs that wish to seek accreditation from a given body must first meet initial eligibility criteria such as being authorized to operate in a given state, offering the types of degrees or programs covered by the accreditor, and enrolling students (e.g., Distance Education Accrediting Commission, n.d.; Middle States Commission on Higher Education, 2011).[2] Colleges can then apply for accreditation after undergoing a self-study process, in which the institution does an internal evaluation based on the accreditor's listed standards and produces a written report that is sent to the accreditor.

The next step in the accreditation process is for a peer review team that generally consists of faculty and administrators from institutions also accredited by the same agency to visit the college, meet with groups of stakeholders, and make determinations based on their visit and the self-study materials. Based on this information, the accreditor will make its decision about the college's accreditation status (Eaton, 2009). Colleges that easily meet the accreditor's standards will receive accreditation for the longest possible period (which can be up to ten years), although most accreditors will require colleges to provide periodic updates or even undergo a less rigorous midterm review.

Colleges that do not receive unconditional reaccreditation can face one of four basic actions that range in severity from minor to major (Sibolski, 2014).[3] An accreditor can place a college on *warning* if it is out of compliance on at least one accreditation standard, or it can place a college on *probation* if the issues are considered more serious. These sanctions can last up to two years if a college has not sufficiently addressed the accreditor's concerns. The third action is a *show cause* ruling, which requires a college to undergo an additional site visit and demonstrate why it deserves continued accreditation; this can also limit a college's ability to make substantial changes without getting approval from the accreditor (e.g., Higher Learning Commission, 2016). The most serious action is a *denial* or *withdrawal* of accreditation, which can then be appealed to the accreditor. If an accreditor denies the appeal, a college can then sue the accrediting body and receive an injunction that temporarily maintains accreditation. However, these law-suits are rarely successful in restoring accreditation beyond the length of the injunction (Kelderman, 2016c).

Regardless of the type of accreditation sought (institutional or program-matic), accreditors generally begin their evaluations by determining whether the college or program meets five broad standards.[4] The first standard is whether a college is able to fulfill its mission, as well as whether that mission is appropriate for the accrediting agency. Whether a college has sufficient control of the institution and adequate governance structures, such as a board that is reasonably independent of the college's funders, is the second standard. The third standard examines whether the college is financially stable enough to continue operating over the length of the accreditation cycle, which is the most common reason for denying accreditation or placing a college on sanctions. For example, 26% of private nonprofit and for-profit colleges in the lowest 5% of financial responsibility scores calculated by the U.S. Department of Education between 2009 and 2014 received sanctions from their accreditors (U.S. Government Accountability Office, 2014).

The fourth standard consists of whether a college has the academic integrity to provide a quality education. This includes factors such as a sufficient number of highly trained faculty members, adequate facilities and libraries, and the presence of other critical academic and student services. Finally, accreditors must include student learning outcomes as a part of the evaluation process. This requirement was first mandated by the federal government in the late 1980s, although explicit performance metrics were not set (Ewell, 2010; Semrow et al., 1992). Colleges in the worst 5% for outcomes such as dropout rates and student loan defaults only faced a 6% likelihood of accreditor sanctions, lending credence to concerns that accreditors are focusing more on financial metrics than academic outcomes (U.S. Government Accountability Office, 2014).

Institutional Accreditation

The federal government currently recognizes 17 accrediting agencies that are classified as institutional accreditors for covering colleges that offer a range of academic or vocational programs (CHEA [Council for Higher Education Accreditation], 2015). Of these agencies, seven are regional accreditors that focus on degree-granting, academically focused colleges and universities, four are national faith-related accreditors that limit membership to colleges with particular religious affiliations and missions, and six are national career-related accreditors that largely accredit vocationally focused colleges.

As discussed in chapter 2, the regional accreditation system first developed in the United States in the late 1800s and spread to cover the entire country by the 1920s. Under this system, a college's accreditor is determined by the state in which the institution is located. There are currently seven regional accreditors serving six regions of the country, with California and Hawaii having separate accreditors for four-year and two-year colleges. These regional accreditors cover the vast majority of public and private nonprofit colleges in the United States. Only a small percentage of for-profit colleges have regional accreditation, but these include behemoths such as Ashford University, Capella University, Grand Canyon University, and the University of Phoenix. Approximately 39% of colleges and 85% of students were accredited by one of the regional agencies in the 2012–13 academic year (CHEA, 2015). Table 5.1 lists the seven regional accreditors and which states they cover.

Regional accreditation is generally seen as the most prestigious form of accreditation, in part because the vast majority of selective four-year colleges are accredited by these agencies. This leads some colleges to note that they

TABLE 5.1   Regional accreditation agencies and states covered

Accreditor name	States covered
Higher Learning Commission	AR, AZ, CO, IA, IL, IN, KS, MI, MO, MN, ND, NE, NM, OK, OH, SD, WI, WV, WY
Middle States Commission on Higher Education	DE, MD, NJ, NY, PA (plus DC)
New England Association of Schools and Colleges	CT, MA, ME, NH, RI, VT
Northwest Commission on Colleges and Universities	AK, ID, MT, NV, OR, UT, WA
Southern Association of Colleges and Schools	AL, FL, GA, KY, LA, MS, NC, SC, TN, TX, VA
Western Association of Schools and Colleges (four-year)	CA, HI
Accrediting Commission for Community and Junior Colleges (two-year)	CA, HI

SOURCE: Accrediting agencies' websites.

Note: Accrediting agencies also include colleges located in outlying areas of the United States and some colleges based in other countries that seek American accreditation. These other locations are not displayed here for the sake of brevity.

have the same accreditor as the most selective private colleges (Marklein, 2010), while a federal investigation found that some for-profit colleges that did not have regional accreditation falsely claimed that they had the same accreditation as Harvard in an effort to recruit students (U.S. Government Accountability Office, 2010). Regional accreditors have also sanctioned some colleges for not meeting the body's standards. Seventy-five of the 456 actions taken by regional accreditors in the 2012–13 academic year were sanctions of some type, with 37 colleges receiving warnings, 26 probation actions, and six terminations (CHEA, 2017). Twenty-six colleges had their regional accreditation terminated between 2000 and 2015 (Fuller & Belkin, 2015a).

A common criticism of the regional accreditation system is that because accreditors are not forced to compete for colleges, there is little incentive for them to set higher standards. Almost 350 of the 1,500 four-year colleges accredited by one of the regional bodies had a graduation rate below (35%) or a student loan default rate above (9.3%) the average of colleges that lost accreditation since 2000 (Fuller & Belkin, 2015a). This has led to proposals to allow regional accreditors to compete for colleges in an effort to break up the "cartels" (e.g., Gillen, Bennett, & Vedder, 2010; Senate Committee on Health, Education, Labor and Pensions, 2015). Even a report from the American Council on Education, the umbrella organization representing nonprofit higher education, stated that "the current regional basis of accreditation is probably not the way America would structure the system if starting from scratch" (ACE National Task Force on Institutional Accreditation, 2012).

NATIONAL ACCREDITORS

Like regional accreditors, national accrediting bodies also accredit entire colleges or universities. But unlike regional accreditors, national accreditors generally limit their membership to colleges with narrower missions—either faith-related accreditors that focus on particular religious traditions or career-related accreditors that focus on accrediting colleges with vocational programs. Faith-related accreditors cover primarily small private nonprofit colleges and included just over 5% of institutions and less than 1% of students in the 2012–13 academic year, while career-related accreditors covered 55% of American colleges (most of which are for-profits) and about 15% of students (CHEA, 2015, 2016). Table 5.2 contains a listing of the four faith-related and seven career-related accreditors, one of which (ACICS) is no longer recognized by the U.S. Department of Education as of mid-2017.

TABLE 5.2 National accrediting agencies and types of colleges covered

Name	Types of colleges covered
Faith-related accreditors	
Association for Biblical Higher Education	All levels of Christian higher education
Association of Advanced Rabbinical and Talmudic Schools	Degree-granting Jewish institutions
Commission on Accrediting of the Association of Theological Schools	Graduate-level seminaries
Transnational Association of Christian Colleges and Schools	All levels of Christian higher education
Career-related accreditors	
Accrediting Bureau of Health Education Schools	Colleges with at least 70% of students or programs in health education
Accrediting Commission of Career Schools and Colleges	Colleges focused on occupational and technical programs
Accrediting Council for Continuing Education and Training	Noncollegiate continuing education and training programs
Accrediting Council for Independent Colleges and Schools*	Nonpublic colleges offering occupational and technical programs
Council on Occupational Education	Colleges offering associates and certificates solely in career and technical education
Distance Education Accrediting Commission	Colleges with the majority of programs offered via distance education
National Accrediting Commission of Career Arts and Sciences	Cosmetology and beauty schools

SOURCE: Accrediting agencies' websites.
Note: ACICS has an asterisk because it is no longer recognized by the U.S. Department of Education.

Faith-related accreditors can be appealing to religious colleges—particularly those with very close ties to a particular denomination—for two different reasons. First, a college's religious mission is an explicit part of the accreditation criteria for faith-related agencies, which can be seen as a positive by governing boards and potential funders that wish to hold the college accountable to its religious identity. For example, the Transnational Association of Christian Colleges and Schools (TRACS) includes foundational standards that mandate a Christian worldview of education, and even go as far as including a definition of Satan that colleges may use in their mission statement. But TRACS also has explicit retention, completion, and job placement rate standards that require colleges to submit a plan for improvement if they are not met. If a college does not have a graduation rate for bachelor's degree students above 50%, it is subjected to additional oversight (TRACS, 2015).

Faith-related accreditors also tend to oversee relatively small colleges, with the average college with faith-related accreditation having just over 300 students (author's calculation using data from CHEA). Research has found that religiously affiliated colleges are sanctioned by regional accreditors at higher rates than other colleges, which is likely due to the small size and shaky financial footings of many religious institutions (Donahoo & Lee, 2008a). Paul Quinn College in Texas, a religiously affiliated historically black college, was initially accredited by the Southern Association of Colleges and Schools (SACS), but the regional accreditor tried to strip its accreditation in 2009. The college sued to keep accreditation, but moved to the faith-related accreditor TRACS in 2011 and kept federal and state financial aid eligibility (Hacker, 2012).

National accreditors are heavily focused on fields of study that directly lead to employment, which are reflected in their additional accreditation criteria beyond the general standards shared by all accreditors. For example, the Accrediting Commission of Career Schools and Colleges (2016) requires that all instructors have teaching experience or formal training in teaching as well as three years of work experience if teaching a vocational topic. The Distance Education Accrediting Commission (n.d.) requires that all students take proctored exams with photo identification on a regular basis in an effort to maintain academic standards in online education programs.

Both types of national accreditors are more likely to sanction their member colleges than regional accreditors, which is not surprising given the smaller size of nationally accredited colleges and the greater financial need of their students. In 2016, faith-related accreditors took 55 actions and career accreditors took 1,234 actions. Fourteen of the 55 actions by faith-related accreditors involved terminating accreditation (either voluntary or involuntary), while there were only four actions involving sanctions. Career accreditors issued 262 sanctions and 25 involuntary denials of accreditation, while 236 actions involved voluntary withdrawals of accreditation (likely due to the contraction of the for-profit sector and the unclear status of ACICS) (CHEA, 2017). However, there are concerns that national accreditors lift sanctions in a much shorter period of time than do regional accreditors, calling the true severity of these sanctions into question (Flores, 2016).

CRITIQUES OF INSTITUTIONAL ACCREDITATION

The current accreditation process by both regional and national bodies faces three main types of critiques in addition to the lack of competition among regional accreditors, as mentioned above. The first critique is that because the accreditation process relies so heavily on faculty members and administrators at peer institutions in the review process, reviewers may go easy on other colleges in exchange for the same treatment at their institution. (The benefit of having reviewers and commissioners from member colleges is that these individuals are more likely to know the circumstances of a particular college than external people.) Cooper (2016) showed that 68% of commissioners of regional accrediting agencies and 62% of commissioners at national agencies worked for colleges that were accredited by that same agency, and the largest accrediting agencies have a higher percentage of commissioners with a potential conflict of interest.[5] Legislation introduced by three Senate Democrats in 2016 sought to ban accreditors from having commissioners from their member institutions (Kreighbaum, 2016b), but this bill has yet to see substantive debate in Congress. A related issue is the relative lack of resources that accrediting agencies have ($75 million across 12 of the largest accreditors in 2013), meaning that efforts to bring in outside reviewers may be financially prohibitive (Flores, 2017).

The second critique is that the process of institutional accreditation restricts innovation by limiting colleges' abilities to try new organizational or delivery methods (e.g., Brown, 2013; Miller, 2014). An example of accreditation potentially limiting innovation occurred with Tiffin University's Ivy Bridge College partnership with for-profit Altius Education. Ivy Bridge operated as an online private two-year college from 2008 to 2013, when the Higher Learning Commission shut down the college amid concerns that too much of the education was outsourced (Fain, 2013). Ivy Bridge then sued the accreditor for $100 million, but the case was dismissed for being filed in the wrong jurisdiction (Thomason, 2015a). However, others contend that colleges are in fact innovating to meet accreditors' standards on student outcomes (Kezar, 2014) and that a streamlined route for provisional accreditation could help foster additional innovation while maintaining sufficient accountability (Gaston, 2014a).

The final critique of accreditation is that the accreditation process is too expensive and time-consuming, particularly for colleges that are in little danger of losing their accreditation. A survey of four-year colleges accredited by three of the six regional bodies found that the average cost of an accreditation cycle was between $300,000 and $450,000, with 70% of this being indirect costs such as the time of faculty (Woolston, 2012). Another study estimated, based on a survey of 13 colleges, that four-year colleges spend $3 billion per year on regional accreditation (Vanderbilt University, 2015). This has led colleges to call for streamlined accreditation processes for colleges that meet certain quality standards (Broad, McPherson, & Rawlings, 2015), although occasionally even prestigious institutions like the University of North Carolina are placed on probation by accreditors for issues of institutional control (Stancill, 2016).

Program Accreditation

The second main type of accreditation is at the program level, in which individual programs are reviewed instead of an entire institution with multiple programs. In the 2016–17 academic year, there were 59 program accreditors that were recognized by CHEA or the U.S. Department of Education. Nineteen of these accreditors were recognized by the U.S. Department of Education, allowing them to grant federal financial aid eligibility to freestanding programs such as an independent law or nursing school, while the remaining 40 program accreditors did not have the ability to authorize their programs to receive federal aid (CHEA, 2017a; U.S. Department of Education, 2017). Essentially, a college with a single focus (such as a freestanding medical school) will get federal financial aid access through its programmatic accreditor, while a research university with a medical school would qualify for federal aid through its regional accreditor.

Program accrediting bodies take two main forms. The first form is mandatory accreditation, in which accreditation is crucial for the credential awarded to have value either in the labor market or to other colleges. A well-known example of programmatic accreditation that is generally mandatory is for law schools, in which the American Bar Association (ABA) is the primary accrediting body. Nineteen states currently limit the ability to take the bar exam to students with a law degree from an ABA-accredited institution in the United States or from a foreign law school (Moeser & Guback, 2016). A few states, such as Alabama and California, also accredit law schools, with student outcomes better than unaccredited colleges but far worse than ABA-accredited institutions. For example, only 20% of people who graduated from unaccredited California law schools actually passed the state's bar exam, far below the state's requirement of 40% and the ABA's requirement of 75% (Song, Kim, & Poindexter, 2015).

Health care–related fields also commonly have mandatory programmatic accreditation. Medical schools must be accredited by the Liaison Committee on Medical Education (a joint effort of the American Medical Association and the Association of American Medical Colleges) in order to grant MDs in the United States and to get federal funds (including financial aid). They must also meet five general institutional capacity requirements and seven curricular requirements that are specific to medical education (Liaison Committee on Medical Education, 2016). Dental programs and osteopathic medicine programs have similar setups, while nursing program accreditation (although mandatory) is split among state and national accreditors.

Accreditation for teacher preparation programs is somewhere between mandatory and voluntary; 21 states required these programs to be accredited as of 2016 (Sawchuk, 2016). The accreditor for teacher education programs, the Council for the Accreditation of Educator Preparation, formed out of the recent merger of two rival accreditors. It requires content knowledge, clinical preparation, diversity and academic preparation of teaching candidates, demonstrated student learning gains, and the use of data to track teaching candidates' outcomes among its standards (Council for the Accreditation of Educator Preparation, 2016). The academic preparation and student learning standards are proving especially controversial among many education schools and contributed to the firing of the accreditor's first president (e.g., Cochran-Smith et al., 2016; Lederman, 2015).

Other programs have accreditation that is completely voluntary, as it is not tied to any licensing or funding requirements. Instead, programs pursue accreditation as a signal of prestige and strength—which was how institutional accreditation also initially began. Programs in engineering and related fields, for example, can also pursue voluntary accreditation through the Accrediting Board for Engineering and Technology (ABET). ABET used to have federal recognition for financial aid purposes, but they withdrew from this status in 2001 (Brittingham, 2009). They currently accredit 714 colleges in 29 countries (ABET, n.d.).

Some disciplines even have multiple voluntary accreditors with different levels of prestige. Business schools can choose from two major programmatic accreditors based on their type of institution, with the Association to Advance Collegiate Schools of Business (AACSB) focusing on research-oriented institutions and the Accreditation Council for Business Schools and Programs (ACBSP) covering teaching-oriented colleges. Both of these voluntary accreditors have global footprints as both American and international institutions see them as a signal of quality. AACSB accredits 777 business schools around the world, and ACBSP accredits business programs at 430 campuses globally (AACSB, n.d.; ACBSP, 2015).

Like institutional accreditation, programmatic accreditation (whether mandatory or voluntary) comes at a significant price tag. A study conducted by Vanderbilt University (2015) estimated that programmatic accreditation cost four-year colleges an additional $3 billion per year on top of institutional accreditation. However, some research suggests that programmatic accreditation does improve student learning outcomes. Volkwein, Lattuca, Harper, and Domingo (2007) examined changes to ABET accreditation standards in engineering schools between 1998 and 2000 and found that graduates' learning outcomes improved and became more consistent following the change in standards. Programmatic accreditors were also willing to take action against subpar programs, with about 6% of the 3,531 actions taken in 2016 involving sanctions (CHEA, 2017b).

Program-level accreditors also face a number of critiques. One is that because accreditors can require that programs maintain certain levels of resources (e.g., Gaston, 2014b; Honan, 1998), colleges have an incentive to shift funds from nonaccredited to accredited programs in an effort to satisfy accreditors. Over time, this can result in substantial resource disparities across programs—and potentially induce other programs to seek out an accreditor if one is available in their discipline in an effort to protect their resources. This can yield less than optimal outcomes for the college as a whole, as their ability to allocate resources as desired is hamstrung by accreditors. Another concern is that the push for prestigious accreditation (such as AACSB) prioritizes research output over teaching quality, displacing faculty with long teaching records (Rogers, 2012).

The critique that accreditors can limit innovation can also apply to programmatic agencies. An example is the University of North Texas, which launched a new law school in downtown Dallas in 2014. It featured two main innovations: tuition far below most other law schools (and students can receive federal aid through the university's regional accreditation) and a focus on enrolling students based on life experience instead of the LSAT scores typically used in admissions.[6] However, the ABA has recommended that the school not be accredited on the grounds of its unusually low LSAT scores, meaning that currently enrolled students will not be able to practice law in Texas (Watkins, 2016). This is in spite of a report by the ABA Task Force on the Future of Legal Education (2014) that recommended that the ABA allow for additional flexibility in law school education in order to reduce student debt and improve outcomes, which is what the North Texas effort is attempting to do.

Accrediting Accreditors

Just like accreditation represents a quality control mechanism for colleges, there are organizations that oversee the accrediting bodies. The first efforts to approve accreditors came in the late 1930s through the formation of a Joint Commission on Accrediting by several higher education associations (Marvin, 1952; Woolston, 2012). This was replaced by the National Commission of Regional Accrediting Agencies and the National Commission on Accrediting (for national accreditors) in the late 1940s (Davenport, 2000). These two organizations merged into the Council on Postsecondary Accreditation (COPA) in 1975, which also branched out to cover specialized accreditors (Young, 1979).

The federal government had required accrediting bodies to be recognized by an approved organization since 1952 after a series of scandals regarding low-quality colleges springing up to receive veterans' benefits. At the time, the federal government chose to use the approved lists of accreditors by the national commissions mentioned above (Conway, 1979; Finkin, 1973). The level of federal involvement increased in 1968 with the formation of an Accreditation and Institutional Eligibility Advisory Committee (Trivett, 1976). This committee took the responsibility of recognizing which accreditors were eligible to receive federal funds, but the federal government still had a great degree of latitude in determining the recognition process. The 1992 reauthorization of the Higher Education Act reflected a great degree of frustration with rising student loan default rates and contained two major changes in the accreditation structure that were focused on additional scrutiny for low-performing colleges (Glidden, 1996).

The first was the establishment of State Postsecondary Review Entities that were designed to scrutinize colleges with the highest default rates. Although these entities were never funded, the reauthorization helped spur the breakup of COPA into two groups with somewhat distinct missions. CHEA focuses on degree-granting institutions and includes about 60 institutional and programmatic accreditors (CHEA, 2017a). Other programmatic accreditors went to the Association of Specialized and Professional Accreditors, which now covers 58 specialized accrediting bodies (Association of Specialized and Professional Accreditors, 2016).

The second was the formation of the National Advisory Committee on Institutional Quality and Integrity, with all members appointed by the secretary of education, to review accreditors every five years under a set of prescribed rules and make accreditation recommendations to the secretary. This committee was later reformulated in 2008 to have appointments made by both parties in Congress as well as by the secretary of education (Basken, 2008). As of late 2016, the U.S. Department of Education recognized 36 accrediting agencies as being eligible to approve colleges to receive federal financial aid, with this group including a mix of institutional accreditors and programmatic accreditors that cover freestanding institutions that focus on a single program (U.S. Department of Education, 2017).

The Changing Landscape of Accreditation

Accrediting bodies have long been under pressure from the federal government, individual states, and the public to hold colleges accountable to higher performance standards, and this pressure has been steadily rising over time. As a result, accreditation reform has played a key role in each of the last three reauthorizations of the Higher Education Act (HEA). The 1992 HEA reauthorization, as discussed above, attempted to form additional review panels at the state level but they were never funded. But the reauthorization explicitly mandated accreditors that require colleges to demonstrate student achievement such as completion, licensing examination passage, and job placement rates, which spurred accreditors to be more explicit in the student learning outcomes colleges were required to demonstrate (Suskie, 2015). The 1998 reauthorization moved these assessment standards to the top of the section on accreditation, while also reducing some requirements regarding when they must conduct investigations and site visits (Flores, 2015).

In preparation for the subsequent HEA reauthorization in the mid-2000s, the U.S. Department of Education formed a Commission on the Future of Higher Education, better known as the Spellings Commission after then secretary of education Margaret Spellings. A series of position papers considered by the commission included ideas to completely overhaul accreditation, such as creating a new public-private partnership to handle accreditation and developing assessments to measure student learning (Dickeson, 2006; Schray, 2006). The committee's final report had less radical language, calling for accreditors to focus more on student learning outcomes and make their decisions readily available to the public (U.S. Department of Education, 2006).

The Department of Education began pushing to implement some of these recommendations in early 2007 by proposing that accreditors set minimum qualitative and quantitative performance standards for student achievement that colleges would have to meet to maintain accreditation (Lederman, 2007). However, this idea was met with fierce opposition from many accreditors and other members of the negotiated rulemaking panel convened to consider the changes. The Department of Education then agreed to replace the language with a broader statement that would take colleges' missions into account when considering student learning (Bollag, 2007). The opposition to these changes reached Congress, which blocked the Department of Education from requiring that accreditors adopt certain performance thresholds or student learning outcomes in the 2008 HEA reauthorization (Flores, 2015).

In the final years of the Obama administration, the idea of requiring so-called bright line standards for accreditors came back to the forefront—this time led by Democrats instead of Republicans. Although congressional hearings on accreditation highlighted frustration with accreditors' perceived low standards, institutional accrediting agencies generally were hesitant to set minimum standards for performance without taking the institution's characteristics into account (Belkin & Fuller, 2015; Nelson, 2013). However, intense political pressure to publish clear and defensible minimum standards has begun to change accreditors' actions.

Although the Department of Education cannot explicitly mandate minimum standards for accreditation, they announced in late 2015 that they would publish additional information on student outcomes by accrediting body in an effort to push accreditors to raise their standards (Kelderman, 2015). The resulting accreditor dashboards, released in mid-2016, contained details on outcomes such as graduation rates, student loan repayment rates and debt burdens, and median earnings ten years after college entry (NACIQI, 2016). The dashboards, inspired by the College Scorecard, allow for easy comparisons to be made across accreditors as well as highlight accreditors with high percentages of lower-performing colleges (Fain, 2016b). Additionally, a bill introduced by three prominent Democratic senators in 2016 would repeal the current provision on the federal government setting minimum outcome standards and require the Department of Education to set a performance floor (Kreighbaum, 2016b).

Accreditors have responded to these political pressures by making some voluntary efforts to set minimum student learning standards in an attempt to maintain more authority over the accreditation process. Both Judith Eaton, the president of CHEA, and Carol Geary Schneider, the recently retired president of the Association of American Colleges and Universities (AAC&U), have called for accreditors and colleges to do more to hold colleges with poorer student outcomes accountable for their performance (Kelderman, 2016a; Thomason, 2015b). The Council of Regional Accrediting Commissions (C-RAC), an umbrella organization that represents the regional accreditors, also announced in 2016 that they would begin to place colleges under additional oversight if their graduation, loan default, and loan repayment rates were below a given threshold. For example, four-year colleges with graduation rates below 25% and two-year colleges with graduation rates below 15% would be subject to additional scrutiny during the accreditation process (Kreighbaum, 2016a).

Accreditors do occasionally revoke colleges' accreditation, with approximately 20 four-year colleges (all private nonprofits) involuntarily losing their regional accreditation between 2003 and 2016 (Fuller & Belkin, 2015b; combined with author's research). Of these 20 colleges, 12 have since closed, with the remaining institutions having merged with another college, found a different accreditor, or remained open without receiving federal financial aid. The loss of accreditation is far more common among national accreditors, with these agencies revoking the recognition of approximately 55 colleges between late 2009 and early 2014 (U.S. Government Accountability Office, 2014).

In spite of pressure from policymakers and the public to tighten accreditation standards, actually revoking a college's accreditation (particularly if the college is not-for-profit) is usually quite difficult. Of the 20 private nonprofits to lose regional accreditation since 2003, six are historically black colleges and universities (HBCUs). HBCUs tend to have weaker financial positions than many predominately white institutions (e.g., Goldrick-Rab, Kelchen, & Houle, 2014), which lead them to be at a higher risk of sanctions by accreditors for financial reasons (Donahoo & Lee, 2008b). But HBCUs also continue to play an outsized role in the education of African American students and have loyal (and vocal) alumni communities, making any closures difficult. Each of the last five HBCUs that saw its accreditation revoked immediately sued their regional accreditor, SACS, to receive injunctions to delay the closure. As noted earlier in the chapter, Paul Quinn College successfully switched accreditors, but the other HBCUs have either eventually lost accreditation or closed within the following few years (e.g., Hawkins, 2013; Wood, 2015).[7]

While revoking the accreditation of small, financially struggling private nonprofit colleges is difficult, doing so for public colleges—regardless of the issues they face—is virtually impossible due to the political implications of that decision. The Accrediting Commission for Community and Junior Colleges (ACCJC) had tried since 2006 to get the City College of San Francisco (CCSF), one of the largest community colleges in the country, to address its concerns about governance and finances. ACCJC was concerned that CCSF was spending too much money on salaries and benefits (which put the college in a bad financial position) and had a provision in the shared governance process that required the faculty senate and board of trustees to reach "mutual agreement" on academic matters. This effectively resulted in allowing both sides to veto the other, creating an impasse when considering changes (Edwards, 2013; Schmidt, 2013a).

ACCJC put CCSF under show cause status in 2012, giving the college nine months to address the issues raised in previous reviews (Fain, 2012). Although the college was able to get a special trustee who was eventually given the ability to veto decisions made by the elected board (Barba, 2016), ACCJC announced in July 2013 that it would revoke CCSF's accreditation within the next year (Schmidt, 2013b). This was immediately followed by a political firestorm, as San Francisco's city attorney sued ACCJC to keep accreditation and House Minority Leader Nancy Pelosi and the U.S. Department of Education both questioned whether ACCJC should be allowed to continue accrediting colleges. ACCJC prepared a report for NACIQI explaining how it had corrected issues in its procedures in an effort to remain a recognized accreditor (Kelderman, 2016b). After years of short-term accreditation extensions, CCSF received an unconditional seven-year affirmation of its accreditation in 2017 (Barba, 2017).

In addition to potential sanctions against ACCJC, NACIQI ended the federal recognition of two other accrediting bodies in the last decade. The first case was the American Academy for Liberal Education (AALE), which was first recognized in 1995 with a focus on encouraging colleges to concentrate on the core liberal arts instead of courses sometimes viewed as trendy (Honan, 1995). But NACIQI soon became concerned about whether AALE had sufficient standards for assessing and evaluating student learning outcomes, and the body recommended in 2007 to deny their continued accreditation. Education Secretary Margaret Spellings subsequently barred AALE from being a recognized accreditor, but AALE appealed the decision and was successful in getting a two-year reprieve (Lederman, 2008). This reprieve was short lived, as Department of Education staff members recommended that AALE be derecognized (Lederman, 2010) and AALE voluntarily withdraw its request for recognition before NACIQI made its final decision (Hebel, 2010). As of late 2016, no freestanding universities in the United States have AALE accreditation (AALE, 2016).

In 2016, NACIQI recommended that the secretary of education terminate the recognition of ACICS, one of the largest national accrediting bodies, in a high-profile hearing. ACICS was the accreditor for some of the Corinthian Colleges and nearly all ITT Technical Institute campuses, both of which collapsed in the mid-2010s over concerns about financial capacity and student outcomes, as well as several other smaller colleges that were accused of fraud. For example, in an influential report titled "ACICS Must Go," former Education Department senior advisor Ben Miller (2016) noted that over half of the approximately $11 billion federal financial aid disbursed by ACICS institutions in the previous three years went to colleges that were under investigation by a state or federal agency. A few days later, Senator Elizabeth Warren (D-MA), a fierce critic of the for-profit industry, all but called for NACIQI to end ACICS's accreditation (Office of Senator Elizabeth Warren, 2016). However, supporters of ACICS noted that when the body did try to revoke the accreditation of Bristol University (a small for-profit in California), the college sued and was successful in regaining accreditation (Fain, 2016a).

The official report written by Department of Education staffers and given to NACIQI committee members recommended that ACICS, which had been recognized by the federal government since 1956, be terminated as a recognized accreditor (U.S. Department of Education, 2016). After hours of debate and discussion, NACIQI members approved the staffers' recommendation in a 10–3 vote—with one Republican-appointed committee member joining Democratic appointees (Fain, 2016c). The Department of Education then agreed with the committee's recommendation (Thomason, 2016), meaning that colleges that were accredited by ACICS had 18 months to find a new accreditor or lose financial aid access for their students.

Conclusion

There are three clear implications of the recent wave of accreditation actions for accountability purposes. First, the federal government is willing to play a larger role in the accreditation process in an effort to protect the billions of dollars in financial aid it provides to students each year. Judith Eaton, president of CHEA, summed up the future well in a statement following NACIQI's decision on ACICS (Eaton, 2016):

> For the accrediting community, the message is clear: The federal government is the principal architect and controlling authority of accreditation. While this role for government in relation to quality assurance is quite common throughout the world, for U.S. accreditors it is a profound change and poses a significant challenge. The bedrock of U.S. accreditation is self-regulation and peer review in the service of institutional autonomy driven by mission and academic freedom. It is now clear that this bedrock has given way: There is no longer any way for accreditors to both be gatekeepers and thus managed and judged by the Department, yet retain an adequate measure of

self-determination in judging quality. As was clearly demonstrated at the NACIQI meeting in relation to all accreditors, nothing that an accreditor does is beyond the purview of NACIQI and thus the federal government.

Second, additional scrutiny from the federal government on accrediting agencies is designed to have them focus their attention on the lowest-performing colleges, but it is far from clear if accreditors will actually be able to follow through and either restructure or close these institutions. It may even be the case that some of the same politicians calling for accreditors to heighten their standards will protest when accreditors attempt to close a college in their district. The example of CCSF highlights the difficulty in holding large colleges that enjoy political support from both sides of the aisle accountable for their performance.

Finally, accreditation has long been criticized for the burden it places on high-performing colleges or programs that are in no real danger of losing their accreditation. Given the increased focus from the federal government and accreditors themselves on colleges below a minimum performance threshold, it is possible that accreditors will focus more of their resources on colleges closer to the threshold. This matches how many other organizations respond to similar incentives to focus on marginal cases, which could help lower-performing colleges improve their outcomes but at the risk of reducing oversight of potential governance or financial issues that may develop at more selective colleges. At the same time, colleges may respond by trying to become more selective in an effort to meet any bright-line performance standards, which could reduce access for disadvantaged students. All of these discussions are likely to occur if—and even when—accreditors start to adopt tougher standards.

CHAPTER SIX

Private-Sector Accountability

To this point in the book, my focus has been primarily on how external agents with the power to influence a college's ability to operate work to hold colleges accountable for their performance—and how colleges respond to those pressures. But although the federal government, state governments, and accrediting agencies can be quite influential in affecting how certain colleges operate, a substantial number of colleges do not have to significantly adjust their practices or priorities in order to meet these entities' performance standards. For example, consider a reasonably well-regarded private nonprofit college. Other than meeting data reporting requirements from the federal and state governments and meeting accreditors' basic conditions for financial stability, governance, and student outcomes, this college generally can set its course without facing existential pressures from external agencies.

For these types of colleges, the private sector (through the use of market-oriented accountability pressures) can often represent the most influential set of actors working to pressure colleges to act in a certain way. Private accountability efforts can be as informal as individuals and families making college choice decisions based on their perception of a college's reputation, which can change quickly in the event of negative events. External advocacy campaigns such as student or alumni protests can also be effective in getting colleges to change their practices to maintain or enhance their reputation. Finally, many colleges (particularly in the four-year sector) are highly attuned to the myriad of private-sector ratings and rankings that have been shown to affect both the composition of the student body and how colleges allocate their resources. In this chapter, I discuss each of these different types of private-sector accountability as well as how colleges respond to these pressures.

Institutional Reputations and Accountability

The most basic form of private-sector accountability is a college's reputation, which includes aspects such as perceived academic quality, the campus environment, and whether former students' outcomes are what students, their families, and alumni would expect. As nonprofit colleges (both private and public) do not have the profit-maximizing objective that for-profit institutions have, many institutions will use any available resource to maximize prestige or reputation (e.g., Winston, 1999). But even for-profit colleges and nonprofit colleges that are less concerned about prestige take care to avoid anything that could negatively affect their reputation, as that could hurt their institutional brand and make recruiting students more difficult.

College choice theories (Cabrera & La Nasa, 2000; Hossler, Schmit, & Vesper, 1999) suggest that a college's reputation can influence students throughout the process of learning about potential postsecondary options, figuring out which colleges to apply to, and then selecting which college to attend. This is backed up by research findings among students considering four-year colleges (who tend to be more mobile and have larger choice sets than other students).[1] For example, a nationwide survey of traditional-age students entering four-year colleges in 2015 showed that three of the top five reasons students chose their college were associated with quality or reputation (Eagan et al., 2016). Empirical research has shown that quality and reputation are associated with a college's size, resources, and selectivity (e.g., Volkwein & Sweitzer, 2006)—factors that colleges may be able to affect, but typically at a high price tag.

The traditional way for colleges to enhance their reputation among prospective students and their families has been through the strategic use of admissions materials to highlight the various strengths of the institution. Residential four-year colleges make sure to carefully market their institution as a diverse environment with a beautiful campus and plentiful extracurricular activities (Saichaie & Morphew, 2014). This perception of quality, as manifested through a college's reputation, is important for establishing a college's brand identity among current students and alumni (Dennis et al., 2016) and is particularly important among international students (e.g., Merchant et al., 2015), who are in high demand due to their ability to pay the full sticker price. Public colleges are also seeking to recruit students from other states in an effort to increase tuition revenue and combat declining real per-student appropriations, even though doing so at selective institutions crowds out minority and low-income state residents (Jaquette & Curs, 2015; Jaquette, Curs, & Posselt, 2016).

A common tool utilized by four-year colleges to enhance their reputation is the use of campus amenities and intercollegiate athletics. Research has shown that students' subjective experiences (which are formed in part by student services) heavily influenced the likelihood that they would donate to their college—both as seniors and as alumni (Freeland, Spenner, & Mc-Calmon, 2015). Increased spending on student services and auxiliary enterprises such as residence halls and recreation centers tend to disproportionately attract relatively low-achieving, high-income students who tend to get relatively small financial aid packages and thus generate tuition revenue (Jacob, McCall, & Stange, 2013).

Even at highly selective colleges, the presence of competitive athletics programs can be a key factor in inducing students to apply and attend (Stevens, 2009)—or even be the way that a student learns that a particular college exists. Athletics success in high-profile sports such as men's basketball and football has been shown to increase both the number of applications the college receives from low-achieving and high-achieving students (Pope & Pope, 2009) as well as alumni donation and engagement (e.g., Anderson, 2012; Martinez et al., 2010). But this comes at a cost, as the majority of Division I programs (the highest level of intercollegiate athletics) run substantial operating deficits (Wolverton & Bauman, 2016) and efforts to shutter or downsize football programs run into opposition from alumni and donors (New, 2016; Scarborough, 2015).[2]

All of these efforts to enhance a college's reputation can quickly be undermined by one academic scandal, inappropriate tweet, or violent crime. An empirical examination of scandals at top-100 research universities between 2001 and 2013 by Luca, Rooney, and Smith (2016) estimated that a scandal with significant media coverage was associated with a 10% drop in applications for the following academic year—similar to dropping ten spots in the U.S. News & World Report college rankings. In many cases, the only way a college receives statewide or national media attention other than athletics is through scandals or corruption—not the way a college wants to show up in the news (Lane, 2007).

Estimates of the effects of adverse publicity at individual colleges are also quite large. Pennsylvania State University has faced a financial hit of at least $237 million following the sexual assault scandal involving former assistant football coach Jerry Sandusky (Scolforo, 2017), while Baylor's sexual assault scandal may end up costing the university $220 million (Ellis, 2016). After a Seton Hall University student was shot in September 2010 in an off-campus incident that garnered national headlines (Baker & Schweber, 2010), the number of undergraduate applications for the following academic year dropped from 11,397 to 6,436 and new first-year students fell from 1,313 to 993 (Beale, 2013). Although applicants and enrollments both recovered the following year, it shows the power of an adverse publicity event on an institution's bottom line.

Colleges' reputations can also be affected through organized advocacy campaigns that are designed to get a college to change its behavior. Some advocacy campaigns are more broadly tied to social trends. These include efforts to get colleges to end relationships with companies doing business with Israel or with Israeli institutions (McMurtrie, 2014), attempts to get colleges to support the Black Lives Matter movement (Brown, Mangan, & McMurtrie, 2016), and campaigns to end ties with companies that are alleged to have unfair or substandard labor practices (Dosh, 2013).

Advocacy campaigns can also be specific to particular colleges. Efforts to fire college presidents or high-profile coaches are relatively common, as their large salaries and public presence makes them frequent targets of critics. Recent presidents to be fired or resign after protests include Kenneth Starr at Baylor amid a sexual assault scandal within the university's football team (Ambrose & Tarrant, 2016), the leaders of both Ithaca College and the University of Missouri–Columbia over alleged weak responses to incidents of racism on campus (Svrluga, 2016a), and the president of Washington's Green River Community College after allegations of unfair labor practices (Long, 2016). In recent years, several college football coaches have been fired with multiple years remaining on their contracts, requiring donors to cover large buyout penalties. Between 2012 and 2014, seven coaches were fired with buyouts of over $5 million each (Schlabach, 2015).

Finally, advocacy campaigns can also have dual missions of trying to get colleges to change their behaviors of their own volition and through appeals to other stakeholders with formal oversight over an institution. One example of this is the Washington, DC–based Education Trust's efforts to highlight colleges where Pell Grant recipients graduated at similar rates to students who did not receive Pell Grants, and shaming colleges that did not provide Pell graduation data to the federal government. In this case, the goal was to both get colleges to focus on equity and to get the U.S. Department of Education to enforce existing laws (Nichols, 2015; Nichols & Santos, 2016). Another example is at Morehouse College in Georgia, where an advocacy campaign to pressure the board of trustees to reconsider its decision not to renew the college president's contract garnered so much media attention that the college's accreditor decided to launch an investigation (Harris, 2017).

College Ratings and Rankings

A more formal method of external accountability is through the development of private-sector ratings and rankings designed to reflect a college's quality or standing based on a set of subjective or objective criteria. Although ratings and rankings are nothing new in American higher education (and colleges respond to some of the modern-day efforts in a similar way to how they did decades ago), the ability of the public to access the information instantaneously as well as the sheer number of organizations doing rankings and ratings has turned this type of accountability into a high-stakes system for many colleges that can determine whether campus leaders keep their jobs. Colleges have also responded to rankings in unintended ways, and in some cases even attempt to game the accountability system in their favor.

CARNEGIE CLASSIFICATIONS

This influential set of college ratings was first released in 1973, when Clark Kerr (former president of the University of California and then head of the Carnegie Commission on Higher Education) attempted to categorize degree-granting colleges based on their degree offerings and missions. The goal of the classifications was to help colleges and policymakers understand which institutions had similar profiles and missions, and that is still one of the purposes they serve today. These classifications are updated roughly every five to seven years and now have separate classifications by degree offerings, program mix, size and setting, and whether a high percentage of students transfer (Carnegie Classification of Institutions of Higher Education, 2016).

An unintended consequence of the Carnegie classifications was that because similar colleges were grouped together, it became obvious that some classifications contained the vast majority of elite institutions. For example, the term "research-one university" quickly became the marker for elite research universities and is still used today in spite of the Carnegie classification system abandoning that term decades ago (Altbach, 2015). Other "striving" colleges are trying to become research universities in an effort to enhance their status (e.g., Brint, Riddle, & Hanneman, 2006; Morphew, 2000). To do this, universities devote a larger percentage of their budgets to research relative to instruction and increase total expenditures (Iglesias, 2014; Morphew & Baker, 2004).

Between the 2010 and 2015 classifications, 43 colleges moved from master's or baccalaureate classifications to doctoral (research), while just nine moved in the other direction (Carnegie Classification of Institutions of Higher Education, 2016). The move to doctoral status is important, as some college rankings (such as *U.S. News & World Report* and *Washington Monthly*) base their classifications on the Carnegie classification system. For the *U.S. News* rankings, master's colleges are separated by region and get far less attention than the national university list. This led Villanova University, which was classified as a master's university in the 2010 Carnegie classifications, to make reaching the Carnegie research status a key strategic goal. They met this goal in the 2013–14 academic year by awarding exactly the minimum 20 research doctorates needed to meet the Carnegie research threshold.[3] The university celebrated its new classification in 2016, with the provost calling it "the dawn of a new age at Villanova" (Anderson, 2016). They celebrated again later in the year when they debuted in the national *U.S. News* rankings in a tie for number 50.

BARRON'S COMPETITIVENESS RATINGS

Another influential set of classifications is the *Barron's* college competitiveness ratings. These ratings, a part of *Barron's* annual *Profiles of American Colleges* publication, group four-year colleges into six main selectivity classifications (as well as a classification for special-focus institutions) based on the percentage of undergraduate students admitted, typical ACT/SAT scores, and high school grades and class rank (Barron's Educational Series, 2016). These classifications, which run from "most competitive" to "noncompetitive," represent a way colleges can be grouped into reasonable sets of peer institutions.[4] The *Barron's* ratings are presented in the media and by foundations in the context of encouraging students to attend more-selective institutions (Jack Kent Cooke Foundation, 2015; Leonhardt, 2013), highlighting the importance of these ratings to colleges.

There has been a clear shift away from less-competitive colleges and toward more-competitive colleges over the last several decades. Table 6.1 shows the number of four-year colleges in each ratings category in 1991, 2001, 2011, and 2016, with the data from the first three periods coming from Hess and Hochleitner (2012) and the most recent data being compiled by my research assistant Olga Komissarova. The number of colleges in the highest selectivity category (most competitive) increased from 44 to 106 in the last 25 years, while the number of colleges in the least selective categories (less competitive and noncompetitive) fell from 467 in 1991 to 248 in 2016. The most competitive category now contains some relatively surprising names,

TABLE 6.1   Trends in *Barron's* competitiveness ratings, 1991–2016

Classification	1991	2001	2011	2016
Most competitive	44	59	87	106
Highly competitive	87	89	105	72
Very competitive	226	265	273	235
Competitive	645	542	687	730
Less competitive	330	342	195	190
Noncompetitive	137	133	80	58
Total	1,469	1,430	1,427	1,391

SOURCES: *Barron's* annual books with data compiled by Hess & Hochleitner, 2012 (1991–2011) and author's research assistant (2016).

Note: Colleges with "plus" designations (such as very competitive+) are combined with the main rating categories. This excludes a small category of "special" colleges with highly specialized academic programs.

such as SUNY Binghamton, Hamilton College, the New College of Florida, and the University of Minnesota, alongside Ivy League universities and elite liberal arts colleges.

CREDIT RATINGS

An often-overlooked accountability metric is a college's creditworthiness, which reflects a college's ability to generate sufficient revenue in the future to pay off current obligations. Colleges that wish to issue bonds will request a rating from one or more of the three main credit rating agencies (Fitch, Moody's, and Standard & Poor's), with the resulting rating affecting the interest rate that bondholders receive and colleges have to pay.[5] For example, the College of Saint Elizabeth and Seton Hall University both issued 30-year loans through the state of New Jersey in fall 2016. Saint Elizabeth, which recently went coed in an effort to stem enrollment losses (Clark, 2015) and does not have a separate credit rating, faced a 4.56% interest rate on its loan. Seton Hall, which has an A3 rating (seventh highest of the 21 possible ratings), received a 3.19% interest rate (New Jersey Educational Facilities Authority, 2016).

Credit ratings agencies have generally been concerned about the future creditworthiness of much of higher education. In 2009, Moody's gave a negative outlook to the higher education sector in the midst of the Great Recession, with a stable rating for elite higher education in 2011 and 2012 (Martin, 2013). Moody's did not change its outlook to stable for all of higher education until 2015 (Global Credit Research, 2015). While nearly all colleges that received ratings were listed as investment grade, this covers only about one-third of all four-year colleges (Moody's Investors Service, 2015). The types of colleges that do not have credit ratings tend to be financially struggling colleges that cannot access capital at reasonable interest rates. Moody's expects that more of these colleges will close in the future, with the predicted rate of private college closures tripling to about 15 per year in the next several years (Woodhouse, 2015).

TYPES OF COLLEGE RANKINGS

Perhaps the best-known form of private-sector accountability comes through the plethora of college rankings and guidebooks that have developed over the past several decades. Since *U.S. News & World Report* published its initial set of college rankings in 1983, dozens of organizations with various policy preferences and definitions of quality have developed their own rankings of colleges and individual programs. (I've been in this game since 2012 as the methodologist for *Washington Monthly* magazine's rankings.) Although many colleges will not publicly admit paying attention to rankings, they do feel pressure to improve their standing due to rankings' influence on public perception of quality (e.g., Espeland & Sauder, 2007). For example, one dean compared the release of the *U.S. News* law school rankings to when she "used to live in an apartment that had roaches" (Sauder & Espeland, 2009, 69). My employer, Seton Hall University, has a prominent page on its institutional website listing its rankings from over 20 different providers (Seton Hall University, 2016).

Table 6.2 summarizes nine of the best-known institutional-level rankings that are specific to American colleges and universities. Most of these rankings are focused on four-year colleges, with only the Payscale rankings regularly including two-year colleges. The decision to focus on four-year colleges is likely for two main reasons. First, because the median community college student attends college just eight miles from their home (Hillman & Weichman, 2016), a national ranking of two-year colleges has less value and is less likely to attract readers than a ranking of selective colleges.[6] Second, available data on two-year colleges have traditionally been of lower quality than in the four-year college sector. For example, the federal graduation rate metric (which only includes first-time, full-time, degree-seeking students) initially covers most first-time students at four-year colleges, but it immediately excludes 37% of two-year students because they were starting college part-time (National Center for Education Statistics, 2016).

The *U.S. News* rankings have been tweaked repeatedly over the last three decades, but the general components of reputation (measured through surveys of fellow college administrators and guidance counselors), graduation

TABLE 6.2   Summary of major American college ranking providers

Organization	Rankings began	Colleges ranked	Main criteria
The Economist	2015	1,275 4-year colleges	Actual vs. predicted earnings of former students
Forbes/Center for College Affordability and Productivity	2008	660 higher-performing 4-year colleges	Earnings, prominent alumni, student reviews of faculty, student outcomes
Kiplinger's	1999	300 higher-performing 4-year colleges	Selectivity, affordability, graduation rates, student debt
Money	2014	705 higher-performing 4-year colleges	Educational quality, affordability, labor market outcomes and well-being
Payscale	2008	381 2-year colleges, 963 4-year colleges	Midcareer earnings of graduates
Princeton Review	1992	381 higher-performing 4-year colleges	62 "best" lists based on student surveys (main list is not ranked)
U.S. News & World Report	1983	1,374 4-year colleges	Graduation rates, reputational surveys, selectivity, institutional resources
Wall Street Journal/ Times Higher Education	2016	1,000 4-year colleges	Institutional resources, student engagement, student outcomes and reputation, diverse environment
Washington Monthly	2005	1,406 4-year colleges	Social mobility, research, community and national service

SOURCES: College rankings organizations' websites.
    Notes: This is not a complete list of organizations doing college rankings and also does not cover program-level rankings. *Kiplinger's* did not begin annual rankings until 2007, and *U.S. News* did not begin annual rankings until 1988.

rates, selectivity, and institutional resources have been fairly similar across time. The *Princeton Review* rankings—the next-oldest set of continuously operating rankings—are based on reputational surveys from students and currently have 62 lists of top-20 colleges in a wide range of categories that cover virtually all parts of the college experience. *Princeton Review*, like

Kiplinger's, Money, and *Forbes*, limit their rankings to the top half or quarter of four-year colleges on a predetermined set of quality metrics.

A newer set of rankings has focused on the economic returns to college, relying on data sources that have become available over the last decade. The first consistent source of graduates' earnings came from Payscale, which debuted its rankings based on midcareer earnings in 2008. Although the data are self-reported by the site's users and are not necessarily a perfect measure of earnings, the Payscale rankings did bring the return on investment into the conversation.[7] The release of the College Scorecard dataset by the U.S. Department of Education in 2015 made earnings data available for a wider number of colleges, and included dropouts as well as graduates. Several rankings, including the *Economist,* the *Wall Street Journal, Money,* and *Washington Monthly,* have already incorporated the data into their rankings.

Another recent trend in college rankings (as well as in higher education research) is to use more rigorous empirical methods to ascertain whether colleges are doing a good job educating their students at a reasonable cost. There are two main ways rankers and researchers have attempted to do this. The first is through the use of a "value-added" framework to estimate effectiveness. Unlike in K–12 education, most value-added estimates in higher education do not have repeated scores on the same measure (such as standardized test scores). Instead, value-added estimates for outcomes such as graduation rates and earnings are predicted by first using regressions controlling for institutional characteristics and then comparing these to the actual metrics. (e.g., Cunha & Miller, 2014; Kelchen & Harris, 2012; Kurlaender, Carrell, & Jackson, 2016; Rothwell & Kulkarni, 2015). These value-added estimates are now components of the *U.S. News, Money*, and *Washington Monthly* rankings, among other providers.

The future of American college rankings may lie in more sophisticated mathematical methods to estimate quality or effectiveness. One potential technique is called data envelopment analysis, in which regression techniques are used to estimate whether a college is operating efficiently compared to similar institutions (e.g., Archibald & Feldman, 2008; Eckles, 2010; Eff, Klein, & Kyle, 2012). Another potential method could be through the use of revealed preferences. Avery, Glickman, Hoxby, and Metrick (2013) examined survey data from over 3,000 high-achieving students on where they were accepted and where they attended to see which colleges they preferred. This yielded Harvard as the top four-year college, with California Institute of Technology, Yale University, Massachusetts Institute of Technology, and Stanford University all in the top five.

In addition to college ranking systems that are focused solely on the

TABLE 6.3   Summary of major global college ranking providers

Organization	Rankings began	Colleges ranked	Main criteria
Academic Ranking of World Universities	2003	500	Alumni awards, faculty awards, citation counts, publications in top science journals
Center for World University Rankings	2012	1000	Alumni awards and employment, faculty awards, citation counts and patents
QS World University Rankings	2004	916	Reputation among other academics and employers, student/faculty ratios, citation counts, internationalization
Times Higher Education	2009	978	Teaching and research reputation, citation counts, internationalization
U.S. News & World Report	2014	750	Research reputation, number of publications, citation counts, internationalization

SOURCES: College rankings organizations' websites.

Note: All universities included in these rankings are research-focused four-year institutions. This excludes program-specific rankings as well as broader ratings such as U-Multirank that do not allow for the calculation of explicit rankings.

United States, there are a number of prominent global efforts to rank colleges beginning with the Academic Ranking of World Universities in 2003 and continuing through U.S. News & World Report's first foray into the global rankings market in 2014. As illustrated in Table 6.3, these ranking systems are primarily focused on a relatively small percentage of research universities and give the most weight to research quantity and quality.[8] The heavy emphasis on research metrics, such as the number of publications in top venues, the frequency with which publications are cited, and the awards received by faculty, is likely because these metrics are available across a large number of countries. However, these methods are criticized for their focus on the sciences and a lack of coverage of publications in languages other than English (e.g., van Raan, van Leeuwen, & Visser, 2011).

In addition to the more empirically focused set of institutional-level rankings both inside and outside the United States, there are a large number of other rankings and guides. Numerous publications rank individual graduate programs, such as the *U.S. News* suite of rankings and the National Research Council rankings that separately rank multiple programs and publications such as *Businessweek* and Above the Law that focus on a single discipline. There are also a sizable number of lesser-known rankings in various programs that do not always make their methodology transparent—or even available. An example of an empirically dubious ranking system comes from a website called Teacher.org, which ranks graduate programs in educational leadership based solely on data on undergraduate students (Teacher.org, 2016).

Other types of college rankings do not claim to be as empirically rigorous, but still get the attention of colleges and the public. A website called Thrillist highlighted subjective rankings nicely: "We based these mostly on our completely subjective gut feelings about whether we'd want to go to these schools, the tolerability of the student body and alums, and other random things that will drive you crazy if you try and parse them in a logical manner" (Lynch & Alexander, 2015). A BuzzFeed contributor created a ranking of the "sexiest, smartest colleges" by combining Forbes's academic rankings with a hotness index from an online dating site (North, 2013). Readers of the site were not amused and gave the post a rating of "fail." *Playboy* put out a list of top party schools for years, listing "the top 10 colleges with a higher degree in modern revelry" (*Playboy*, 2015).

Princeton Review also does annual party school rankings (and "stone-cold sober school" rankings) that get a lot of attention. The University of Wisconsin-Madison's response to being ranked as the top party school was to note the academic strengths of the university along with the negative implications of excessive drinking (Kingkade, 2016). Meanwhile, Brigham Young University (which is controlled by the Church of Jesus Christ of Latter-day Saints and where drinking alcohol is not allowed) celebrated its nineteenth consecutive year atop the "stone-cold sober" rankings by putting the designation on its creamery's chocolate milk bottles (Jones, 2016). The range of rankings has also led to publications such as *Slate* and the *New Republic* ranking the value of each college rankings system, which was then spoofed in a piece in the *Atlantic* titled "Ranking the College Ranking Rankings" (Meyer, 2013).

EFFECTS OF CHANGING RANKING POSITIONS

Although just 17% of college presidents surveyed by Gallup, Inc. (2016) said that college rankings were a very important metric of evaluating a president, the reality is that few selective four-year colleges systemically ignore college rankings for long periods of time (e.g., Friedrich, 2011; Rivard, 2014). At these institutions, moving up in the various college rankings (typically *U.S. News*) has become a key strategic goal. For example, Seton Hall University (ranked 118th by *U.S. News* in 2016) has set a strategic goal of being a top-5 Catholic university and a top-75 national university, up from being a top-100 university in the previous strategic plan (Marshall, 2016).

The Kentucky legislature and the University of Kentucky made a compact in 1997 to become a top-20 public research university by 2012 and the university requested an additional $260 million in funding over this time period. The state provided some of this funding, but Kentucky's ranking barely budged over this time (Fowles, Frederickson, & Koppell, 2016). Some institutions, such as Arizona State University and Virginia Commonwealth University, have gone as far as tying presidential pay or bonuses to their performance in the rankings (Jaschik, 2007; Thompson, 2003).

Northeastern University, which was ranked 162nd in the national *U.S. News* rankings in 1996, embarked upon a systemic effort to rise in the rankings. The university's new president, Richard Freeland, planned to replicate the *U.S. News* rankings formula in an effort to move up the largest number of spots in the rankings at the lowest price. Northeastern proceeded to finesse class sizes, moving to the Common Application to get more applications, and increasing public relations efforts to move up in the peer assessments (Kutner, 2014). Freeland's efforts got Northeastern up to 98th by 2006, and they were 39th in the 2017 rankings. But the net price at Northeastern for students with family incomes below $30,000 per year was $18,240 in 2013–14, raising concerns about affordability and contributing to a ranking of 238 by *Washington Monthly*.

Success stories like Northeastern's are fairly uncommon, as any college trying to improve their performance in the rankings quickly realizes that rankings are a competition. In order to move up one spot in the rankings, a college must displace another institution that likely has the same goal. This has led to very little movement toward the top of the rankings. Between 2002 and 2010, at most one new college entered the top 10 each year and two entered the top 50 (Ortagus, 2016). In addition, the correlation between the 2003 and 2012 rankings for national universities was 0.968 and 0.930 for liberal arts colleges (Fowles, Frederickson, & Koppell, 2016). Changes in the rankings are so slow to happen because reputational surveys are heavily influenced by past rankings and also affect future assessments (Bastedo & Bowman, 2010; Bowman & Bastedo, 2011). This makes quick rises in the rankings even more difficult.

Another reason for stability in the rankings is that moving up is an incredibly expensive proposition that requires increased spending across the entire institution (e.g., Kim, 2015). For a research university ranked in the mid-30s, moving up one spot would require increasing SAT scores by 100 points, increasing graduation rates by 2%, increasing alumni giving rates by 3%, or spending $7,400 more per student per year—a difficult proposition (Gnolek, Falciano, & Kuncl, 2014). This helps to explain why the probability of a top-50 college moving by more than four spots in a given year is very low (Grewal, Dearden, & Lilien, 2008).

Yet colleges endeavor to move up in the rankings because of the growing importance of rankings in the college choice processes of certain students. In fall 1995, 9% of incoming freshmen at baccalaureate/master's colleges and 13% attending research universities noted that rankings were "very important" in making the decision to attend that college (Sax et al., 1996). By fall 2005, those percentages rose to 13% and 22%, respectively (Pryor et al., 2006) and to 15% and 26% in fall 2015 (Eagan et al., 2016). Fully two-thirds of a national sample of SAT takers who were seniors in high school reported using rankings to at least some extent (Art & Science Group, 2013).

A body of research has shown that higher-income and higher-achieving students are particularly responsive to college rankings. At the most selective universities, 38% of first-year students said that rankings were a "very important" consideration in 2015, higher than the percentage of students who rated price and graduation rates as very important (Eagan et al., 2016). Griffith and Rask (2007) examined admissions data and concluded that students (particularly those with the ability to pay the full sticker price without receiving any financial aid) considering highly selective colleges are more likely to attend a higher-ranked college after controlling for other factors, particularly among full-pay students. About 15% of students in the bottom half of the income distribution reported that rankings were very important in their college choice decision, compared to nearly 25% in the top quartile (Espinosa, Crandall, & Tukibayeva, 2014). Further evidence is provided by Hurwitz and Smith (2016), who found that students from high schools in wealthy areas were more likely to send their SAT scores to colleges with higher earnings in the College Scorecard dataset.

A college's position in the *U.S. News* rankings has been shown to be associated with changes in a college's student characteristics.[9] Multiple studies have shown that colleges that rose in the rankings—and particularly if they made the top 25 or top 50—had significantly higher numbers of applications, lower acceptance rates, and higher standardized test scores than colleges that did not rise (Alter & Reback, 2014; Bowman & Bastedo, 2009; Luca & Smith, 2013; Meredith, 2004; Monks & Ehrenberg, 1999; Ortagus, 2016). Yet moving up in the rankings is also associated with decreases in African American student enrollment, raising concerns about equity and diversity (Ortagus, 2016).

Rankings can also affect a college's financial position. Public colleges in a lower *U.S. News* ranking tier had lower out-of-state tuition levels than higher-tier colleges eight years later after controlling for other factors (Bastedo & Bowman, 2011), a significant concern for institutions looking to balance their budgets through nonresident tuition. Monks and Ehrenberg (1999) found that selective private colleges that suffered small drops in the rankings did not respond by reducing tuition, but they did have to offer students additional grant aid in order for them to come. This resulted in a 0.3% drop in net tuition revenue for each one-point fall in the rankings.

There is research evidence that colleges that had large drops in the rankings increased their tuition in an effort to appear more prestigious—an example of the "Chivas Regal effect" in which consumers value a good more because of its high price tag (Askin & Bothner, 2016). However, this study did not consider net tuition revenue, which means that these colleges could have substantially increased grant aid as well as tuition. Finally, Holmes (2009) found that as a college's *U.S. News* ranking rose, donation amounts by young alumni significantly increased, highlighting another mechanism through which rankings could affect institutional finances.

CRITIQUES OF RANKINGS

Those with knowledge of higher education generally do not consider rankings to be a perfect measure of a college's performance. For example, nearly 90% of college admissions counselors at least somewhat agreed that the *U.S. News* rankings offer misleading conclusions about the quality of individual colleges (National Association for College Admission Counseling, 2011). As the methodologist for *Washington Monthly*'s annual college rankings since 2012, I have lost count of the number of e-mails I have received from public relations staffers and provost's offices about their college's performance. While many of these critiques are quite thoughtful, others are not as well considered. I still remember an e-mail I received from the president of a small midwestern college in 2012 that had the following section (whose name I will withhold in spite of the letter being published in the magazine): "What kind of Rube Goldberg-inspired formula would lead to this result? Sorry, folks, but you've discredited yourselves with such mathematical nonsense. In the future you'd better stick to subjects that you know something about. Math and ranking methodologies sure aren't among them."

Although colleges frequently complain about their position in the rankings, fewer colleges are willing to fully opt out of the rankings because of the attention these rankings receive. About 70% of colleges that are included in the *U.S. News* rankings actively promote their ranking in some form (National Association for College Admission Counseling, 2011), although sometimes lower-ranked colleges will note that they are included in the rankings instead of noting their ordinal ranking (Luca & Smith, 2015). In the 2000s, the presidents of about 70 colleges (primarily small liberal arts colleges) signed a letter saying they would refuse to promote their *U.S. News* rankings, but would still provide data to the magazine in order to be included in the rankings (Education Conservancy, 2007).[10]

More colleges are opting out of the reputational survey component of the *U.S. News* rankings while staying in the main rankings. Participation rates have fallen from 67% in 2005 to about 50% in 2015, forcing *U.S. News* to average multiple years of data to increase precision (Jaschik, 2015). Only a small number of colleges fully opt out of the *U.S. News* rankings, as that likely lowers their ranking due to how *U.S. News* treats missing data. Reed College in Oregon (ranked 87th by *U.S. News*) is the most prominent to opt out of all cooperation, which it has done since 1995, although it alleges that its rank would be higher if it provided information (Lydgate, 2015). Other less-selective colleges that refused to participate in the rankings in 2016 included Delta State University, Paine College, Northwestern State University, and Viterbo College.

Colleges that participate in the rankings have a number of valid concerns and complaints about rankings. First of all, many of the metrics included in college rankings only serve as proxies for the true items of interest (Longden, 2011), and metrics such as student engagement (aside from unrepresentative opinion surveys) are not well captured in most college rankings (Pike, 2004). For example, retention and graduation rates are often used as a rough measure of the college's academic quality and represent an even rougher measure of student learning. Value-added metrics, which attempt to compare colleges to institutions with similar characteristics, help to address concerns about outcomes being correlated with student demographics.

The use of per-student expenditures as a ranking criterion, as is the case in the *U.S. News* rankings, has been widely criticized as a weak proxy for academic quality because the funds could be used on an array of educational and non-educational purposes. John Duffy, a professor at George Washington University's law school, eloquently made this point in a *New York Times* interview: "I once joked with my dean that there is a certain amount of money that we could drag into the middle of the school's quadrangle and burn, and when the flames died down, we'd be a Top 10 school. As long as the point of the bonfire was to teach our students. Perhaps what we could teach them is the idiocy in the US News rankings" (Segal, 2011). The availability of new data sources is helping to reduce the need for proxy measures in some cases. The release of the updated College Scorecard dataset in 2015 made data on postcollege earnings—a key outcome of interest for many students and families—available to additional rankings providers. The large-scale (although not necessarily representative) survey of students in the new *Wall Street Journal/Times Higher Education* rankings also bears watching as an improvement in estimating student engagement and satisfaction at a larger number of colleges.

Another valid critique of college rankings is that even though students respond to small changes in a college's ranking, these changes are generally not statistically significant or educationally meaningful (Clarke, 2002; Kelchen & Harris, 2012). Dichev (2001) estimated that about 70%–80% of the annual change in the *U.S. News* rankings is due to random noise such as measurement and estimation errors rather than meaningful changes in a college's performance. Gnolek, Falciano, and Kuncl (2014) noted that among colleges near the top of the *U.S. News* rankings, movements of fewer than four spots should be considered "noise."

Finally, colleges are also concerned that other institutions are reporting inaccurate data to college rankings providers. In a survey of college admissions officers, only 1% of respondents admitted to falsely reporting admissions data to college rankings providers, but 93% thought that other colleges do so (Jaschik & Lederman, 2014). Indeed, in the 2012–13 academic year, five colleges admitted giving out false data to *U.S. News*—either through an honest mistake or with an intent of deception (Jaschik, 2013). But since data provided to college rankings providers (or the federal government, for that matter) are not audited to guarantee accuracy, the rate of inaccurate data may be higher than reported.

Efforts to Game College Rankings

Because the annual release of college rankings has become a high-stakes event for many selective four-year colleges, theories of how organizations respond to incentives (see chapter 1 for a summary) would suggest that colleges would attempt to improve their positioning without changing their day-to-day activities. This results in a number of efforts to game the ranking system, thus leading to the classic performance paradox (Van Thiel & Leeuw, 2002) in which the rankings system can become a weaker measure of a college's performance over time unless the metrics used to rank colleges are also updated on a regular basis. These efforts can range from the fairly mundane to outright fraud, and I include some examples in this section.

Colleges will work to tweak their practices to meet incentives provided by rankings providers while still fulfilling their missions, with a particular focus on manipulating metrics that are close to the threshold set in rankings systems. Because some key metrics used in college rankings, such as standardized test scores and retention/graduation rates, are based on first-time, full-time students who began in the fall semester, colleges have an incentive to admit only the students with the highest likelihood of success in the fall semester. For example, the University of Maryland enrolls nearly one-fifth of its new students during the spring semester, and these students have average SAT scores 100 points lower than fall admits (Anderson, 2014). This strategy does help improve the university's *U.S. News* ranking, but it also helps Maryland increase its diversity and operate at capacity after some students do not return for the spring semester. This allows the university to simultaneously meet goals of encouraging social mobility and looking good in prestige-based rankings.

An unusually frank conference presentation by a former institutional research analyst at Clemson University, Catherine Watt (2009), highlighted other ways colleges will subtly change their practices in response to the rankings criteria. Clemson was trying to reach its 2001 strategic goal of being a top-20 public university by 2011, up from 38th in 2001 (Office of the President, 2007). Watt's presentation listed some of the easy ways to improve the university's *U.S. News* ranking, such as manipulating classes in the 18–21 and 49–52 student ranges (as the key thresholds are at 20 and 50 students), pushing less-prepared students into not enrolling full-time in the first semester, and mailing Clemson materials to other presidents in an effort to enhance the university's reputation. A far more controversial admission in Watt's presentation was that the university always had its administrators rate all institutions other than Clemson below average on *U.S. News*'s peer assessment survey (Watt, 2009). Yet even by taking these steps, Clemson was in a three-way tie for 25th by 2011—and they did not win the football championship, which was also a part of their strategic goal, until 2017.

Watt also said about Clemson's efforts to manipulate reputation surveys:

"I'm confident my president is not the only one who does that" (Lederman, 2009). Further investigations revealed that she was correct. University of Florida president Bernie Machen gave his institution (and a small number of elite institutions) the highest "distinguished" ranking, while giving most others in Florida the lowest rankings of "adequate" or "marginal" (Crabbe, 2009). *Inside Higher Ed* filed open records requests for the reputational surveys of 48 public colleges and got 18 responses with some revealing findings. At the University of Wisconsin–Madison, the administrator who completed the survey ranked 260 of 262 colleges (all but Wisconsin and where the administrator's son was attending college) as adequate. Only three of the 18 universities that released surveys did not rank themselves as distinguished (Lee, 2009). In 2012, a marketing firm (likely working on behalf of a college) sent out a survey titled "U.S. News and World Report Peer Assessment Survey Participant" in an effort to get college presidents to explain how they would rate a dozen selective research universities and the particular factors that would affect their rating. None of the universities on the survey would acknowledge sending it out (Jaschik, 2012).

Perhaps the most extreme attempt by a college to manipulate its rankings and look good on a key market-based accountability mechanism came in 2015, when Mount St. Mary's University's new president, Simon Newman, surveyed all incoming students during orientation. Although the survey was ostensibly about helping students discover factors associated with motivation and success, e-mails obtained by the university's student newspaper revealed that the true intention of the plan was to identify 20–25 students who would be dismissed before the date of record for the semester—meaning these students would not show up in the cohort used to calculate retention and graduation rates. The goal of the plan was to immediately increase retention by 4%–5% (Schisler & Golden, 2016).

Other faculty and administrators immediately objected to Newman's plan, and the president was unhappy. He told an administrator that "you just have to drown the bunnies . . . put a Glock to their heads." This got reported by the college newspaper (Schisler & Golden, 2016), which started a firestorm on campus. Newman responded by firing the newspaper's faculty adviser and a tenured faculty member and initially ignored an overwhelming vote of the faculty asking him to resign for his actions. He eventually resigned six weeks after the newspaper broke the story amid national scrutiny, in part because the college's accreditor got involved and threatened sanctions over concerns with leadership, integrity, and admissions practices (Svrluga, 2016b).

Conclusion

Colleges face a large and growing number of private-sector accountability pressures that are far more intense than they were decades ago. While reputation and prestige have always been concerns for many institutions (particularly four-year colleges), the never-ending news cycle and instantaneous nature of modern communications have placed colleges into a position in which they must be able to immediately respond to protests, crises, or other threats to a college's reputation. The rapid dissemination of information can also complicate interactions with other stakeholders who can hold colleges accountable for their performance, such as federal and state governments or accrediting agencies.

The recent proliferation of college rankings and ratings, many of which prioritize different outcomes, further complicate the accountability landscape. While *U.S. News & World Report* is still the dominant rankings provider in the United States, the wide range of both institutional-level and program-level rankings can be used by stakeholders to hold colleges accountable for their preferred outcomes. The improved availability of outcomes data through the federal government—and the likelihood of additional improvements that would allow for even more detailed private-sector rankings—will force colleges to further prioritize which accountability metrics are the most important to respond to and which ones are less important to stakeholders and funders.

A good example of rising private-sector accountability pressures and the interaction with public-sector accountability is the awkward situation the University of North Carolina found itself in after the state's Republican governor signed legislation requiring individuals to use bathrooms consistent with their gender at birth. The Obama administration's Department of Justice sued to block the law and listed the university as a defendant, while system president Margaret Spellings (former secretary of education for George W. Bush) said that she would not enforce the law (Mytelka, 2016).

The university has faced intense pressure from both supporters and opponents of the law, which ratcheted up even further when both the National Collegiate Athletic Association (NCAA) and the Atlantic Coast Conference announced that they were moving all championship events from the state for the 2016–17 academic year as a result of the law (Beaton, 2016). Republican lawmakers initially responded by doubling down on the law and criticizing the NCAA for not giving Baylor University stricter penalties for its sexual assault scandal (Peralta, 2016) before finally acceding to pressure to repeal the law in April 2017. The NCAA then "reluctantly" lifted its ban on postseason events in North Carolina, as they were still concerned about the legislature's ability to resume restrictions on which bathrooms an individual can use (Tracy, 2017). The continuing tension between Republican legislators who supported the original bill and key private-sector organizations and student groups fighting to make sure the bill never comes back has the potential to affect the university's funding and autonomy, leaving the university to walk a fine line of pacifying the legislature while also satisfying key constituencies.

CHAPTER SEVEN

Institutional Accountability Policies and Practices

IN ADDITION TO the external forms of accountability that have been discussed in the previous four chapters, colleges work to hold themselves accountable internally. This type of self-accountability can serve three main purposes. First, college leaders typically seek to build trust among the institution's various stakeholders, such as students and their families, faculty, staff, and alumni. Having clear procedures in place regarding how decisions are made and who is accountable for the results can potentially help build support for institutional leaders, as well as help with the transition process when new leadership enters a college. The second purpose of internal accountability systems is the potential for a more efficient use of scarce resources. If the performance of faculty, staff, and administrators can be monitored by others, it is possible that individuals will work harder toward the organization's goals. By publicizing performance, colleges could also reallocate funds toward high-need areas and thus improve student success or reduce inefficient spending.

The third and final purpose of internal accountability—one that is often overlooked—is that transparent and effective efforts by colleges to hold themselves accountable can be used as tools to satisfy external stakeholders (such as state or federal governments or accrediting bodies) that wish to hold colleges accountable for their performance. Given that many stakeholders are charged with monitoring a large number of institutions at the same time, a college that has a strong self-regulation structure may be subject to fewer additional oversight requirements. This gives the institution more autonomy to operate as it sees fit.

Internal accountability structures can include several components. All colleges, regardless of whether they are public, private nonprofit, or for-profit, will have a leadership structure that is usually headlined by at least one governing board. Tenured and tenure-track faculty members at most public and private nonprofit colleges usually have some power through academic freedom and the shared governance process, while unionized faculty and staff at a sizable number of (mainly public) colleges also have the potential to hold college leaders accountable for their performance while pushing back against external accountability pressures that they deem unwise. Students can also exercise power through shared governance at some institutions and can highlight their views of faculty teaching quality through the course evaluation process.

However, these internal forms of accountability can also make the institution less accountable to the public if students, faculty, and administrators put their interests ahead of the best interests of other stakeholders. In this chapter, I discuss the components of internal accountability structures across the American higher education system and how they seek to hold faculty, staff, and administrators accountable for their performance. I also provide several examples of what happens when different stakeholders both inside and outside a college have differing views of performance and how that affects how a college operates.

Governing Boards

A college's governing board (and in some cases multiple boards) represents the final decision-making body of the institution. While these boards may still answer to other organizations such as state boards of higher education or accrediting bodies, they have the ability to hire and fire college presidents, enter into contracts for new facilities, and finalize academic policies and procedures. The structures of governing boards vary considerably across public, private nonprofit, and for-profit colleges due to the different stakeholders for each type of college. For that reason, I examine the characteristics and effectiveness of governing boards by institutional type.

PUBLIC COLLEGES AND UNIVERSITIES

Public institutions are governed by a board of trustees for an individual college or an entire system of higher education. These boards, which average 12 members (AGB Editor, 2016), are generally composed of members with some level of accountability to the public. The vast majority of governing board members at public four-year colleges are political appointments, similar to other state boards and commissions. A survey by Schwartz (2010a) found that 77% of trustees were appointed by the governor, typically with the consent of the state Senate.[1] States vary in the requirements they impose regarding geographic, political, racial/ethnic, or gender diversity of their trustees in an effort to ensure the trustees are broadly representative of the state as a whole. For example, the University of Missouri requires that each of the state's eight congressional districts have a member on the nine-member board of curators and that at most five curators have the same partisan affiliation (University of Missouri System, 2016). These requirements are not always followed in practice; Kentucky and Wyoming have had boards with far more members of the governor's political party than allowed (McNair, 2015; Todd, 2014).

Four states (Colorado, Nebraska, Nevada, and Michigan) have at least some trustees at four-year colleges elected by popular vote, which is a typical way to select school board members in K–12 education and a fairly common way to select community college trustees. While political appointments to governing boards typically match the governor's ideology to the extent possible, trustee elections at the two-year level generally do not include partisan labels. At the four-year level, candidates in Colorado and Michigan run with partisan affiliations while candidates in Nebraska and Nevada do not. Partisan affiliation can affect how colleges operate; the University of Colorado's Board of Regents is elected in partisan races and selected a former Republican gubernatorial nominee to be the university's president in 2008 on a party-line vote (Kuta, 2016).

At the vast majority of public colleges, there is one governing board with most members being either appointed or elected as above. But three colleges, all of which have private roots, have unusual governance structures. Clemson University's board has seven self-perpetuating seats, where current members with lifetime terms get to select new members, and six seats appointed by the state legislature as a stipulation of the donation that founded the institution (Clemson University, 2015). Rutgers University, which was initially founded as Queen's College in 1766, has a 41-member board of trustees that has responsibility over portions of the university that existed prior to the institution becoming public in 1956 in addition to a 15-member board of governors that is more typical of public universities (Rutgers, 2016). Finally, the University of Vermont has a 25-member board with nine self-perpetuating trustees, nine legislative appointments, three gubernatorial appointments, two students, the state's governor, and the university's president (University of Vermont, 2015).

Politically appointed board members come to colleges with distinct strengths and weaknesses. The greatest strength of political members is that they often have strong relationships with the governor and legislature, and thus can potentially help a public college make a stronger case for its priorities and perhaps even additional funding. Nearly two-thirds of all board members are in business or other professional fields outside of education (such as law or medicine), which can be advantageous in building relationships with the community and raising funds (Schwartz, 2010a). The drawback of having such well-connected trustees, conversely, is the inevitable possibility of conflicts of interest that can force trustees to recuse themselves from votes (Bastedo, 2009b).

Because politicians select the vast majority of governing board members, trustees at public colleges represent another type of state oversight over higher education in addition to the types of accountability discussed in chapter 4. State policymakers can use the trustee selection process to impose their own policy preferences, which may differ from what colleges prefer to do. The concern of so-called activist trustees (e.g., Bastedo, 2005, 2009a) has risen substantially in recent decades (Zumeta, 2001). This charge is typically levied against trustees who affiliate with the American Council of Trustees and Alumni (ACTA), an organization founded in 1995 amid dissatisfaction in primarily conservative circles with the dominant Association of Governing Boards of Universities and Colleges (AGB) that has traditionally represented governing board members. ACTA, with members at nearly 1,300 colleges, encourages trustees to actively work to support the liberal arts and hold colleges accountable for their performance (ACTA, 2015). AGB accuses ACTA of being an activist organization, while ACTA accuses AGB of being too supportive of college presidents and therefore not being an independent voice seeking to push colleges to improve their performance (ACTA, 2016; Legon, 2014).

Yet in spite of the political differences that may exist between trustees and presidents, they have similar views of the shared governance process. Respondents to a survey by Lounder (2016) indicated that they would like the shared governance process to operate more as a way to align priorities among institutional stakeholders such as faculty, staff, and students and less as a method of consultation or a way to set rules of engagement. This would give more power to boards and the presidents.

Political appointments to governing boards also raise concerns about the qualifications of trustees, particularly as states vary substantially in the amount of vetting and orientation given to potential board members. Unfortunately, there is little rigorous empirical research examining the implications of trustee qualifications. Minor (2008) examined the five states with the most rigorous trustee selection processes and the five least rigorous processes and found that states with the most rigorous processes tended to have higher-performing institutions, although this relationship is certainly not causal.

Another concern with politically appointed trustees is that they may feel pressure to grant special favors to the politicians who helped them obtain their positions. A prime example of this happened at the University of Illinois in the late 2000s, where an open records request filed by the *Chicago Tribune* revealed that at least 800 applicants were flagged for special consideration due to their ties to legislators or trustees. Some of the admitted applicants had test scores so low that the university had to admit additional students in order to not affect their ranking (Cohen, St. Clair, & Malone, 2009a). An independent review commission appointed by the governor of Illinois recommended that all nine members of the board of trustees resign (State of Illinois Admissions Review Commission, 2009), and seven members and the board's president did resign (Malone, St. Clair, & Cohen, 2009) along with the university's president (Cohen, St. Clair, & Malone, 2009b).[2]

Concerns about the qualifications of some trustees and disagreements with state policymakers about the goals of higher education have led public college presidents to have limited confidence in their governing boards. A 2013 survey by Gallup and *Inside Higher Ed* revealed that only 20% of presidents at four-year public colleges were very confident that their boards governed well and that 68% would like to replace at least some board members. This compares to four-year private colleges, where 45% were very confident in their boards and only 33% wanted to replace board members (Rivard, 2013). Board members themselves are not always confident in their knowledge of important issues; nearly 30% of both public and private college respondents to an AGB survey said boards did not understand academic freedom, shared governance, tenure, or accreditation well (Hodge-Clark, 2014).

In addition to externally selected trustees, some colleges have internal constituents such as faculty, staff, and students on their governing boards. In 2010, 13% of public college governing boards had at least one voting faculty member and 7% had at least one voting staff member. Half of public colleges had at least one student with a vote, while 28% more had a nonvoting member (Schwartz, 2010a). This gives stakeholders a direct voice in the governance process at the highest level and can help inform trustees' discussions (e.g., Middleton, 2010), but it also raises the potential for conflicts of interest as internal trustees may act in their own best interest instead of the college as a whole. AGB officially opposes having internal stakeholders as voting members, although it does not support taking away the voting rights of faculty if one already exists (AGB, 2010; Schwartz, Skinner, & Bowen, 2009).

Is the possibility of a conflict of interest a legitimate concern? It is difficult to tell from the rather sparse body of literature in this area. On the one hand, a survey of faculty trustees by Ehrenberg, Patterson, and Key (2012) found that a majority of respondents indicated that their role as faculty representative was equal to or greater than their role representing the college as a whole, which would support the conflict of interest narrative. On the other hand, Kaplan (2004) concluded that faculty membership on a governing board was associated with lower faculty salaries instead of the higher salaries that might be hypothesized.

PRIVATE NONPROFIT COLLEGES

The governing board structures of private nonprofit colleges vary more than those at public colleges, with colleges tightly controlled by a particular religious denomination often having different structures than nondenominational colleges. The average board size of 29 members (AGB Editor, 2016) thus obscures a great deal of variation in how private colleges' boards are structured. There is one commonality across most private colleges that is not true for many public colleges: many of their board members are large donors. In 2010, 49% of private colleges required contributions from board members (Schwartz, 2010b), and trustees are often selected to serve by their fellow trustees on the basis of their ability to contribute. The ability to raise funds is particularly important at private research universities, where a disproportionate percentage of their trustees also serve on large corporations' boards (Pusser, Slaughter, & Thomas, 2006; Slaughter et al., 2014).

The typical structure of a nonsectarian private institution is to have one governing board that draws the majority of its membership from two different sources. Self-perpetuating trustees are the most common types of trustees at most private colleges, with many institutions also allowing alumni to directly elect trustees. At 42% of private colleges, at least one member of the alumni association was guaranteed a vote (Schwartz, 2010b), while other colleges allow alumni to select trustees outside of the alumni association. Additionally, in 2010, 8.5% of private colleges had at least one voting student, 14.9% had a voting faculty member, and 19.5% had a voting staff member (Schwartz, 2010b).

An additional characteristic of private colleges' boards is that they can vary in size instead of the fixed number of trustees at public colleges. For example, Princeton's board can have between 23 and 40 members, with alumni electing 13 alumni trustees, New Jersey's governor and Princeton's president holding ex officio seats, and the remaining trustees are elected by the board (Trustees of Princeton University, 2012). Princeton's board currently has 40 members, meaning that a majority of trustees are elected by the other trustees instead of by alumni. Another example is the University of Rochester, which allows the board to determine the number of trustees (currently 51) without specifying a range. Rochester also has "life trustees," former trustees who can attend meetings but not vote (University of Rochester, 2015).

Colleges that are actively affiliated with a religious denomination will generally reserve a number of board seats for members of that denomination. Baylor University elects three-fourths of its board of regents via self-perpetuating seats, while the Baptist General Convention of Texas elects the other one-fourth of members (Baylor University, n.d.). Some Catholic institutions have two governing boards, with one board being the legal owner of the institution (and having more members selected by the Catholic Church) and the other board serving more as a planning and advisory board. Loyola Marymount University, Providence College, and Seton Hall University (my employer) all use this two-board model. At Seton Hall, the 16-member board of trustees has legal authority over the university and also elects the 32 to 46 members of the board of regents after consulting with the other regents (Seton Hall University, 2016).

The heavy reliance on self-perpetuating trustees at private nonprofit colleges has significant implications for accountability and institutional effectiveness. The advantage of allowing trustees to select new members is that it can potentially improve collegiality among members and keep the institution focused on its mission, the latter of which is very important at colleges affiliated with a religious denomination. However, self-perpetuating boards can also suffer from groupthink and an unwillingness to adapt to changing student demographics or economic realities (Longanecker, 2006).

A microcosm of the debate between self-perpetuating and elected boards can be found at Dartmouth College, which had a highly publicized governance dispute in the 2000s. At that time, the board of trustees had 18 members, with eight elected by alumni, eight elected by the rest of the trustees, and two ex officio members. Alumni elections had traditionally been rather sleepy affairs, with the alumni association's preferred slate of candidates typically cruising to victory. But between 2004 and 2007, conservative and libertarian alumni upset about the direction of the college successfully defeated four consecutive candidates proposed by the alumni association (Lewin, 2007). After conducting a study finding that the board needed additional (wealthy) members to thrive, trustees approved adding eight new self-perpetuating members in 2007—thus ensuring that the current direction of the board could not be radically altered by alumni (Jaschik, 2007).

Another example of the pressures faced by trustees at many private colleges with modest endowments is the near closing of Sweet Briar College in Virginia in 2015. The board's March 2015 announcement that the small women's college would be closing at the end of the academic year came as a surprise to the campus community as well as most higher education observers. At that time, the college was financially stable, but the board wanted to have an orderly closure and make sure all obligations were paid before declining enrollment placed the college under severe fiscal pressure (Jaschik, 2015b). The board saw itself operating in the best interest of the college and its students by giving students the opportunity to transfer in a relatively orderly fashion.

The alumnae of the college were upset with the board's decision, claiming that efforts had not been made to save the college before the decision to close was announced. They started a group called Saving Sweet Briar, which then sued the college's trustees to stop the closure. The alumnae were able to get an injunction from a Virginia court in June to keep the college open (Svrluga, 2015). Later that month, Saving Sweet Briar was able to negotiate a settlement with the state's attorney general that gave them control of the college and a new president and governing board conditional on alumnae raising $12 million within 60 days (which they then did) (Kapsidelis, 2015; Stolberg, 2015). However, enrollment in fall 2016 stood at about 325 students, up from 240 students in fall 2015 but down from 560 in 2014 (Pounds, 2016), suggesting that Sweet Briar's fate is far from secure.

Do the characteristics of higher education governing boards have any relationship with institutional effectiveness? There is very little research in this area, which is surprising given a growing body of literature on other aspects of governing boards. Hermalin (2004) examined the literature on higher education and governing boards and noted the lack of a relationship between size of the boards and performance in both higher education and the corporate world, although most studies reviewed were anecdotal and not empirical. Brown (2013) found that a higher percentage of trustees elected by alumni at private colleges was associated with increased student SAT scores, higher graduation rates, and higher levels of efficiency after controlling for other factors. This provides some evidence that trustees selected by a group more external to the institution (alumni instead of current trustees) may result in a more effective organization.

FOR-PROFIT COLLEGES

Governing boards at publicly traded for-profit colleges tend to look more like boards of directors in the corporate world than those at public or private nonprofit colleges. (Small, privately held for-profit colleges typically do not have an external board of trustees.) In 2009, the typical governing board at a for-profit college had nine members, which is similar in size to public colleges. However, the median board member got paid over $100,000 for their service (Field & Fain, 2011), while board members in nonprofit higher education are typically just compensated for their expenses. An analysis of corporate boards in the S&P 500 by Spencer Stuart (2015) showed that these boards averaged ten members, with average annual compensation of $277,237.

Individuals on for-profit colleges' governing boards tend to be primarily from the corporate world, with some having significant experience in higher education; the CEO of the company is also typically on the board. For example, three of the largest publicly traded for-profit college chains (as of 2016)—Apollo Education Group (the University of Phoenix), DeVry University, and Kaplan University—all have at least one trustee with experience as an administrator or leader of a traditional college. In early 2016, DeVry made news by inviting the current presidents of the University of Arizona and University of California, Davis to serve on their board, a decision that did not sit well with some on their home campuses (Wexler, 2016). Davis chancellor Linda Katehi resigned her position on the DeVry board within days, but Arizona president Ann Weaver Hart remained on the board and eventually left the university presidency one year early amid criticism of her decision (Jung, 2017).

HOLDING PRESIDENTS ACCOUNTABLE

In recent years, governing boards at many colleges have given more scrutiny to the performance of their presidents. A survey of presidents who had served at least ten years revealed that 56% of respondents indicated that dealing with accountability pressures had become more important since they first took the position. A higher percentage of presidents listed accountability as a rising pressure rather than other areas of concern such as fundraising, enrollment management, and budgeting (ACE [American Council on Education], 2012). These growing pressures have possibly contributed to the declining tenure of college presidents, which has fallen from 8.5 years in 2006 to 6.5 years in 2016 with even shorter tenures at public four-year institutions (Gagliardi et al., 2017). Presidents' contracts have also become more formal and structured in recent years, with specific performance bonuses now common in longer-term contracts (Thomas & Van Horn, 2016).

The changing nature of a college presidency has affected who is selected to be president, as well as who even wants to be considered for the job. The traditional path to a college president has been to rise through the academic ranks from tenured faculty member to department chair to dean and then provost before becoming a president. While this is still the most common path to the presidency, fewer provosts are interested in becoming presidents due to the increased visibility of the position and less time to focus on core academic priorities (Jaschik & Lederman, 2014; Wilkins, 2012). As a result, a growing number of presidents are taking nontraditional paths to the presidency. The percentage of presidents who came from outside higher education rose from 10% in 1986 to 13% in 2006 to 20% in 2011 before falling back to 15% in 2016, with the increases primarily coming at private non-profit and for-profit colleges (Gagliardi et al., 2017; Corrigan, 2002).

Although still relatively uncommon, a small number of large public universities have hired nontraditional presidents in recent years in an effort to build an entrepreneurial culture and to improve relations with legislators and governors. In the last decade, Florida State University, the University of Colorado, the University of Iowa, and the University of North Carolina have all hired leaders with political or business experience but without traditional academic backgrounds. This fits in with efforts to instill academic capitalism, which is generally defined as encouraging universities to become entrepreneurial by seeking to gain additional resources and partnering with the private sector (e.g., McClure, 2016; Slaughter & Rhoades, 2004). These efforts have generally been met with praise by conservative state legislators but have been opposed by some faculty members who are concerned about whether colleges are prioritizing corporatization over staying true to their mission of educating undergraduate students (e.g., Gerber, 2014; Ginsberg, 2011; Schultz, 2015).

A particularly controversial nontraditional pick to be a university's president was the University of Iowa Board of Regents' 2015 decision to select businessman Bruce Harreld to lead the institution. In 2006, the university's Faculty Senate had voted no confidence in the leadership of the board of regents after the board's president terminated a presidential search without (in their view) adequately consulting the faculty. The search that followed yielded a traditional academic, Sally Mason, as the next president; she served until 2015 amid good relations with the faculty (Finkin & Decesare, 2016). The board of regents selected Harreld in 2015, in spite of faculty considering him unqualified and the other three candidates highly qualified; this led the faculty senate to vote no confidence in the board five days later. The American Association of University Professors (AAUP) then censured the university in 2016 for the low number of faculty representatives on the search committee (Charis-Carlson, 2016).

Faculty Governance

As detailed in chapter 2, the role of faculty in the governance process (and hence, their role in the landscape of higher education accountability) has changed considerably over the history of American higher education. Faculty members' ability to participate in the shared governance process without repercussion was strengthened by the AAUP (1940) statement on academic freedom and tenure. This statement, which was written by an organization striving to represent faculty members and has been adopted by most colleges, noted that faculty members have the freedom to follow their research interests, unless clearly stated up front at religious institutions. More directly relevant to the shared governance process, a second statement from the AAUP in conjunction with the ACE and the AGB concluded that faculty should have the primary responsibility in determining curriculum and instruction, and that the governing board and faculty should work together to select a new president (AAUP, n.d.).

The shared governance process, which has traditionally been fairly strong at most public and private nonprofit colleges, is designed to be a counterbalance to pressures from administrators, trustees, and other external agents. This provides an opportunity for faculty members to make sure the institution remains focused on teaching and learning when other groups try to change the college's priorities. However, the shared governance process is often criticized for protecting the interests of faculty members or moving too slowly in response to challenges that may require faster courses of action (Benjamin, 2007; Bok, 2013). Therefore, shared governance should at times be viewed both as a blessing and a curse with respect to accountability.

Although some colleges give their faculty a vote on the governing board, the typical mechanism for faculty authority is through a faculty senate. A 2009 survey of governing board chairs, provosts, and presidents revealed that 90% of colleges that responded had an institution-wide faculty senate, although the influence of the faculty senate varied considerably. Among colleges with faculty senates, just 13% of institutional leaders called the senate "policy-making," but 59% called it "policy-influencing" and 29% called it "advisory" (Schwartz, Skinner, & Bowen, 2009).

This system of shared governance is under pressure at many colleges as full-time, tenure-track and tenured faculty are steadily being replaced by larger percentages of part-time and/or full-time, non-tenure-track faculty. The tenure system provides strong protections to faculty who wish to speak their minds on issues of institutional governance, but the long-term costs of committing to one person for potentially decades to come is more than many colleges wish to bear. In 2013, a majority of faculty in all segments of higher education were either part-time or non-tenure track. For example, at private research universities, the percentage of tenure-track or tenured faculty (on a head count basis) fell from 50% in 1993 to 35% in 2013 and from 62% to 49% at public research universities (Finkelstein, Conley, & Schuster, 2016). Community colleges have a very low percentage of tenure-line faculty, and the tenure system is basically nonexistent at for-profit colleges.

If administrators and trustees were given the chance to do so, many would prefer to move away from the tenure system in an effort to maintain fiscal flexibility and to be able to incentivize faculty to focus on the administration's priorities instead of their own. A majority of college provosts, particularly at private colleges and community colleges, would prefer long-term contracts to tenure (Jaschik & Lederman, 2016). Additionally, private college presidents viewed tenure as negotiable instead of essential (Jaschik, 2016). Deans and department chairs are also more likely to agree that tenure should be modified or eliminated than do faculty (e.g., Premeaux, 2008) and department chairs view the collegiality portion of some colleges' tenure criteria as a way to protect lower-performing faculty (Rothgeb, 2014). However, tenure can serve as a key tool to attract and recruit top faculty, potentially at lower salaries than they would earn under a system of long-term contracts.

A number of studies have explored the implications of tenure-line faculty on a range of outcomes of interest to colleges. The body of literature that has garnered the most attention is on the teaching effectiveness of tenured/tenure-track faculty relative to contingent faculty. The challenge with this research is that the types of institutions examined and the definition of contingent faculty (ranging from adjuncts teaching a small number of classes to full-time, non-tenure-track faculty members) varies substantially across studies, which helps to explain relatively mixed results. Several studies of two-year and four-year colleges found negative implications of using lower-paid part-time faculty compared to full-time faculty on graduation and transfer rates (Eagan & Jaeger, 2009; Jaeger & Eagan, 2009; Umbach, 2007). Ehrenberg and Zhang (2005) noted a negative relationship between using non-tenure-line faculty and graduation rates at four-year colleges, with the most notable relationship at public comprehensive universities. However, Bettinger and Long (2010) found null to slightly positive effects of adjuncts on STEM (science, technology, engineering, and math) students' course choices at an Ohio public university and Figlio, Schapiro, and Soter (2015) concluded that contingent faculty were associated with higher learning gains for students in first-year classes at Northwestern University than tenured or tenure-track faculty, although it should certainly be noted that Northwestern is far from a representative institution.

In addition to raising concerns about granting faculty lifetime tenure, some policymakers have questioned whether the incentives present in tenure systems align with state public policy goals and the best interest of taxpayers. One example of this is the balance among teaching, research, and service—the three main components of a full-time faculty member's job at four-year universities (community colleges rarely have research expectations). Although there are no reliable longitudinal data sources of faculty teaching loads due to different questions being asked on national surveys over time, the perception is that teaching loads have gone down over time as faculty members feel a push to focus more on research.[3] For example, although the University of Missouri–Columbia requires faculty members to teach either 60 students or four classes each year, nearly half of all faculty members received a waiver to have a reduced teaching load—much to the chagrin of leading state lawmakers (Keller, 2015).

Although the data on teaching trends are inconclusive, it is clear that faculty members at four-year colleges are placing a larger focus on research. Between 1988 and 2004, the proportion of faculty members with no publications in the past two years fell from 55% to 32% (Finkelstein, Conley, & Schuster, 2016). Research expectations for tenure and promotion have risen over time, even at master's-level institutions and liberal arts colleges with formerly high teaching loads and low research expectations (e.g., Fairweather, 2005; Youn & Price, 2009) and in spite of concerns about mission (e.g., Gonzales, 2013). Many presidents of four-year colleges support the increasing focus on faculty research, as successfully increasing research expenditures and graduate degree production can allow them to be considered research universities under the influential Carnegie classifications and to become more prestigious (Brint, Riddle, & Hanneman, 2006; Morphew, 2000).[4] But this effort to focus on research comes at a price to other stakeholders. Colleges "striving" to become research universities increased total expenditures (potentially affecting the price students pay) and spent relatively less money on instruction than nonstriving colleges (Iglesias, 2014; Morphew & Baker, 2004).

In addition to tenure and the tradition of shared governance, another key internal accountability component at some colleges is the faculty union. Faculty unionization can affect accountability by clearly specifying the roles of faculty relative to administrators and creating streamlined grievance policies, although the exact topics covered in collective bargaining agreements vary across colleges (Bucklew, Houghton, & Ellison, 2013). In 2012, 26%

of full-time and 21% of part-time faculty were represented by collective bargaining agreements, with the percentage of full-time faculty who were unionized ranging from 60% at community colleges to just 3% at private nonprofit colleges. Public-sector unionized faculty are heavily concentrated in five states, with California, Illinois, Michigan, New Jersey, and New York having nearly two-thirds of the unionized faculty in American higher education (Berry & Savarese, 2012). In 26 states with what are known as "right-to-work" laws, employees have the ability to fully opt out of a union if desired, reducing the power of faculty unions in these states (National Conference of State Legislatures, 2016).

Tenure-track and tenured faculty can generally only unionize at public colleges due to a 1980 Supreme Court decision (*National Labor Relations Board v. Yeshiva University*), in which full-time tenure-line faculty at private colleges are considered managers due to their role in the shared governance process and thus cannot unionize (Suntrup, 1981). Although the exact definition of "manager" has proven contentious over time, the court decision has generally kept tenure-line private college faculty from unionizing. Full-time, non-tenure-track faculty at private colleges who are not performing religious duties can unionize as a result of a 2014 National Labor Relations Board (NLRB) ruling considering them not to be managers (Jaschik, 2015a), and unions are actively organizing adjunct faculty members in a number of metropolitan areas (Flaherty, 2013).

The empirical research on faculty unionization at public colleges provides some intriguing findings. Unionized faculty at regional public universities and two-year colleges tend to have higher salaries than those who are not unionized (Katsinas, Ogun, & Bray, 2016; Thornton & Curtis, 2012), with no effects at doctoral universities (Thornton & Curtis, 2012). But one recent study attempting to control for additional characteristics and living costs has found null effects (Hedrick et al., 2011). Unionized faculty members at public colleges are more likely to have more decision-making power than nonunionized faculty, suggesting that unions are effective in amplifying the faculty voice (Porter, 2013). Finally, there is some evidence that unionization is associated with improved efficiency and effectiveness, although this could be because unions may be formed during tough economic times (Cassell & Halaseh, 2014).

Colleges and policymakers have tools at their disposal to hold faculty members accountable for their performance. In order to receive tenure or be promoted, eligible faculty must receive approval from tenured faculty members, administrators, and finally the governing board. In most cases, administrators and trustees defer to faculty recommendations, but 54% of college presidents reported denying tenure to at least one faculty member over issues of scholarly competence (Jaschik & Lederman, 2015). A high-profile recent example of this occurred at Lafayette College in Pennsylvania, where the college's president denied tenure to assistant professor Juan Rojo (who then went on a high-profile hunger strike) after two faculty bodies approved his tenure application over concerns about his teaching (Flaherty, 2016).

In rare cases, trustees may deny tenure applications or fail to approve hiring decisions. The University of Illinois's board made national news in 2014 for revoking a tenured job offer to Steven Salaita, a professor who resigned a tenured position at Virginia Tech to take a similar position at Illinois. Salaita faced scrutiny from the Illinois board due a series of tweets about the Israeli-Palestinian conflict that upset many advocates for Israel, and the board eventually voted not to offer him a job (Mackey, 2014). The AAUP censured Illinois over this case (AAUP, 2015), although the university eventually agreed to pay Salaita a $600,000 settlement (Cohen, 2015).

Another potential mechanism to hold faculty accountable for their performance is through merit pay, in which colleges tie at least a portion of salary increases to research, teaching, and/or service productivity. Merit pay (particularly when based on research output) can also serve as a way to help retain star faculty members who may be receiving other job offers. A review of the literature by McCrea and Deyrup (2016) finds mixed evidence of merit pay's effectiveness in improving faculty productivity, with the particular details of merit systems appearing to affect systems' efficacy.

The University of Wisconsin System has been a flashpoint of disputes between faculty and administrators and policymakers in recent years. This began soon after Republican governor Scott Walker took office in 2011, when he announced a bill that would end faculty members' right to unionize that the previous Democratic governor signed into law just two years earlier (Stripling, 2011) as well as requiring graduate student unions to annually certify. This led to months of massive protests in Madison, but the legislation passed and was followed in 2015 by a right to work law that has survived legal challenges (Glauber, 2016).

In 2015, Wisconsin legislators and Governor Walker removed tenure protection from state statutes and ordered the University of Wisconsin System's Board of Regents to write new tenure protections into the board's policies (Helfing, 2015). While tenure policies in most states are made at the board level instead of in state statutes (Schmidt, 2015), the changes upset faculty—particularly when the regents' tenure policy was less favorable to faculty then the previous version. The new tenure rules did not guarantee that faculty would have guaranteed input into decisions to cut academic programs and tenured faculty and the definition of termination being changed to "emergency" instead of "exigency" for financial reasons, a weaker standard that the AAUP opposes (Schmidt, 2016). Additionally, the UW System implemented a post-tenure review process that is conducted by administrators instead of fellow tenured faculty members, as is normally the case (Herzog, 2016).

Faculty backlash to the changes has been substantial, but to this point generally ineffective in changing policies. Eight of 14 UW System faculty senates voted no confidence in the board of regents and the UW System's president (Kremer, 2016), moves that raised the ire of conservative politicians. The speaker of the state assembly called the votes "a big mistake" (Schneider, 2016), while Governor Walker said that "some faculty bodies . . . appear more interested in protecting outdated 'job for life' tenure than about helping students get the best education possible" (Savidge, 2016). Other faculty decided to leave, with the number of faculty members at Madison receiving counteroffers to potentially stay after getting an outside job offer rising from 37 in 2014–15 to 96 in 2015–16 (Gardner, 2016).

Student Governance

Student government is an often-neglected aspect of higher education accountability, but it can play an important role, particularly in public higher education. As noted earlier in this chapter, a majority of public colleges have at least one student on their governing board, which offers a direct voice in the governance structure. Students may also have control over at least a portion of their fee dollars used for student activities, although students' ability to change their fees may be limited by fee caps. But many other colleges will at least informally include students in the shared governance process through regular meetings with student government leaders or placing students on key institutional committees. Wisconsin provides an unusual example of a strong student voice, as state statues guarantee that students have representation in institutional governance and that they get to determine their representatives (Wisconsin State Legislature, 2016).

Students can also have influence in the governance process through lobbying activities and making their voices heard in demonstrations, as noted in chapter 6. For example, the resignation of the University of Missouri–Columbia's chancellor and system president in 2015 largely was due to student protests against alleged racism on and near the university's campus as well as graduate students' concerns about their health insurance subsidy being cut. These protests gained national attention after one graduate student went on a hunger strike, students camped out on the university quadrangle, and the football team (with the coach's support) announced that they would boycott a game at the cost of $1 million to the university if the system president did not resign (Kelderman, 2015). First-year undergraduate enrollment at Mizzou fell by over 1,400 students the following year while other Missouri universities saw enrollment growth. Minority student enrollment and university donations both declined significantly, as individuals both supporting and opposing the protestors made their voices heard (Keller, 2016).

Undergraduate and graduate students alike have a voice in holding faculty members accountable through the course evaluations that they complete. It is common to consider student evaluations of faculty members in making decisions to retain faculty who are not tenure-eligible or to grant tenure to assistant professors. While systemically low evaluations can certainly indicate an inadequate teacher, there is a body of empirical research finding that student evaluations are correlated with the faculty member's race/ethnicity, gender, or field of study (e.g., MacNell, Driscoll, & Hunt, 2014; Reid, 2010). There is also some evidence that student evaluations are higher in courses in which students perform better, even though their grades in subsequent classes may not benefit (Braga, Paccagnella, & Pellizzari, 2014; Carrell & West, 2010). In spite of the concerns with student evaluations, an Iowa legislator proposed a bill (which was later dropped) that would require the state's public universities to fire the faculty with the lowest teaching evaluations—and would also allow students to vote on which one of the five faculty just above the minimum threshold they would like to fire (Will, 2015).

Depending on the institution they attend, graduate students who are also university employees (through a teaching or research assistantship) may be able to unionize in an effort to gain better pay and benefits as well as more clout in institutional decision making. As of 2012, 25% of graduate student employees at public universities were unionized, with concentrations highest in the same states that have a strong faculty union presence (Berry & Savarese, 2012). There is little research on the implications of graduate student unions, but one study did find that unionization is associated with increased compensation at public universities while not substantially affecting the student/advisor relationship that is a crucial part of graduate education (Rogers, Eaton, & Voos, 2013).

Although graduate student unionization at public colleges consistently has been around for decades (particularly in states without right-to-work laws), the ability of graduate students at private colleges to unionize has been dependent on the political party of the American president. In the first case in 1972, the Nixon-appointed NLRB ruled that graduate students at

Adelphi University could not unionize because their primary job was as students instead of employees. (Graduate students at public universities are subject to state laws regarding unionization, which can supersede NLRB decisions.) A Clinton-appointed NLRB allowed New York University students to unionize in 2000, but then a Bush-appointed majority reversed the decision in 2004 after an appeal from Brown University (Rogers, Eaton, & Voos, 2013). The Obama-appointed NLRB reversed itself again by allowing Columbia University grad students to unionize in August 2016 (Thomason, 2016). The credit rating agency Moody's immediately responded to the NLRB decision by calling the likely compensation increases for graduate students, particularly at lesser-endowed institutions, "credit negative" (*Inside Higher Ed*, 2016). However, this decision appears likely to be reversed again during the Trump administration.

Voluntary Associations

The final type of accountability system that colleges use to hold themselves accountable for their outcomes is through the use of voluntary associations. As discussed in chapters 2 and 5, accreditation of colleges and universities was an outgrowth of voluntary associations before institutional accreditation became tied to federal financial aid. Some types of program-level accreditation (such as for business schools) still serve as measures of prestige rather than as a necessary condition for funding. But there are other types of associations or affiliations that can be used to demonstrate some metric of interest for both internal and external constituencies.

An example of a voluntary affiliation coming from the higher education community (instead of a private organization such as the LEED ratings for energy efficiency) that could interest both faculty and prospective students are quality assurance programs for online courses. For example, the Quality Matters organization was founded in 2003 to provide external reviews of online and blended courses in an effort to improve the quality of instruction in this new delivery method. The system has nearly 1,000 participating colleges (Quality Matters, 2016), and there is some evidence that undergoing Quality Matters review may be associated with improved student outcomes (Adair & Shattuck, 2015; Legon & Runyon, 2007).

Groups of colleges have also created three large-scale voluntary accountability systems in an effort to highlight their outcomes to their own campuses as well as to policymakers who may be considering imposing additional accountability. The University and College Accountability (U-CAN) system from the National Association of Independent Colleges and Universities

(NAICU) contains some additional information on over 800 private non-profit colleges that is not currently available in federal data (NAICU, 2014). However, metrics such as student learning outcomes are not present in the U-CAN data.

The Student Achievement Measure, started by the Association of Public and Land-Grant Universities (APLU) and supported by the Gates Foundation and the Carnegie Corporation, presents information not currently available in federal data on graduation rates of part-time and transfer students for about 600 (mainly public) colleges (Student Achievement Measure, 2013). Finally, the Voluntary System of Accountability was started by the APLU and the American Association of State Colleges and Universities to provide information on student learning outcomes and other metrics of interest for about 275 public four-year colleges (APLU, n.d.).

Conclusion

Colleges have always faced pressures from internal stakeholders such as students, faculty, and trustees to hold themselves accountable for their performance. However, the growing impatience of trustees and students combined with a shrinking portion of American faculty members taking on governance responsibilities has changed the landscape of internal accountability and how colleges respond to outside pressure. Colleges are also increasingly aware of these external forces, as evidenced by the growing voluntary efforts by colleges to publicize their outcomes and justify their value to an increasingly skeptical public. Whether these internal efforts will be sufficient to hold external accountability pressures remains to be seen, but all signs point to external stakeholders heightening the pressure on colleges regardless of their internal accountability frameworks. In the next chapter, I will discuss what has been learned from decades of high-stakes accountability policies in higher education and other related areas—and how colleges' efforts to preemptively hold themselves accountable can help shape the structures of new accountability frameworks.

CHAPTER EIGHT

Ten Lessons Learned from Accountability Policies

A S THE FINANCIAL STAKES tied to accountability in higher education become larger, it is important to look back at lessons learned from previous and current accountability efforts in order to design more fair and effective accountability systems in the future. Some of these lessons are apparent from past efforts to implement accountability in higher education, while others are drawn from other publicly supported areas such as K–12 education and health care. In this chapter, I detail ten of the most important considerations to take into account when considering new higher education accountability systems.

Lesson 1: In Order to Be Effective, Accountability Systems Must Be Reasonably Aligned with a College's Mission and Capacities

Individual accountability systems may make perfect sense when viewed in isolation but are unlikely to be effective if they do not align with both a college's mission and its ability to make changes. College rankings are very effective at influencing the actions of selective public and private colleges (e.g., Alter & Reback, 2014; Bastedo & Bowman, 2011; Holmes, 2009) because these institutions have made increasing their prestige a top strategic goal—and have the ability to make substantial investments in efforts to rise in the rankings. Similarly, many colleges will readily comply with accreditors' guidelines for institutional improvement because institutions believe in improving student learning outcomes and are able and willing to target scarce resources on student success.

If either the mission or capacity component is missing, accountability systems are unlikely to have their desired effect. Efforts to tie state funding to students' future earnings, for example, have the potential to be effective at vocationally focused institutions. The Texas State Technical College system took the unusual step of asking the state to tie nearly all of its funding to a metric of how much money its former students earned above the minimum wage; this formula was phased in starting in the 2014–15 academic year (Selingo & Van Der Werf, 2016). This model would be unlikely to change behavior to the same extent at transfer-focused community colleges or liberal arts colleges, where workforce training is but one part of the college's mission and students are likely to go on and pursue additional degrees that delay labor market entry.

Similarly, college rankings are unlikely to influence colleges' behavior if the rankings metrics are not at least somewhat aligned to a college's mission. The *U.S. News & World Report* college rankings are far less likely to induce colleges with a long tradition of public service and broad access to increase selectivity and prioritize research. Patricia McGuire, longtime president of access-oriented Trinity Washington University, wrote an opinion piece in the *Los Angeles Times* asking colleges to ignore *U.S. News* because the rankings do not align with the public good (McGuire, 2007). Reputational factors also are far less relevant for colleges that have a mission of serving students within a local area, such as commuter-oriented four-year colleges and community colleges.

In other cases, the goals of an accountability system may be well aligned with a college's mission and priorities, but the capacity to make improvements may be limited. Research on state performance funding systems (see chapter 4 for more details) has consistently found that lesser-resourced colleges frequently struggle with making the types of changes needed to improve college completion rates due to factors such as a lack of advising resources and inadequate student data systems. Some states have implemented "stop-loss" systems that are designed to reduce penalties for colleges while they make changes, but additional funding to build capacity is less common. The lack of capacity has been noted as a key reason performance funding systems have had at most a muted effect on improving student outcomes (e.g., Hillman, 2016).

Lesson 2: Data Limitations Restrict the Ability to Accurately Measure Many Short-Term Outcomes of Interest

Whether or not a governmental body, accrediting agency, or private-sector organization is trying to develop an accountability system, the same set of metrics is typically used. Many systems use either graduation rates or the number of students who receive credentials as key outcomes of interest, as these metrics are easily calculated and are of interest to most stakeholders. The federal government is also moving toward a more complete set of definitions regarding graduation rates beyond the traditional cohort of first-time, full-time students used in many current accountability systems.

Other metrics of interest, such as earnings, student debt burdens, and student loan repayment rates of former students, are newly available at the national level or greatly improved through the use of the College Scorecard dataset. However, even these metrics are restricted to a portion of all college students because only students receiving federal financial aid are a part of this dataset. The College Scorecard includes 70% of all students, with percentages ranging from 62% at community colleges to 90% at for-profit colleges. Students who did not receive federal financial aid tend to have higher family incomes (nearly $18,000 for dependent students), suggesting a somewhat biased sample even if there is overlap between the distribution of aided and nonaided students (Council of Economic Advisers, 2015).

The vast majority of data elements available at the federal level are only available for broad subgroups of students, such as by race/ethnicity and gender. Data for more narrow subgroups of students (or by academic program) typically are not available at the federal level due to the ban on so-called student unit record datasets placed in the 2008 Higher Education Act reauthorization (Laitinen & McCann, 2014). States tend to have more detailed higher education data, as nearly every state has a unit record data system and 42 states either currently link or will link at least some of their postsecondary education systems to workforce data (Armstrong & Zaback, 2016). But a majority of state systems exclude students attending private nonprofit colleges within the state and are generally unable to track students who move to other states after college or are self-employed. In Virginia, for example, about 30% of graduates did not show up in the state's dataset with wages 18 months after completing a bachelor's degree (State Council of Higher Education for Virginia, n.d.).[1]

Lesson 3: It Is Important to Consider Proxy Variables for Outcomes That Take Years to Unfold or Are Difficult to Measure

According to a nationally representative survey of first-year students at four-year colleges, 70% of respondents considered the ability of college graduates to make more money on average as a very important factor when deciding to attend college (Eagan et al., 2016). Although one of the key reasons students attend college is to gain long-term economic security, it is typically difficult to use a potentially measurable outcome such as long-term earnings as a key component in an accountability system because of the long lag period between when students enter college and when their eventual outcomes are observed.

One potential way that stakeholders can incorporate longer-term economic outcomes into accountability systems is to rely on the correlation between shorter-term and longer-term metrics. For example, policymakers may not want to wait ten years to observe the earnings of former students that are now available in the College Scorecard, instead preferring to use a measure of earnings six years after college entry. The correlations between these two earnings measures was above 0.94 for both two-year and four-year colleges in the initial College Scorecard data release, suggesting that a shorter-term earnings metric generally captures colleges' performance over a slightly longer period. If the correlations between shorter-term and even longer-term earnings outcomes are reasonable (or can be enhanced by controlling for differences in student body characteristics over time), stakeholders can be more confident in the utility of shorter-term outcomes as a proxy for longer-term outcomes.

Other important metrics, such as quality of life, civic engagement, and happiness, have traditionally been extremely difficult to measure across colleges for two reasons. First, these metrics do not always have agreed-upon definitions even if particular components (such as charitable contributions and voting rates) can be measured. Second, systemically collecting data on these outcomes is an expensive endeavor that requires an organization with the ability to get data across colleges. There are some efforts to collect data on the non-economic outcomes of higher education among former students that appear promising. One prominent example is the Gallup-Purdue Index, which began annual surveys in 2014 of nearly 30,000 bachelor's degree recipients across the age distribution. These surveys cover five types of well-being that would be of interest to stakeholders: community, financial, physical, purpose, and social (Gallup, 2015). Although colleges' individual results are not made available to the public at this point, these elements could provide the framework of a broader accountability system in which colleges are required to participate in an outcomes-based survey and make results available to the public.

Lesson 4: Data Used in Accountability Systems Should Be Audited for Quality Assurance

A little-known aspect of American higher education data is that many commonly used data elements in accountability systems are not audited to make sure the reported values are actually correct. For example, the federal government does not check colleges' submissions to the Integrated Postsecondary Education Data System (IPEDS) for quality, although are some safeguards built into the system that require colleges to verify and/or explain reported values that are either significantly changed from the prior year or an unusual value (NCES, n.d.). Colleges also have the ability to go back and correct errors in IPEDS data the following year (NCES, 2016), which typically results in minor changes to the IPEDS dataset following its initial release.

Data provided by colleges to accreditors or college rankings providers are also not audited. These data sources can have both intentional and unintentional data errors, particularly when metrics are either new or complicated. In many years, *U.S. News* removes multiple colleges from its main rankings for reporting incorrect admissions data, with some of the errors being quite substantial. In 2013, the magazine revealed that one college reported data that resulted in an admissions rate of 27% instead of 89% and another college had been reporting SAT scores based on a subset of its students for more than a decade (Morse, 2013). Currently, no college rankings system conducts an audit of the data it collects, although the *Times Higher Education* rankings has brought in an independent auditor to verify that its calculations are accurate given the data it uses even though the data are not audited (Baty, 2016).

The American Bar Association (the accrediting agency for law schools) recently implemented stricter standards for determining job placement rates, and law schools are struggling to meet the requirement that 95% of graduates' employment files have sufficient documentation. The accreditor audited ten randomly selected law schools and found that only five of the schools were able to account for 95% of files. Two schools had documentations for just over half of all graduates, with one of the schools apparently creating records on a retroactive basis just before the audit took place (Seltzer, 2016).

Two steps would help to improve the quality of data collected and reported for accountability purposes. If a college must self-report data to various stakeholders, a small percentage of colleges' submissions should be audited for quality each year. This could be less onerous than the current process used by the U.S. Department of Education's Office of Federal Student

Aid, which requires colleges to verify for a certain percentage of their students that the financial information students submitted on the Free Application for Federal Student Aid (FAFSA) is accurate (Federal Student Aid, n.d.). Over 60% of Pell recipients currently have their FAFSAs verified (Federal Student Aid, 2016a), while just 0.7% of individual taxpayers had their returns audited in 2014 (Internal Revenue Service, 2016). An audit rate of 0.7% would represent about 50 colleges per year, which may prove sufficient to judge data quality.

For data sources that are compiled by organizations other than a college (such as by a state or federal government), it is important to give colleges an opportunity to verify that the data are accurate. This can both catch any errors in the data and potentially increase the buy-in from colleges when implementing an accountability system. An example of a verification process is how Federal Student Aid conducts the process for releasing cohort default rates on federal student loans. Colleges receive an opportunity to verify default rates calculated by the U.S. Department of Education and challenge any students who they feel were classified in error (Federal Student Aid, 2016b).

Lesson 5: The "Performance Paradox" Makes Assessing True Performance Difficult

The performance paradox, a key theory in the field of public administration, suggests that as a set of specified outcomes are measured and tracked over time, the correlation between these indicators and overall performance weakens as institutions adapt to optimize their performance on what is being measured at the expense of what is not being measured (Van Thiel & Leeuw, 2002). This is a corollary of Campbell's Law, which states that "the more any quantitative social indicator is used for social decision-making, the more subject it will be to corruption pressures and the more apt it will be to distort and corrupt the social processes it is intended to monitor" (Campbell, 1979, 85). Completely eliminating incentives to game the system seems to be infeasible (particularly given the cost of constantly changing accountability programs), but stakeholders wishing to hold colleges accountable need to take two main steps in order to mitigate this concern.

First, they should set clear definitions for outcomes that reduce the incentive for *parking*—reclassifying students into a group that is not counted in order to improve performance without changing core practices. Fields outside of higher education, such as job placement assistance (Koning & Heinrich, 2013) and K–12 education (e.g., Chakrabarti, 2013; Figlio, 2006), have shown evidence of parking. Within higher education, efforts to limit the group of first-time, full-time students to only those who are most likely to persist and graduate (e.g., Anderson, 2016; Schisler & Golden, 2016) reflect potential cases of parking. An accountability system that requires colleges to justify substantial changes to their cohort of students subject to accountability metrics could help reduce this concern.

Second, the set of outcomes being measured in an accountability system needs to be both reasonably broad and not tightly correlated with each other to make focusing on one metric unlikely to generate large changes in measured performance. For example, focusing solely on cohort default rates as a metric of postcollege financial performance provides colleges with an incentive to push defaults outside the period of measurement rather than take more difficult steps to improve students' economic circumstances (Blumenstyk & Richards, 2011). The ability to use multiple metrics can reveal if colleges are attempting to focus solely on one metric. An analysis I conducted with Amy Li at the University of Northern Colorado showed that student demographics, institutional control, and state-level economic conditions explain substantially more variation in student loan repayment rates (which were not tracked during the period of the study) than default rates (which were tracked), providing additional evidence of the performance paradox (Kelchen & Li, 2017).

A good path forward for considering multiple outcomes comes from new research by Minaya and Scott-Clayton (2016), who examined the outcomes of multiple cohorts of students who attended Ohio public colleges and universities. Instead of relying just on one outcome (such as graduation or transfer rates), they also examined full-time, full-year employment rates, annual earnings, the percentage of individuals working in public service fields, and the percentage of former students who claimed unemployment insurance. They found fairly weak correlations across many of these measures and with the relationships changing over time, highlighting the importance of using a number of metrics over a period of several years.

Lesson 6: Avoid Accountability Systems That Are Too Complex

Although accountability systems that rely on one or a very small number of metrics are susceptible to the performance paradox, systems that use too many metrics are also unlikely to be effective. (In order to generate the desired response from a college, it must know how to respond!) The classic example of an incomprehensible accountability system was South Carolina's effort to create a high-stakes performance funding system in the late 1990s. This system sought to tie all state funding to a score based on 37 different metrics within three years of adopting the program, but it instead collapsed due to confusion from colleges and legislators (Dougherty & Natow, 2015).

If an accountability system needs to have a larger number of metrics, each of the metrics should be clearly justified. College rankings systems often have a large number of metrics; for example, the *Washington Monthly* rankings that I compile have up to 18 metrics depending on the type of institution (Kelchen, 2016). We attempt to make these rankings comprehensible to colleges by posting the methodology and sharing the data files with colleges upon request, which are good ideas for trying to make complex systems easier to understand. But it is likely the case that colleges focus on just a few of the 18 metrics when figuring out how to respond to the rankings.

A special concern with complex accountability systems comes when there are value-added or input-adjusted components, which attempt to isolate a college's contribution to student outcomes after controlling for other factors (e.g., Bailey & Xu, 2012; Horn & Lee, 2016). While value-added systems can often help less-selective colleges justify their value, the public and institutional leaders often struggle to understand complex statistical models. Researchers responsible for developing value-added models for policymakers and the private sector must be transparent in their methods and work with colleges to understand the results. Additionally, care must be taken to distinguish institutional-level value-added models in higher education from their often-controversial counterparts in K–12 education that are designed to estimate individual teachers' effectiveness (e.g., Koedel, Mihaly, & Rockoff, 2015).

Lesson 7: Unless Appropriate Safeguards Are Put in Place, Colleges May Respond to Accountability Systems by Restricting Access

There is a sizable body of literature in higher education that finds that colleges engage in *creaming* activities—becoming more selective in the admissions process—when confronted with accountability pressures. There is some evidence that colleges have increased admissions requirements and become less diverse in response to state performance funding systems (Kelchen & Stedrak, 2016; Umbricht, Fernandez, & Ortagus, 2017). Some community colleges (particularly those serving a higher percentage of minority students) have opted out of the federal student loan program in response to cohort default rate metrics (Cochrane & Szabo-Kubitz, 2016); denying access to federal loans has been shown to adversely affect students' academic success (Wiederspan, 2016).

Some accountability systems have taken steps to try to reduce creaming by explicitly rewarding colleges that serve students whose success is far from guaranteed. Approximately 18 of the 34 states with performance funding policies in effect provide additional weights to the outcomes of Pell recipients, minority students, adult students, and/or students from rural areas (author's calculation using data from National Conference of State Legislatures [2015], Snyder & Fox [2016], and state websites). In order for these incentives to change institutional behavior, two conditions must hold: colleges both must be aware that these incentives exist and they must be large enough to alter institutions' behavior.

Properly setting the size of bonuses to reduce creaming requires better data than many higher education systems currently possess. Although minority and first-generation students tend to require remedial coursework at higher rates than other students (Sparks & Malkus, 2013), relatively little is known about the costs of additional services needed to help disadvantaged students succeed in college at higher rates. Efforts to determine the true costs of running individual courses through activity-based costing systems are in their infancy (Massy, 2016), making it difficult to determine the appropriate incentive required.[2] Additionally, some colleges may require incentives above the additional cost of educating disadvantaged students in order to change their behavior if they value the prestige of having a more selective admissions process.

Lesson 8: As More Money Is at Stake in Accountability Systems, Colleges Will Target Their Resources toward Cases on the Margin.

Accountability systems that are based on whether a college is able to meet a certain quality threshold give colleges a strong incentive to focus their resources on a small number of cases. A body of literature in K–12 education has found that schools disproportionately focus on "bubble kids" who are close to the cutoff for passing a standardized test (e.g., Booher-Jennings, 2005; Neal & Schanzenbach, 2010). In higher education, efforts to meet retention or graduation thresholds could also encourage colleges to focus on students who are just on the margin of dropping out at the expense of students whose success is far less likely. Regional accrediting bodies' recent moves to conduct additional oversight of colleges with graduation rates below a certain threshold (Kreighbaum, 2016) may provide additional incentives to focus on the marginal cases.

The focus of students on the margin of success means that students with the lowest probability of success are likely to receive less attention than under a lower-stakes accountability system. But this sort of policy can still have benefits from an equity perspective, as a larger percentage of resources would still go to students from disadvantaged backgrounds. Policies that give extra weight to the performance of disadvantaged students, as is the case in some states' performance funding systems, can also help to direct more resources to students with greater levels of need.

One way to reduce colleges' incentives to focus on a small group of students is to get rid of the all-or-nothing threshold present in several current accountability systems. For example, the current federal cohort default rate system goes from no financial sanctions with a 29% default rate to the potential loss of all federal financial aid with a 30% default rate. A potential way to hold colleges accountable for their outcomes while avoiding this threshold effect would be to require colleges to pay a percentage of all students' defaulted loans above a certain amount. This type of risk-sharing proposal for federal student loans would give colleges the same incentive to care about every student's loan status, meaning that they would try to reduce defaults until the cost of helping an additional student avoid default became larger than the potential sanction.

Lesson 9: Holding Individual Faculty and Staff Members Accountable Is a Difficult Task in Higher Education

State governments and school districts have tried to hold teachers in K–12 education accountable for student learning for decades. Although the efforts have often been controversial (e.g., Darling-Hammond, 2010), they are far easier to do in K–12 education than in higher education for two main reasons. First, while an elementary school teacher might deliver a majority of a student's instruction in a given year, a college professor may teach just one or two of the 40-plus courses that a student takes while pursuing a bachelor's degree. Determining an individual professor's contribution toward a student's education is much harder as a result, and makes individual-based incentives for teaching difficult to use.

Second, higher education employees—particularly tenured faculty members—often enjoy levels of autonomy that are higher than employees in other public-sector areas. (This is not true for contingent faculty, who are essentially at-will employees.) Part of this is a result of the shared governance process at most nonprofit colleges and universities, while the often-decentralized nature of higher education also contributes to autonomy. This means it is important to get faculty and staff to support the goals of accountability systems if there is to be any hope that employees will change their behaviors under the lack of any real incentives. While it may be possible to reduce faculty members' autonomy, this is likely to be a slow and painful process for colleges considering this path.

Lesson 10: New Accountability Systems Should Be Implemented Gradually

Because of the number of potential pitfalls to implementing effective accountability systems discussed earlier in this chapter, it is important to roll out new systems over a period of time. If financial stakes are tied to a new system, the amount of money at stake should gradually be increased over a period of several years to allow colleges to make adjustments. A four-year college may need six or more years to fully implement changes in response to a system that encourages higher graduation rates, as the time needed to recruit and admit students should also be included in the calculations.

Gradually implementing sanctions or rewards also provides time for colleges to try new policies or practices without the threat of financial ruin. Accountability systems can be designed with components that encourage colleges to implement new practices by allowing institutions to submit improvement plans. If a college follows an approved plan but outcomes do not improve, sanctions could be postponed because the college made a good-faith effort to improve. The drawback of this type of plan is that it takes additional funds to operate, even though the increased buy-in from stakeholders may make the price tag worthwhile. It also may be difficult to implement in unstable political or economic environments, as colleges may decide not to make any changes if they do not believe the accountability system will be around several years from now.

CHAPTER NINE

The Future of Higher Education Accountability

C OLLEGES ARE INCREASINGLY SUBJECT to a wide range of accountability policies and pressures from a variety of organizations seeking to influence their behavior. Although some of these stakeholders have been holding colleges accountable to some extent for decades, these pressures are becoming stronger and more instantaneous. The days in which colleges could wait several weeks before responding to requests from journalists, legislators, or accrediting agencies are long gone, as colleges must now be ready to address issues immediately before they become crises.

Higher education accountability is currently entering a period of great uncertainty. At the federal level, the recent election of Donald Trump and the overdue reauthorization of the Higher Education Act are likely to result in some types of accountability being rolled back while potentially creating new systems that affect different types of colleges. The accreditation system is also in flux, as accreditors are facing strong pressures from federal policymakers and the public alike to increase standards. States are generally increasing their scrutiny of colleges' performance, while private companies and individuals are leveraging the power of new data sources and social media to encourage colleges to focus on certain metrics and to become more transparent in their operations.

In this concluding chapter, I look ahead at the future of higher education accountability policies and practices over the next decade. I begin by summarizing the current landscape of accountability across four main external sources: the federal government, state government, accreditors, and the private sector. I then conclude the book by asking five questions that will influence the directions in which higher education accountability will move in the future.

Colleges' Vulnerability to Accountability Pressures

Some accountability pressures are much stronger for different types of colleges, while other colleges can primarily focus their responses on one main accountability pressure. In table 9.1, I classify each of these pressures into high, medium, and low categories for six different types of colleges based on institutional control and performance on metrics such as graduation rates.

Not surprisingly, for-profit colleges tend to face the strongest accountability pressures from multiple sources. The federal government has recently implemented gainful employment regulations that disproportionately affect the for-profit sector, with 98% of the programs that failed in the first data release in 2017 being at proprietary colleges (see chapter 3 for more details). The federal government's recent decision to derecognize the Accrediting Council for Independent Colleges and Schools—one of the largest accreditors of for-profit colleges—represents both an intensification of federal accountability and a push toward closer scrutiny from other accrediting agencies (Camera, 2016). The Trump administration will likely reduce accountability pressures on for-profit colleges, as evidenced by the Department of Education's 2017 decision to renegotiate both gainful employment regulations and a set of borrower defense to repayment regulations that had yet to take effect but would have made it easier for former students to sue a college if it misrepresented itself in any way (Kreighbaum, 2017). However, as of this writing the full implications of a Trump presidency are unknown.

States, particularly those with Democratic leaders, are also increasing their oversight of the for-profit sector. This is evidenced by attorneys general in a number of states filing lawsuits against colleges accused of fraudulent

TABLE 9.1   Summary of accountability pressures by type of college

Type of college	Federal	State	Accreditor	Private sector
High-performing public 4-year	Low	Medium	Low	High
Low-performing public 4-year	Medium	High	Medium	Low
Community college	Low	Medium	Medium	Low
High-performing private 4-year	Low	Low	Low	High
Low-performing private 4-year	Medium	Low	High	Low
For-profit college	Medium	Medium	High	Low

behavior (National Consumer Law Center, 2014; U.S. Department of Justice, 2015). Additional accountability pressures may even come from local communities; for example, the Milwaukee city council passed a bill that would require any for-profit colleges receiving local development funds to meet Obama-era federal accountability metrics (Smith, 2017).

Private-sector accountability regarding for-profit colleges primarily occurs through advocacy campaigns and protests from organizations such as the Debt Collective that want to see for-profit colleges shut down or substantially reformed. In a well-publicized event in 2015, Debt Collective protestors targeted the annual conference of the National Association of Student Financial Aid Administrators (NASFAA) as a way to highlight alleged abuses in the for-profit sector (Stratford, 2015a). However, these pressures appear to affect only a small percentage of for-profit colleges.

Public colleges face a somewhat different set of accountability pressures than private nonprofit institutions. State governments have increased their scrutiny of public colleges through mechanisms such as limiting tuition and fee increases and tying a percentage of appropriations of funding to outcomes, while state oversight over private nonprofit colleges is much more limited (Kelly, James, & Columbus, 2015). Higher-performing public and private colleges face relatively little scrutiny from the federal government or accrediting agencies unless they are accused of fraudulent behavior or facing federal investigations for sexual assault under Title IX.[1]

Both public and private colleges with poorer academic outcomes tend to face additional scrutiny from the federal government and accrediting agencies, with the pressures being stronger for private colleges because of the precarious financial constraints lower-performing private colleges often find themselves in without a backstop of state support. After the U.S. Department of Education pulled its recognition of the Accrediting Council for Independent Colleges and Schools (ACICS) in 2016 and regional accreditors moved toward implementing minimum standards for graduation rates (Kreighbaum, 2016), colleges with lower financial and academic performance will see additional scrutiny from accreditors going forward.

Community colleges tend to face somewhat lower levels of accountability pressures than most other sectors, with accreditation being a potential exception. Community colleges do tend to have higher student loan default rates than other sectors (Federal Student Aid, 2016), but they are affected less by federal cohort default rate metrics than for-profit colleges because a much smaller percentage of their students borrow. Likewise, gainful employment regulations affect a far smaller percentage of programs than in the for-profit sector. State performance-based funding systems do affect both four-year and two-year colleges, but these systems seem to put less funding at stake than in the four-year sector. Finally, private-sector accountability sources such as college rankings rarely include community colleges.

The only sector of higher education that can truly concentrate on responding to one set of accountability pressures is high-performing private non-profit colleges. These institutions can nearly exclusively focus on private-sector accountability systems such as college rankings that primarily affect elite institutions. These colleges are also particularly concerned about their reputation and are spending large amounts of money to recruit their desired student bodies. Flagship public universities in states with relatively hands-off legislatures or state higher education boards can also operate in the same way, although they do need to placate policymakers in order to get state appropriations.

Five Questions for Future Accountability Systems

Colleges will probably face additional accountability pressures in the future due to a combination of increased efforts to improve higher education productivity while government funding for higher education will remain fairly constant on a per-student basis. In this landscape of competing accountability pressures, I present five key questions that policymakers and other stakeholders will need to consider when developing or revising higher education accountability systems.

QUESTION 1: WILL ACCOUNTABILITY POLICIES BE IMPLEMENTED AT THE INSTITUTIONAL LEVEL OR AT THE PROGRAM LEVEL?

Most accountability efforts in higher education have traditionally been at the institutional level, but program-level efforts are becoming more common. Rankings of individual programs within colleges (particularly at the graduate level) have been around for nearly a century (e.g., Foster, 1936; Hughes, 1925). Today, there are numerous private-sector rankings of graduate-level programs in fields such as business, law, political science, and education. Another key set of program-level accountability policies is through the programmatic accreditation process, which is often required for federal financial aid eligibility or state licensure.

The federal government's ability to implement program-level accountability has typically been limited by available data for individual programs. However, the ability to do teacher-level accountability in K–12 education (e.g., Stevens & Kirst, 2015) places pressure on policymakers to provide more granular accountability systems in higher education. But the federal government's gainful employment regulations that took effect in 2017, which are based on the debt-to-earnings ratios of graduates of individual programs, represent a first step toward program-level accountability. If the College Scorecard dataset expands to include program-level outcomes in addition to institutional-level outcomes (which is technically feasible and has been discussed at technical review panels), both the federal government and private organizations could implement more granular accountability systems.

State governments already have detailed information on program-level outcomes through their rapidly improving student unit record data systems. With conservative governors and legislators already questioning the value of subsidizing students in certain liberal arts fields (e.g., Kiley, 2013), the conditions are in place for state performance-based funding (PBF) systems to focus on program-level outcomes instead of institutional-level outcomes. The increasing availability of data could also encourage the development of additional program-level accreditors, most likely as a metric of prestige rather than a condition for financial aid eligibility.

A move to program-level accountability in nonvocational fields would raise several concerns for how to adequately measure outcomes. Some of these issues include how to count students who enter college without having declared a major, how to handle students who go on to graduate school instead of immediately entering the labor force, and what to do when students graduate with multiple majors. A move to program-level accountability could potentially change colleges' internal organizational structures, with delegation of authority to individual programs being quite likely.

This sort of decentralization would likely encourage the use of responsibility center management (RCM), in which individual colleges are responsible for generating their own revenue (Strauss & Curry, 2002). RCM may have the potential to help institutions become more efficient and meet goals in other accountability systems such as state PBF by giving power to deans and department chairs to adjust as they see fit (Kosten, 2016). Yet RCM is criticized for encouraging duplicitous course offerings and administrative positions within a college as every unit scrambles to maximize revenue at the possible expense of other departments within the same institution (e.g., Hearn et al., 2006).

QUESTION 2: SHOULD ACCOUNTABILITY POLICIES
BE TARGETED TOWARD THE LOWEST-PERFORMING
COLLEGES, OR SHOULD THEY BE DESIGNED TO
ENCOURAGE IMPROVEMENT FROM ALL COLLEGES?

The majority of current accountability policies are focused on setting minimum quality thresholds for institutions that seek funding or accreditation. In some cases, these systems affect a very small number of colleges. In 2016, just 63 of 4,759 colleges participating in the federal student loan system had cohort default rates above 30% that would subject them to additional scrutiny in the future (author's calculation using Federal Student Aid data). Ten colleges were facing the loss of at least some federal financial aid due to consistently high default rates, and only 11 colleges actually had their eligibility for federal financial aid stripped between 1999 and 2015 (U.S. Senate Committee on Health, Education, Labor & Pensions, 2015a). More prestigious colleges and the associations that represent them have encouraged the federal government to allow accrediting bodies to expedite reviews of their institutions in an effort to allow accreditors to target low-performing institutions (Belkin & Fuller, 2015; Broad, McPherson, & Rawlings, 2015).

Conversely, accountability systems that only affect the lowest-performing institutions are unlikely to induce the vast majority of colleges to change their behaviors. Student academic preparation and graduation rates are highly correlated; among four-year colleges, the correlation between standardized test scores and six-year graduation rates is over 0.8 (author's calculation using Integrated Postsecondary Education Data System [IPEDS] data). This means that some colleges may be offering little added value to students while still generating outcomes that are adequate enough to avoid sanctions. Some accountability systems have recognized differences in student characteristics in their outcome metrics. Most college rankings systems have incorporated at least a small value-added component that rewards institutions that are relatively successful in serving the students they enroll, and about half of all PBF systems give additional weight to serving low-income, minority, adult, or underprepared students (National Conference of State Legislatures, 2015).

A potential flashpoint in the targeting of accountability systems is likely to occur in the debate regarding risk sharing for federal student loans, particularly among minority-serving institutions. Students attending historically black colleges and universities (HBCUs), a group of institutions with strong political support in Washington, tend to have some of the highest student debt burdens in the country. In my calculations using the most recent College

Scorecard data, 18 of the 20 four-year public and private nonprofit colleges with highest debt burdens are HBCUs. Yet many of these burdens are likely due to the limited financial resources of both the students attending HBCUs and of the colleges themselves (Goldrick-Rab, Kelchen, & Houle, 2014).[2]

Bipartisan risk-sharing legislation introduced by Senators Jeanne Shaheen (D-NH) and Orrin Hatch (R-UT) in 2015 sought to require colleges to pay up to 20% of the loan balances of students who did not pay down any principal. This would have disproportionately affected HBCUs due to their lower repayment rates and higher debt burdens. Other proposals, such as my own (Kelchen, 2015; Kelly, 2016; Webber, 2015), would either compare colleges to their peers or provide bonuses for colleges that graduate lower-income students. This would help encourage all colleges to improve rather than focusing on colleges such as HBCUs that serve larger numbers of lower-income students.

QUESTION 3: TO WHAT EXTENT SHOULD HIGHER
EDUCATION FUNDING BE TIED TO OUTCOMES
COMPARED TO ENROLLMENT?

Although state PBF policies have gained popularity and now cover a majority of American colleges, the vast majority of higher education funding is still tied to a combination of enrollment and historical allocations. Using the Lumina Foundation's definition of outcomes-based funding, Snyder (2015) estimated that only five states tied more than $1,000 per full-time equivalent student funding (or 10% of overall state funding) to outcomes. In 2016, an additional two states reached the 10% threshold of performance funding (Snyder & Fox, 2016).

Federal funding for higher education is almost exclusively based on enrollment, which is a function of the voucher system used to grant all federal financial aid aside from the approximately $2 billion dedicated to the relatively small campus-based aid programs (work-study and the Supplemental Educational Opportunity Grant). These campus-based programs do tend to disproportionately benefit students attending the most selective colleges (Kelchen, 2017), but this is a function of historical allocations rather than an explicit effort to fund colleges based on their outcomes. There have been proposals to tie campus-based aid to outcomes from higher education advocates and the Obama administration (Huelsman & Cunningham, 2013; NASFAA, 2013b; Nelson, 2012), but those proposals have yet to make significant progress in Congress.

Efforts to tie funding to outcomes raise two key concerns that must be considered when implementing higher-stakes systems. The first concern is whether colleges can effectively control the outcomes of interest. This is a particular issue in the community college sector, where 71% of students who transferred to a four-year college did not earn a credential before transferring (Jenkins & Fink, 2016). In this case, colleges should be rewarded for a combination of successful transfers and course progressions in addition to the number of completions. Open-access four-year colleges may be able to move the needle somewhat on degree completions, but performance funding systems should at least consider differences in student characteristics and institutional resources when setting performance goals. Funding based on completions also threatens to upend the traditional budget model at many four-year colleges, in which students in lower-division classes subsidize students taking upper-division classes that are more expensive to operate (Conger, Bell, & Stanley, 2010).

Funding colleges based on the number of students enrolled at what is called the date of record (typically around the end of the second week of the term, after which students cannot withdraw from courses without facing a penalty) rather than degree completions may reduce in fewer incentives to gain state funding systems. College faculty and administrators have reported pressures to lower academic standards and become more selective in states with PBF systems (e.g., Dougherty & Natow, 2015). But funding based on enrollment could remove this incentive and potentially encourage colleges to open their doors to more students if funding is sufficient.

QUESTION 4: WHO SHOULD BE RESPONSIBLE FOR DETERMINING WHETHER A COLLEGE IS ACADEMICALLY AND FINANCIALLY VIABLE?

Colleges are formally held accountable for their performance through what is sometimes known as the regulatory triad—the federal government, state governments, and accrediting bodies (Crow, 2009). The federal government has traditionally focused on issues of financial capacity, while state governments have concentrated on consumer protection issues and accreditors have worked with colleges to ensure minimum quality standards. But as dissatisfaction with colleges' performance has increased, it has become increasingly unclear where the role of one of these agencies ends and the next agency's role begins.

The federal government has taken a larger role in the quality control process in recent years, as evidenced by the decision to deny ACICS's accreditation, attempts to place financial restrictions on financially unstable for-profit colleges, and legislative pushes to set minimum standards for colleges' performance. Yet not all federal efforts have been as successful. The Obama administration's efforts to explicitly rate colleges through the Postsecondary Institution Ratings System were quietly abandoned in 2015 (Blumenstyk, 2015), and a longstanding system of requiring private colleges with low scores on a financial responsibility metric to submit a letter of credit in order to be considered financially stable has been repeatedly criticized for inaccurate methods (NAICU [National Association of Independent Colleges and Universities], 2012).

The federal role in the regulatory triad may recede somewhat in the next few years, as the Trump administration is likely to focus more on refining the financial responsibility metric to identify the least fiscally stable colleges rather than wading into issues of academic quality. Republicans in Congress may also push for what they consider the "cartel" of regional accreditors to be broken in an effort to allow competition and spur the creation of heightened academic standards (Peters, 2015; U.S. Senate Committee on Health, Education, Labor, & Pensions, 2015b). This could return accreditors to their more traditional role of academic gatekeepers rather than judging colleges based on their fiscal health. Finally, some states—particularly those with Democratic attorneys general—may use threats of legal action to continue to push for-profit colleges to change practices that they deem unethical.

QUESTION 5: IS THERE THE NECESSARY POLITICAL WILL
TO CLOSE COLLEGES THAT DO NOT MEET
PERFORMANCE STANDARDS?

The last several years have seen a sharp contraction in the for-profit college sector, with enrollment falling by 28% between the 2010–11 and 2014–15 academic years (author's calculation using IPEDS data). The number of for-profit colleges in the United States fell from 3,360 to 3,197 between the 2013–14 and 2014–15 academic years alone, and large chains like ITT Technical Institute and Corinthian Colleges have closed their doors in recent years. Supporters of for-profit colleges have loudly complained that the Obama administration's policies have contributed to their decline (Schneider & Klor de Alva, 2014; Vedder, 2016), with the valuations of the seven largest for-profit chains falling from $51 billion in 2009 to about $6 billion in mid-2016 (Hensley-Clancy, 2016). Publicly traded colleges then rallied to reach 52-week highs in stock prices immediately after Donald Trump's election in 2016 (Dynarski, 2016).

A great deal of media attention has been paid to nonprofit colleges that are at risk of closing due to financial instability. A much-publicized report from analysts at Moody's Investors Service predicted that the number of nonprofit colleges closing each year would rise from an average of five per year between 2004 and 2014 to about 15 per year in 2017 (Woodhouse, 2015). In 2016, 13 nonprofit colleges closed (Brown, 2016), which reflects the largest number of closures since at least 1999. This represents a tiny portion of American higher education, with most closed colleges having fewer than 1,000 students. Even Sweet Briar College, which famously reversed its decision to close in 2015, had just 561 students at the time the closure was attempted (Seltzer, 2016a).

Closing a college that is on the verge of financial insolvency is an incredibly difficult task, as evidenced by Sweet Briar, Dowling College, Morris Brown College, and several other colleges that have tried to stay afloat in recent years with various levels of success. But there is very little conversation about whether private nonprofit or public colleges with very poor student outcomes should either be closed or restructured. For example, a *Wall Street Journal* feature article highlighted 11 accredited four-year colleges (eight of which were public or private nonprofits) that had six-year graduation rates for first-time, full-time students below 10% (Fuller & Belkin, 2015). The Education Trust (2014) has highlighted over 100 colleges it considers "dropout factories" for graduating fewer than 15% of its students, while an analysis by Hiler and Hatalsky (2016) called 85% of four-year public colleges "dropout factories" for having graduation rates below 67%—the definition of dropout factories in K–12 education.

Several years ago, it appeared that accrediting bodies may have been willing to revoke the accreditation of colleges with poor academic outcomes in addition to colleges that were struggling financially. But the longstanding saga of the City College of San Francisco, which resulted in the college's accreditor facing additional oversight from the state government and threats from influential members of Congress after it attempted to pull its accreditation due to severe governance issues (Dudnick, 2014; Hammill, 2014), is likely to scare accreditors that may have been otherwise willing to recommend a virtual death sentence of revoking accreditation. It is far more politically feasible to keep struggling colleges accredited and on probation rather than try to revoke accreditation except in the most egregious cases.

Federal and state policymakers also face significant difficulties in trying to close the lowest-performing colleges. An example of this is when the U.S. Department of Education retroactively revised cohort default rates for between two dozen and three dozen colleges just on the threshold of facing sanctions in 2014 (Field, 2014) and for another dozen colleges in 2015 (Stratford, 2015b). One reason is that policymakers are vulnerable to coordinated lobbying campaigns by their constituents, particularly as colleges are often the largest employer in their community. It is even more difficult to recommend closing a college when students may not have any nearby options in their field of study. Hillman (2016) has shown that a sizable percentage of adults, particularly those in rural areas, with high proportions of racial/ethnic minorities, or with lower educational levels, are less likely to have access to multiple in-person college options than students living in wealthier urban or suburban areas. In other cases, there may be multiple colleges in a given area, but not all colleges may offer a student's program of interest or be accessible given a student's academic preparation (Blagg & Chingos, 2016).

Closing community colleges is even more difficult, as the typical community college student lives just eight miles from their campus (Hillman & Weichman, 2016) and community colleges often receive local funding in addition to state and federal aid. Although students have an increasing number of high-quality online options available that can help to reduce these "education deserts," not all students are interested in studying online (and for vocational fields, it may not be practical) and high-speed Internet access is not available in all parts of the country. When deciding to close a college in an education desert, accreditors and policymakers should consider whether a low-quality college is better or worse than no college at all.

At the state level, Georgia is taking a different path to improve struggling colleges by merging together institutions. This has faced a great deal of opposition from stakeholders, in part because of proposals to merge colleges with different missions and student populations (Jaschik, 2015; Rivard, 2013), but this is likely easier than trying to shutter a campus. Among the six mergers of Georgia colleges in recent years is Georgia Perimeter College, a community college with a 6% graduation rate, with Georgia State University. The hope is that Georgia State's experience improving its graduation rate will help Georgia Perimeter students (Smith, 2016). There is some empirical research supporting the state's merger frenzy; a working paper by Russell (2016) found that students attending merged colleges were more likely to persist in college than students attending similar colleges that were not merged while per-student spending remained flat.

Concluding Remarks

At this point, it would be possible for me to conclude this book on the depressing reality that shuttering some of America's worst colleges is virtually impossible. But I remain somewhat optimistic that accountability efforts can at least marginally improve the behavior of some of these colleges. Rather than recommending the complete shutdown of colleges, accreditors, states, or the U.S. Department of Education could instead require that low-performing colleges implement school improvement plans similar to what has been in place in K–12 education. Both the No Child Left Behind Act (McClure, 2005) and the Every Student Succeeds Act (Klein, 2016) tied federal Title I funds to implementing improvement plans, with differing levels of control by the federal and state governments. By requiring significant or complete changes in leadership, it could be possible to make large-scale institutional changes in an effort to try to improve colleges without being able to close them.

The private sector could also play an important role in turning around struggling colleges. Nonprofit organizations dedicated to improving student outcomes could partner with colleges to share best practices in student success as well as potentially providing additional resources. Foundations could work to develop or support organizations connecting colleges that are at financial or academic risk of closure, such as the Yes We Must Coalition of 35 small private nonprofit colleges that has received support from multiple foundations (Yes We Must Coalition, 2016) and another group of 15 small liberal arts colleges supported by the Endeavor Foundation (Seltzer, 2016b).

A number of colleges will work proactively to develop their own accountability metrics in an effort to demonstrate value to other stakeholders and to avoid having high-stakes accountability systems that they dislike being placed upon them. Existing efforts such as the Voluntary System of Accountability, which provides information on student learning outcomes (Voluntary System of Accountability, n.d.), and the Student Achievement Measure, which includes more comprehensive information on graduation rates than is currently available from the federal government (Student Achievement Measure, 2013), represent ways that colleges are trying to demonstrate their value. But in an environment in which colleges are pressured to be fiscally accountable for their students' outcomes, a group of about 100 liberal arts colleges that have pledged to make graduates' loan payments if they meet certain eligibility criteria and earn low salaries as a sort of money-back guarantee (Belkin, 2017).[3]

In the decade ahead, I see accountability pressures continuing to rise at the expense of the autonomy many colleges and universities have traditionally enjoyed. Although federal accountability pressures may ebb and flow depending on the partisan balance in Washington, states, accreditors, the private sector, and internal stakeholders are unlikely to trust colleges to the extent that they did several decades ago. New accountability measures will continue to develop in the years ahead and have increasing power over a college's bottom line. It is in the best interest of colleges to be proactive and to work to develop these metrics with stakeholders whenever possible in an effort to create reasonable accountability systems that seek to improve colleges' performance, recognize their particular mission, and guard against unintended consequences. This is a tall task to be sure, but I am optimistic that the next generation of accountability metrics will be substantial improvements over the ones present today.

Introduction: The Rationale for Accountability in Higher Education

1. As a technical note (and one that frustrates higher education finance researchers), the Gallup/Purdue survey inappropriately used "cost" when "price" would have been more accurate. The price of an education is what students and their families pay, while the cost refers to how much money it takes to provide the education regardless of who pays for it.

2. Some students do not apply to a particular college because the sticker price (before grant aid) of that college is too high (e.g., Grodsky & Jones, 2007; Hesel & Meade, 2012).

Chapter One: The Theoretical Underpinnings of Accountability

1. See Miller (2005) for a review of the literature on monitoring in public-sector organizations.

2. While it is quite likely that unobserved student characteristics explain some of the differences across colleges, given its magnitude it is difficult to envision these characteristics explaining the entire gap in graduation rates.

3. See Christensen and Gazley (2008) for an excellent review of how to determine and analyze capacity in the field of public administration.

4. Some accountability systems, such as college rankings, also reward colleges for their inputs. For example, the *U.S. News & World Report* rankings reward colleges for selectivity, while the *Washington Monthly* rankings reward colleges for economic diversity. I will return to the topic of rankings in more detail in chapter 6.

5. Author's calculation using Integrated Postsecondary Education Data System (IPEDS) data.

6. Kelly's analysis excludes more than 2,000 postsecondary institutions whose highest credential awarded is a certificate, understating the number of institutions with a stake in higher education policy.

7. In the interest of full disclosure, I have received funding through both ACE and NASFAA to conduct research projects.

8. For example, the correlation between ACT/SAT scores and six-year graduation rates among four-year colleges was approximately 0.87 between 2011–12 and 2013–14 (author's calculations using IPEDS data).

Chapter Two: The Historical Development of Higher Education Accountability

1. There is currently another college named The College of New Jersey. The institution formerly known as Trenton State College adopted the name in 1996 over objections from some members of the Trenton State community as well as a potential lawsuit from Princeton University (Stout, 1996). The two colleges eventually reached a settlement that allowed Trenton State to take the TCNJ name (Thelin, 2011).

2. Although Rutgers and William and Mary are now public institutions, they were private for most of their histories. William and Mary became public in 1906 and Rutgers became fully public in 1956 (College of William and Mary, n.d.; Rutgers University, n.d.).

3. William H. Woodard, the defendant, was appointed by the state government to be the secretary of the board of overseers.

4. There are two accrediting bodies in some western states: the Western Association of Schools and Colleges (which covers four-year colleges) and the Accrediting Commission for Community and Junior Colleges (which covers two-year colleges). All other regional accreditors cover both sectors.

Chapter Three: Federal Accountability Policies

1. An estimated $18 billion in tax credits are also awarded directly to students instead of to colleges, but these funds do not come until several months after a student enrolls in college.

2. These data are scheduled to become available to the public in late 2017.

3. The net price of attendance is officially defined as the total cost of attendance (tuition, fees, room/board, books, and other living expenses) less all grant aid received.

4. Colleges must also be accredited by a recognized accrediting agency in order to receive federal financial aid dollars. See chapter 5 for more details on accreditation as an accountability tool in higher education.

5. Data on nonprofit college closures came from Ray Brown's excellent *College History Garden* blog, which tracks closures: https://collegehistorygarden.blogspot.com/2015/11/college-closures-since-2009.html.

6. Because of this, there is no research up to this point on how being subject to HCM affects colleges.

7. Some other colleges owned by DeVry, such as the Ross University School of Veterinary Medicine, receive closer to 85% of their total revenue from federal sources other than veterans' benefits (Smith, 2016).

8. APSCU changed its name to Career Education Colleges and Universities in 2016 (Fain, 2016).

Chapter Four: State Accountability Policies

1. This analysis excludes student loan dollars, as the expectation is that students will repay these obligations.

2. New Jersey's 1994 changes also influenced Arkansas college officials, who successfully lobbied their legislature to make a similar change to a less-powerful commission in 1997 (McLendon, 2003b).

3. However, McLendon, Hearn, and Mokher (2009) did not find a significant relationship between governance structures and appropriations at public colleges.

4. The period of analysis ended before Illinois's recent stopgap budgets for higher education.

5. Because Nebraska has a unicameral, officially nonpartisan legislature while all other states have two legislative chambers with partisan affiliations being allowed, Nebraska is traditionally excluded from this body of literature.

6. See chapter 1 for a more complete treatment of how public-sector accountability systems have spread over the past several decades in areas other than higher education.

7. Two interesting studies provide insights into what students and their families might be doing with some of the merit aid dollars. Cornwell and Mustard (2007) highlighted a jump in new car sales in high-income Georgia counties after that state's merit aid program began, while Cowan and White (2015) showed that large merit aid programs were associated with an increase in binge drinking among male students.

8. Pell Grant–eligible students attending select private colleges in Colorado can qualify for a grant equal to half of the public college grant (College Opportunity Fund, n.d.). Graduate education and other services were directly funded by the state through performance contracts, which is why Colorado only funded 11.7% of total higher education expenditures via grant aid in 2015 (National Association of State Student Grant and Aid Programs, 2015).

9. Recall that unit record datasets are currently not allowed at the federal level.

10. I would like to thank my research assistant, Olga Komissarova, for her tireless work reviewing states' websites.

11. I have received support from all three organizations for prior research, although none for my work on performance funding.

12. My calculations used data from the National Conference of State Legislatures (2015), Snyder & Fox (2016), and state websites.

13. New York, New Jersey, and Pennsylvania are ineligible as they are not a part of a regional education compact.

14. See chapter 5 for a more complete discussion of accreditation and ACICS's fight to maintain federal recognition.

Chapter Five: Accreditation and Accountability

1. See chapter 2 for a more detailed discussion on the historical development of accreditation.

2. Although I use "colleges" below, most of the language that follows also applies to individual programs that are seeking accreditation.

3. The terminology here has been agreed upon by all regional accreditors and generally reflects the types of potential sanctions that other accreditors also use. However, accreditors have somewhat different criteria that trigger placing a college into one of these categories (Flores, 2016).

4. To support grouping accreditors' individual standards into five classifications, I examined two regional and two national accreditors. Although national accreditors had additional standards specific to the type of colleges they accredited, all four bodies had standards that fit into the groups summarized in this chapter (ACCJC, 2014; Accrediting Commission of Career Schools and Colleges, 2016; Middle States Commission on Higher Education, 2011; TRACS, 2015).

5. Middle States is a notable exception, as just 6% of its commissioners had a potential conflict of interest (Cooper, 2016).

6. University of North Texas's law school went from being a freestanding institution to a professional school within its Dallas campus in 2015, which allowed it to gain federal financial aid access (UNT Dallas College of Law, 2015).

7. Paine College in Georgia had its accreditation reinstated via injunction in 2016 while its lawsuit was pending (Quinn, 2016).

Chapter Six: Private-Sector Accountability

1. Informal accountability via a college's reputation has a different meaning among students who are placebound or living in "education deserts" (Hillman, 2016) and thus do not have as large of a college choice set as other students. In that case, the student's decision may be between going to the local community college or an open-access four-year public university or not attending at all.

2. It is worth noting that 21 colleges that have ended Division I football programs in the last several decades have not seen significant changes to their reputation (Hutchinson, Rascher, & Jennings, 2016).

3. This excludes professional doctorates in fields such as law and medicine.

4. Three of the categories (competitive, very competitive, and highly competitive) also have "plus" distinctions, which do not seem to get as much attention when the ratings are discussed. For this reason, I combine colleges with a plus distinction with other colleges in the same competitiveness band.

5. Standard & Poor's and Moody's rate similar numbers of private nonprofit colleges, Moody's rates the majority of public colleges, and Fitch is a relatively uncommon ratings provider in higher education (White, Harvey, & Ludwig, 2014).

6. There are some efforts to rate and/or rank a segment of community colleges. For example, the Aspen Prize program regularly recognizes ten high-performing

community colleges and awards one college a $1 million prize, while *Washington Monthly*'s ranking of best community colleges for adult learners listed the top 100 institutions based on their flexibility for students as well as their outcomes for adult students.

7. It is entirely possible that people who report earnings to Payscale tend to have higher earnings than the typical graduate, but as long as the selection issue is present regardless of where a student attended, the order of the rankings is still preserved.

8. For a more thorough summary of the international rankings landscape, see Hazelkorn (2017).

9. For a more detailed treatment of how colleges respond to rankings, see Morphew and Swanson (2011).

10. Other rankings, such as *Forbes, Money,* and *Washington Monthly*, are based on data that are available from sources other than the individual colleges, meaning that colleges cannot opt out of these rankings by refusing to provide data.

Chapter Seven: Institutional Accountability Policies and Practices

1. Members of governing boards are called "trustees," "regents," "governors," or even "curators" or "visitors" at different colleges. I use the terms interchangeably in this chapter.

2. One of the two trustees who refused to resign, James Montgomery Sr., was reappointed in 2013 and continues to serve to this day.

3. One well-publicized paper in 2013 claimed that tenure-line faculty members' teaching loads fell by 25% between 1987 and 2003, but it was later withdrawn due to comparability of the data across survey waves (*Inside Higher Ed*, 2013).

4. See chapter 6 for a more thorough discussion of the Carnegie classification system and its influence on institutional behavior.

Chapter Eight: Ten Lessons Learned from Accountability Policies

1. Thanks to Tod Massa at the State Council of Higher Education for Virginia (which has perhaps the best public-facing state higher education data interface) for pointing me to this resource.

2. The Delaware Cost Study (four-year colleges) and National Community College Cost and Productivity Project (two-year colleges) provide information about program-level costs, but have limitations regarding course-level costs.

Chapter Nine: The Future of Higher Education Accountability

1. For up-to-date information on which colleges are facing Title IX investigations regarding sexual assault, I highly recommend the *Chronicle of Higher Education*'s tracking website at http://projects.chronicle.com/titleix.

2. Currently, colleges cannot restrict student borrowing below federal limits if

there is space in a student's financial aid package. Both NASFAA (2013a) and the U.S. Senate Committee on Health, Education, Labor and Pensions (2015a) have called for colleges to have the ability to limit student borrowing in certain cases, which is likely to be included in Higher Education Act reauthorization.

3. Much of the price tag of these loan repayment plans is paid for by the federal government, as income-driven repayment plans will reduce loan payments to as little as zero dollars per month.

REFERENCES

Introduction: The Rationale for Accountability in Higher Education

American Council of Trustees and Alumni. 2013. *Are they learning? A college trustee's guide to assessing academic effectiveness.* Washington, DC: Author.

Arum, R., and J. Roksa. 2011. *Academically adrift: Limited learning on college campuses.* Chicago: University of Chicago Press.

Benjamin, R. 2013. *Does college matter? Measuring critical-thinking outcomes using the CLA.* New York: Council for Aid to Education.

Bok, D. 2006. *Our underachieving colleges: A candid look at how much students learn and why they should be learning more.* Princeton, NJ: Princeton University Press.

Brand, J. E., and Y. Xie. 2010. Who benefits most from college? Evidence for negative selection in heterogeneous economic returns to higher education. *American Sociological Review* 75 (2): 273–302.

Carlson, A. 2016. *SHEF: FY 2015 state higher education finance.* Boulder: State Higher Education Executive Officers Association.

Carnevale, A. P., T. Jayasundera, and A. Gulish. 2016. *America's divided recovery: College haves and have-nots 2016.* Washington, DC: Georgetown University Center on Education and the Workforce.

Cochrane, D. F., and D. Cheng. 2016. *Student debt and the class of 2015.* Oakland, CA: The Institute for College Access and Success.

Delaney, J. A., and W. R. Doyle. 2011. State spending on higher education: Testing the balance wheel over time. *Journal of Education Finance* 36 (4): 343–68.

Delisle, J. 2014. *The graduate student debt review.* Washington, DC: New America.

Dynarski, S. 2015, August 31. Why students with smallest debts have the largest problem. *New York Times.* http://www.nytimes.com/2015/09/01/upshot/why-students-with-smallest-debts-need-the-greatest-help.html.

Eagan, K., E. B. Stolzenberg, A. K. Bates, M. C. Aragon, M. R. Suchard, and C. Rios-Aguilar. 2016. *The American freshman: National norms for fall 2015.* Los Angeles: Cooperative Institutional Research Program, University of California, Los Angeles.

Field, K. 2012, January 25. State of the Union speech leaves many questions unanswered. *Chronicle of Higher Education.* http://www.chronicle.com/article/State-of-the-Union-Speech/130464.

Gallup. 2016. *Americans value postsecondary education: The 2015 Gallup-Lumina Foundation study of the American public's opinion on higher education.* Washington, DC: Author.

Ginsberg, B. 2011. *The fall of the faculty: The rise of the all-administrative university and why it matters.* Cambridge: Oxford University Press.

Goldrick-Rab, S., R. Kelchen, and J. N. Houle. 2014. *The color of student debt: Implications of federal loan program reforms for black students and historically black colleges and universities.* Madison: Wisconsin HOPE Lab.

Gose, B. 2008, November 21. Gates fund creates plan for college completion. *Chronicle of Higher Education.* http://www.chronicle.com/article/Gates-Fund-Creates-Plan-for/25063.

Grodsky, E., and M. T. Jones. 2007. Real and imagined barriers to college entry: Perceptions of cost. *Social Science Research* 36: 745–66.

Hanover Research. 2016. *McGraw-Hill Education 2016 workforce readiness survey.* New York: McGraw-Hill Education.

Hebel, S. 2009, May 1. Lumina's leader sets lofty goals for fund's role in policy debates. *Chronicle of Higher Education.* http://www.chronicle.com/article/Luminas-Leader-Sets-Lofty/28674.

Hebel, S., and J. Selingo. 2009, February 26. Obama's higher-education goal is ambitious but achievable, leaders say. *Chronicle of Higher Education.* http://www.chronicle.com/article/Obamas-Higher-Education-Goal/117386.

Helfing, K. 2015, June 18. Walker's latest target: College professors. *Politico.* http://www.politico.com/story/2015/06/scott-walker-targets-college-professors-unions-wisconsin-119124.

Hershbein, B., and M. Kearney. 2014. *Major decisions: What graduates earn over their lifetimes.* Washington, DC: Hamilton Project.

Hesel, R. A., and D. C. Meade Jr. 2012, September 14. A majority of students rule out colleges based on sticker price. *College Board and Art and Science Group StudentPOLL.* http://www.artsci.com/studentpoll/v9n1/index.html.

Jaschik, S. 2013, January 7. Least stressful job? Really? *Inside Higher Ed.* https://www.insidehighered.com/news/2013/01/07/claim-college-professor-least-stressful-job-infuriates-faculty.

———. 2015, April 13. UCLA faculty approves diversity requirement. *Inside Higher Ed.* https://www.insidehighered.com/news/2015/04/13/ucla-faculty-approves-diversity-requirement.

Kane, T. J., and C. E. Rouse. 1995. Labor-market returns to two- and four-year college. *American Economic Review* 85 (3): 600–14.

Kensing, K. 2013, January 3. The ten least stressful jobs of 2013. *CareerCast.* http://www.careercast.com/jobs-rated/10-least-stressful-jobs-2013.

Ludwig, M. 2011, July 11. Higher ed reformers target the elusive "lazy professors." *Houston Chronicle.* http://www.chron.com/news/houston-texas/article/Higher-ed-reformers-target-the-elusive-lazy-2080715.php.

Ma, J., S. Baum, M. Pender, and M. Welch. 2016. *Trends in college pricing.* Washington, DC: College Board.

Matthews, D. 2016. *A stronger nation 2016.* Indianapolis: Lumina Foundation.

Nguyen, M. 2012. *Degreeless in debt: What happens to borrowers who drop out.* Washington, DC: Education Sector.

OECD (Organisation for Economic Co-operation and Development). 2016a. Population with tertiary education. Accessed November 20, 2016 from https://data.oecd.org/eduatt/population-with-tertiary-education.htm.

———. 2016b. Education at a glance 2016: OECD indicators. Paris: Author.

Oreopoulos, P., and U. Petronijevic. 2013. Making college worth it: A review of the returns to higher education. *Future of Children* 23 (1): 43–65.

Redden, E. 2016, November 14. International student numbers top 1 million. *Inside Higher Ed.* https://www.insidehighered.com/news/2016/11/14/annual -open-doors-report-documents-continued-growth-international-students-us -and-us.

Reed, M. 2008. *Student debt and the class of 2007.* Oakland, CA: Institute for College Access and Success.

Rubin, C. 2014, September 19. Making a splash on campus. *New York Times.* http://www.nytimes.com/2014/09/21/fashion/college-recreation-now-includes -pool-parties-and-river-rides.html.

Scally, J., and D. Lee. 2016. 2016 *Student loan update.* Federal Reserve Bank of New York. Accessed June 20, 2017. https://www.newyorkfed.org/medialibrary /interactives/householdcredit/data/xls/sl_update_2016.xlsx.

Schleifer, D., and R. Silliman. 2016. *What's the payoff? Americans consider problems and promises of higher education.* New York: Public Agenda.

Shapiro, D., A. Dundar, P. K. Wakhungu, X. Yuan, A. Nathan, and Y. Hwang. 2015. *Completing college: A national view of student attainment rates—Fall 2009 cohort.* Herndon, VA: National Student Clearinghouse Research Center.

Sidhu, P., and V. Calderon. 2014, February 26. Many business leaders doubt U.S. colleges prepare students. *Gallup.* http://www.gallup.com/poll/167630/business -leaders-doubt-colleges-prepare-students.aspx.

Stancill, J. 2015, April 18. Lawmakers back away from increased course loads for UNC professors. *News and Observer.* http://www.newsobserver.com/news /politics-government/politics-columns-blogs/under-the-dome/article19828554 .html.

Taylor, P., K. Parker, R. Fry, D. Cohn, W. Wang, G. Velasco, and D. Dockterman. 2011. *Is college worth it? College presidents, public assess value, quality, and mission of higher education.* Washington, DC: Pew Research Center.

U.S. Department of Education. 2016. 2014–2015 federal Pell Grant program end-of-year report. Accessed November 22, 2016 from http://www2.ed.gov/finaid /prof/resources/data/pell-2014-15/pell-eoy-2014-15.html.

Weber, L. 2014, April 27. Apprenticeships help close the skills gap. So why are

they in decline? *Wall Street Journal*. http://www.wsj.com/articles/SB10001424
05270230397830457947350194364261.

Woodhouse, K. 2015, June 15. Lazy rivers and student debt. *Inside Higher Ed.*
https://www.insidehighered.com/news/2015/06/15/are-lazy-rivers-and-climbing
-walls-driving-cost-college.

Chapter One: The Theoretical Underpinnings of Accountability

Aldrich, H. E., and D. Herker. 1977. Boundary spanning roles and organization
structure. *Academy of Management Review* 2 (2): 217–30.

Aldrich, H. E., and J. Pfeffer. 1976. Environments of organizations. *Annual Review of Sociology* 2: 79–105.

Alter, M., and R. Reback. 2014. True for your school? How changing reputations
alter demand for selective U.S. colleges. *Educational Evaluation and Policy Analysis* 36 (3): 346–70.

Anderson, N. 2014, February 2. U-Md.'s unusual admissions approach: One out
of every five freshmen starts in spring term. *Washington Post.* https://www
.washingtonpost.com/local/education/u-mds-unusual-admissions-approach
-one-out-of-every-five-freshmen-start-in-spring-term/2014/01/31/21d99a64
-8794-11e3-916e-e01534b1e132_story.html.

Archibald, R. B., and D. H. Feldman. 2008a. Explaining increases in higher education costs. *Journal of Higher Education* 79 (3): 268–95.

———. 2008b. Graduation rates and accountability: Regressions versus production frontiers. *Research in Higher Education* 49 (1): 80–100.

Armstrong, E. A., and L. T. Hamilton. 2013. *Paying for the party: How college
maintains inequality*. Cambridge, MA: Harvard University Press.

Baker, J. 2014, September 23. Adjustment of calculation of official three year cohort default rates for institutions subject to potential loss of eligibility. *Office
of Federal Student Aid*. http://ifap.ed.gov/eannouncements/092314Adjustment
ofCalculationofOfc3YrCDRforInstitutSubtoPotentialLossofElig.html.

Bailey, M. J., and S. Dynarski. 2011. Inequality in postsecondary education. In
Whither opportunity?, edited by G. Duncan and R. Murnane, 117–32. New
York: Russell Sage Foundation.

Bailey, T., and D. Xu. 2012. *Input-adjusted graduation rates and college accountability: What is known from twenty years of research?* Washington, DC: HCM
Strategists.

Ballou, D., M. G. Springer, D. F. McCaffrey, J. R. Lockwood, B. M. Stecher, L.
Hamilton, and M. Pepper. 2012. Point/counterpoint: The view from the trenches
of education policy research. *Education Finance and Policy* 7 (2): 170–202.

Bastedo, M. N., and N. A. Bowman. 2011. College rankings as an interorganizational dependency: Establishing the foundation for strategic and institutional
accounts. *Research in Higher Education* 52 (1): 3–23.

Baumol, W. J. 1967. Macroeconomics of unbalanced growth: The anatomy of
urban crisis. *American Economic Review* 57 (3): 415–26.

Benjamin, L. M. 2008. Bearing more risk for results: Performance accountability and nonprofit relational work. *Administration and Society* 39 (8): 959–83.

———. 2010. Funders as principals: Performance measurement in philanthropic relationships. *Nonprofit Management and Leadership* 20 (4): 383–403.

Booher-Jennings, J. 2005. Below the bubble: "Educational triage" and the Texas accountability system. *American Educational Research Journal* 42(2): 231–68.

Bowen, H. R. 1980. *The costs of higher education: How much do colleges and universities spend per student and how much should they spend?* Washington, DC: Jossey-Bass.

Bowman, N. A., and M. N. Bastedo. 2009. Getting on the front page: Organizational reputations, status signals, and the impact of *U.S. News and World Report* on student decisions. *Research in Higher Education* 50 (5): 415–36.

Box, R. C. 1999. Running government like a business: Implications for public administration theory and practice. *American Review of Public Administration* 29 (1): 19–43.

Brackett, A. 2016. Public college lobbying and institutional appropriations: The role of lobbying in state higher education budgets. Doctoral dissertation, Seton Hall University.

Buurman, M., and R. Dur. 2012. Incentives and the sorting of altruistic agents into street-level bureaucracies. *Scandinavian Journal of Economics* 114 (4): 1318–45.

Campbell, D. A., and K. T. Lambright. 2016. Program performance and multiple constituency theory. *Nonprofit and Voluntary Sector Quarterly* 45 (1): 150–71.

Chakrabarti, R. 2013. Accountability with voucher threats, responses, and the test-taking population: Regression discontinuity evidence from Florida. *Education Finance and Policy* 8 (2): 121–67.

Cheslock, J. J., and D. B. Knight. 2015. Diverging revenues, cascading expenditures, and ensuing subsidies: The unbalanced and growing financial strain of intercollegiate athletics on universities and their students. *Journal of Higher Education* 86 (3): 417–47.

Chiang, H. 2009. How accountability pressure on failing schools affects student achievement. *Journal of Public Economics* 93 (9/10): 1045–57.

Christensen, R. K., and B. Gazley. 2008. Capacity for public administration: Analysis of meaning and measurement. *Public Administration and Development* 28 (4): 265–79.

Cohen, P., and C. Bray. 2016, February 8. University of Phoenix owner, Apollo Education Group, will be taken private. *New York Times*. http://www.nytimes.com/2016/02/09/business/dealbook/apollo-education-group-university-of-phoenix-owner-to-be-taken-private.html.

Courty, P., D. H. Kim, and G. Marschke. 2011. Curbing cream-skimming: Evidence on enrollment incentives. *Labour Economics* 18: 643–55.

Courty, P., and G. Marschke. 1997. Measuring government performance: Lessons from a federal job-training program. *American Economic Review* 87 (2): 383–88.

———. 2004. An empirical investigation of gaming responses to explicit performance incentives. *Journal of Labor Economics* 22 (1): 23–56.

———. 2008. A general test for distortions in performance measures. *Review of Economics and Statistics* 90 (3): 428–41.

Croston, T., and C. Hall (writers), and T. Garcia (director). 2008, November 9. No Bobby left behind. Television series episode. *King of the hill*, M. McJimsey (producer). Los Angeles: 20th Century Fox Television.

Cullen, J. B., and R. Reback. 2006. Tinkering toward accolades: School gaming under a performance accountability system. Cambridge, MA: National Bureau of Economic Research Working Paper 12286.

Cunha, J. M., and T. Miller. 2014. Measuring value-added in higher education: Possibilities and limitations in the use of administrative data. *Economics of Education Review* 42: 64–77.

Dal Bo, E. 2006. Regulatory capture: A review. *Oxford Review of Economic Policy* 22 (2): 203–25.

Davis, J. H., F. D. Schoorman, and L. Donaldson. 1997. Toward a stewardship theory of management. *Academy of Management Review* 22 (1): 20–47.

Dee, T. S., W. Dobbie, B. A. Jacob, and J. Rockoff. 2016. The causes and consequences of test score manipulation: Evidence from the New York Regents examinations. Cambridge, MA: National Bureau of Economic Research Working Paper 22165.

Dee, T. S., B. A. Jacob, and N. L. Schwartz. 2013. The effects of NCLB on school resources and practices. *Educational Evaluation and Policy Analysis* 35 (2): 252–79.

Deming, D. J., and D. Figlio. 2016. Accountability in US education: Applying lessons from K–12 experience to higher education. *Journal of Economic Perspectives* 30 (3): 33–56.

Desrochers, D. M., and S. Hurlburt. 2016. *Trends in college spending: 2003–2013.* Washington, DC: American Institutes for Research.

Dickinson, D., and M. Villeval. 2008. Does monitoring decrease work effort? The complementarity between agency and crowding-out theories. *Games and Economic Behavior* 63 (1): 56–76.

Dixit, A. 1999. Incentives and organizations in the public sector: An interpretive review. *Journal of Human Resources* 37 (4): 696–727.

Dougherty, K. J., S. M. Jones, H. Lahr, R. S. Natow, L. Pheatt, and V. Reddy. 2016. *Performance funding for higher education.* Baltimore: Johns Hopkins University Press.

Dougherty, K. J., and R. S. Natow. 2015. *The politics of performance funding for higher education: Origins, discontinuations, and transformations.* Baltimore: Johns Hopkins University Press.

Dougherty, K. J., R. S. Natow, and B. E. Vega. 2012. Popular but unstable: Explaining why state performance funding systems in the United States often do not persist. *Teachers College Record* 114 (3): 1–41.

Dur, R., and R. Zoutenbier. 2014. Working for a good cause. *Public Administration Review* 74 (2): 144–55.

Eberts, R., K. Hollenbeck, and J. Stone. 2002. Teacher performance incentives and student outcomes. *Journal of Human Resources* 37 (4): 913–27.

Eckles, J. E. 2010. Evaluating the efficiency of top liberal arts colleges. *Research in Higher Education* 51 (3): 266–93.

Eff, E. A., C. C. Klein, and R. Kyle. 2012. Identifying the best buys in U.S. higher education. *Research in Higher Education* 53 (8): 860–87.

Elmore, R. F., C. H. Abelmann, and S. H. Fuhrman. 1996. The new accountability in state education reform: From process to performance. In *Holding schools accountable: Performance-based reform in education*, edited by H. E. Ladd, 65–98. Washington, DC: Brookings Institution.

Ethiraj, S. K., and D. Levinthal. 2009. Hoping for A to Z while rewarding only A: Complex organizations and multiple goals. *Organization Science* 20 (1): 4–21.

Ewing, A. M. 2012. Estimating the impact of relative expected grade on student evaluations of teachers. *Economics of Education Review* 31: 141–54.

Figlio, D. N. 2006. Testing, crime and punishment. *Journal of Public Economics* 90 (4/5): 837–51.

Florida Board of Governors. n.d. Florida Board of Governors performance funding allocation. Accessed June 19, 2017. http://www.flbog.edu/board/office/budget/_doc/performance_funding/Allocation-Year-1-2014-15-Summary.pdf.

Frey, B. S. 2012. Crowding effects on intrinsic motivation. *Renewal* 20 (2/3): 91–98.

Gabriel, T. 2010, June 10. Under pressure, teachers tamper with tests. *New York Times*. http://www.nytimes.com/2010/06/11/education/11cheat.html.

Gailmard, S., and J. W. Patty. 2007. Slackers and zealots: Civil service, policy discretion, and bureaucratic expertise. *American Journal of Political Science* 51 (4): 873–89.

Gallup. 2015. Great jobs, great lives: The relationship between student debt, experiences and perceptions of college worth. Washington, DC: Author.

Gerrish, E. 2016. The impact of performance management on performance in public organizations: A meta-analysis. *Public Administration Review* 76 (1): 48–66.

Goodman, S. F., and L. J. Turner. 2013. The design of teacher incentive pay and educational outcomes: Evidence from the New York City bonus program. *Journal of Labor Economics* 31 (2): 409–20.

Herzog, K. 2016, February 4. UW-Madison spent $8 million to fend off raids on faculty. *Milwaukee Journal-Sentinel*. http://www.jsonline.com/news/education/uw-system-regents-to-take-up-tenure-plan-thursday-friday-b99664273z1-367677251.html.

Hillman, N. W., D. A. Tandberg, and A. H. Fryar. 2015. Evaluating the impacts of "new" performance funding. *Educational Evaluation and Policy Analysis* 37 (4): 501–19.

Holmstrom, B. 1979. Moral hazard and observability. *Bell Journal of Economics* 10 (1): 74–91.

———. 1982. Moral hazard in teams. *Bell Journal of Economics* 13 (2): 324–40.

Jacob, B. A., and S. D. Levitt. 2003. Rotten apples: An investigation of the prevalence and predictors of teacher cheating. *Quarterly Journal of Economics* 118 (3): 843–77.

Jacob, B., B. McCall, and K. M. Stange. 2013. *College as country club: Do colleges cater to students' preferences for consumption?* NBER Working Paper 18745. Cambridge, MA: National Bureau of Economic Research.

Jaschik, S. 2013, January 28. How much admission misreporting? *Inside Higher Ed.* https://www.insidehighered.com/news/2013/01/28/bucknells-admission-rai ses-questions-about-how-many-colleges-are-reporting-false.

Jennings, J. L., and A. A. Beveridge. 2009. How does test exemption affect schools' and students' academic performance? *Educational Evaluation and Policy Analysis* 31 (2): 153–75.

Jensen, M. C., and W. H. Meckling. 1976. Theory of the firm: Managerial behavior, agency costs and ownership structure. *Journal of Financial Economics* 3 (4): 305–60.

Kelchen, R., and D. N. Harris. 2012. *Can "value added" methods improve the measurement of college performance? Empirical analyses and policy implications.* Washington, DC: HCM Strategists.

Kelchen, R., and L. J. Stedrak. 2016. Does performance-based funding affect colleges' financial priorities? *Journal of Education Finance* 41 (3): 302–21.

Kelly, A. P. 2014, March 31. The thorny politics of higher education reform. *Forbes.* http://www.forbes.com/sites/akelly/2014/03/31/the-thorny-politics-of -higher-education-reform/.

Kim, J. 2015. The cost of rankings? The influence of college rankings on institutional management. Doctoral dissertation, University of Michigan.

Koning, P., and C. Heinrich. 2013. Cream-skimming, parking, and other intended and unintended effects of high-powered, performance-based contracts. *Journal of Policy Analysis and Management* 32 (3): 461–83.

Kreighbaum, A. 2017, April 13. The (temporary?) U.S. education team. *Inside Higher Ed.* https://www.insidehighered.com/news/2017/04/13/department-edu cation-makes-first-official-senior-hires.

Krieg, J. M. 2008. Are students left behind? The distributional effects of the No Child Left Behind Act. *Education Finance and Policy* 3 (2): 250–81.

Laffont, J., and D. Martimort. 2002. *The theory of incentives: The principal-agent model.* Princeton, NJ: Princeton University Press.

Laffont, J., and J. Tirole. 1991. The politics of government decision-making: A theory of regulatory capture. *Quarterly Journal of Economics* 106 (4): 1089–1127

Lauen, D. L., and S. M. Gaddis. 2016. Accountability pressure, academic standards, and educational triage. *Educational Evaluation and Policy Analysis* 33 (1): 127–47.

Lemke, R. J., C. M. Hoerander, and R. E. McMahon. 2006. Student assessments, non-test-takers, and school accountability. *Education Economics* 14 (2): 235–50.

Levinthal, D. 1988. A survey of agency models of organizations. *Journal of Economic Behavior and Organization* 9 (2): 153–85.

Luca, M., and J. Smith. 2013. Salience in quality disclosure: Evidence from the *U.S. News* college rankings. *Journal of Economics and Management Strategy* 22 (1): 58–77.

Mangan, K. 2016, January 20. A president's plan to steer out at-risk freshmen incites a campus backlash. *Chronicle of Higher Education*. http://chronicle .com/article/A-President-s-Plan-to-Steer/234992.

Martin, R. E., and R. C. Hill. 2013. Involuntary and voluntary cost increases in private research universities. Baton Rouge: LSU Department of Economics Working Paper 2013–05.

———. 2014. Measuring Baumol and Bowen effects in public research universities. Working paper.

McCann, C., and B. Miller. 2014, September 24. Get-out-of-jail-free card for some colleges with high default rates. *EdCentral*. http://www.edcentral.org/get -jail-free-card-ed-colleges-high-default-rates.

McLendon, M. K., J. C. Hearn, and C. G. Mokher. 2009. Partisans, professionals, and power: The role of political factors in state higher education funding. *Journal of Higher Education* 80 (6): 686–713.

McLendon, M. K., C. G. Mokher, and W. Doyle. 2009. "Privileging" public research universities: An empirical analysis of the distribution of state appropriations across research and non-research universities. *Journal of Education Finance* 34 (4): 372–401.

McMurrer, J. 2007. *Choices, changes, and challenges: Curriculum and instruction in the NCLB era*. Washington, DC: Center on Education Policy.

Miller, G. J. 2000. Above politics: Credible commitment and efficiency in the design of public agencies. *Journal of Public Administration Research and Theory* 10 (2): 289–327.

———. 2005. The political evolution of principal-agent models. *Annual Review of Political Science* 8: 203–25.

Moe, T. M. 1984. The new economics of organization. *American Journal of Political Science* 28 (4): 739–77.

Moynihan, D. P. 2008. *The dynamics of performance management: Constructing information and reform*. Washington, DC: Georgetown University Press.

Myerson, R. B. 1979. Incentive compatibility and the bargaining problem. *Econometrica* 47 (1): 61–74.

National Commission on Excellence in Education. 1983. *A nation at risk: The imperative for education reform*. Washington, DC: U.S. Government Printing Office.

Natow, R. S. 2015. From Capitol Hill to Dupont Circle and beyond: The influence of policy actors in the federal higher education rulemaking process. *Journal of Higher Education* 86 (3): 360–86.

Neal, D. 2011. The design of performance pay in education. In *Handbook of the economics of education*, vol. 4, edited by E. A. Hanushek, S. Machin, and L. Woessmann, 495–550. Amsterdam: North Holland.

Neal, D., and D. W. Schanzenbach. 2010. Left behind by design: Proficiency counts and test-based accountability. *Review of Economics and Statistics* 92 (2): 263–83.

Olson, M. 1965. *The logic of collective action: Public goods and the theory of groups*. Cambridge, MA: Harvard University Press.

Pham, L. D., T. D. Nguyen, and M. G. Springer. 2017. Teacher merit pay and student test scores: A meta-analysis. Working paper, Vanderbilt University.

Polikoff, M. S. 2012. Instructional alignment under No Child Left Behind. *American Journal of Education* 118 (3): 341–68.

Prendergast, C. 1999. The provision of incentives in firms. *Journal of Economic Literature* 37 (1): 7–63.

———. 2007. The motivation and bias of bureaucrats. *American Economic Review* 97 (1): 180–96.

Rabovsky, T. M. 2012. Accountability in higher education: Exploring impacts on state budgets and institutional spending patterns. *Journal of Public Administration Research and Theory* 22 (4): 675–700.

Reback, R. 2008. Teaching to the rating: School accountability and the distribution of student achievement. *Journal of Public Economics* 92 (5/6): 1394–1415.

Rojstaczer, S., and C. Healy. 2012. Where A is ordinary: The evolution of American college and university grading, 1940–2009. *Teachers College Record* 114 (7): 1–23.

Rose-Ackerman, S. 1996. Altruism, nonprofits, and economic theory. *Journal of Economic Literature* 34 (2): 701–28.

Rouse, C. E., J. Hannaway, D. Goldhaber, and D. Figlio. 2013. Feeling the Florida heat? How low-performing schools respond to voucher and accountability pressure. *American Economic Journal: Economic Policy* 5 (2): 251–81.

Rutherford, A., and T. Rabovsky. 2014. Evaluating impacts of performance funding policies on student outcomes in higher education. *The ANNALS of the American Academy of Political and Social Science* 655 (1): 185–208.

Shavell, S. 1979. Risk sharing and incentives in the principal and agent relationship. *Bell Journal of Economics* 10 (1): 55–73.

Smallwood, S., and A. Richards. 2011, June 12. How educated are state legislators? *Chronicle of Higher Education*. http://chronicle.com/article/How-Educated -Is-Your/127845.

Spence, M., and R. Zeckhauser. 1971. Insurance, information, and individual action. *American Economic Review* 61 (2): 380–87.

Spooren, P., B. Brockx, and D. Mortelmans. 2013. On the validity of student evaluation of teaching: The state of the art. *Review of Education Research* 83 (4): 598–642.

Springer, M. G. 2008. The influence of an NCLB accountability plan on the distribution of student test score gains. *Economics of Education Review* 27 (5): 556–63.

Springer, M. G., J. F. Pane, V. Le, D. F. McCaffrey, S. F. Burns, L. S. Hamilton, and B. Stecher. 2012. Team pay for performance: Experimental evidence from the Round Rock pilot project on team incentives. *Educational Evaluation and Policy Analysis* 34 (4): 367–90.

Steinberg, R. 2010. Principal-agent theory and nonprofit accountability. In *Comparative corporate governance of non-profit organizations*, edited by K. J. Hopt and T. von Hippel, 73–125. New York: Cambridge University Press.

Stigler, G. J. 1971. The theory of economic regulation. *Bell Journal of Economics and Management Science* 2 (1): 3–21.

Stratford, M. 2014, September 24. Reprieve on default rates. *Inside Higher Ed.* https://www.insidehighered.com/news/2014/09/24/education-dept-tweaks -default-rate-calculation-help-colleges-avoid-penalties.

Sundaramurthy, C., and M. Lewis. 2003. Control and collaboration: Paradoxes of governance. *Academy of Management Review* 28 (3): 397–415.

Tandberg, D. A. 2010a. Interest groups and governmental institutions: The politics of state funding of public higher education. *Educational Policy* 24 (5): 735–78.

———. 2010b. Politics, interest groups and state funding of public higher education. *Research in Higher Education* 51 (5): 416–50.

Tandberg, D. A., and N. W. Hillman. 2014. State higher education performance funding: Data, outcomes, and policy implications. *Journal of Education Finance* 39 (3): 222–43.

Titus, M. A., A. Vamosiu, and K. R. McClure. Forthcoming. Are public master's institutions cost efficient? A stochastic frontier and spatial analysis. *Research in Higher Education.*

Tversky, A., and D. Kahneman. 1991. Loss aversion in riskless choice: A reference-dependent model. *Quarterly Journal of Economics* 106 (4): 1039–61.

Umbricht, M. R., F. Fernandez, and J. C. Ortagus. 2017. An examination of the (un)intended consequences of performance funding in higher education. *Educational Policy* 31 (5): 643–73.

Van Puyvelde, S., R. Caers, C. Du Bois, and M. Jegers. 2012. The governance of nonprofit organizations: Integrating agency theory with stakeholder and stewardship theories. *Nonprofit and Voluntary Sector Quarterly* 41 (3): 431–51.

Van Thiel, S., and F. L. Leeuw. 2002. The performance paradox in the public sector. *Public Performance and Management Review* 25 (3): 267–81.

Weatherley, R., and M. Lipsky. 1977. Street-level bureaucrats and institutional innovation: Implementing special-education reform. *Harvard Educational Review* 47 (2): 171–97.

Williamson, O. E. 1981. The economics of organization: The transaction cost approach. *American Journal of Sociology* 87 (3): 548–77.

Chapter Two: The Historical Development of Higher Education Accountability

AAUP (American Association of University Professors). 1940. 1940 statement of principles on academic freedom and tenure. Washington, DC: Author.

———. 1962. Disclaimer affidavit: Non-participating and disapproving colleges and universities. *AAUP Bulletin* 48 (4): 331.

Altschuler, G. C., and S. M. Blumin. 2009. *The GI Bill: A new deal for veterans.* New York: Oxford University Press.

An Act to Establish a Department of Education. 1867. Public Law 39-73, 14 Stat 434.

Angulo, A. J. 2016. *Diploma mills: How for-profit colleges stiffed students, taxpayers, and the American dream.* Baltimore: Johns Hopkins University Press.

Babcock, C. 1911. *A classification of universities and colleges with reference to bachelor's degrees.* Washington, DC: U.S. Government Printing Office.

Beck, A. H. 2004. The Flexner Report and the standardization of American medical education. *Journal of the American Medical Association* 291 (17): 2139–40.

Becker, C. L. 1943. *Cornell University: Founders and the founding.* Ithaca, NY: Cornell University.

Bicha, K. D. 1990. Professor, preceptress, and pupil: Academic life at Galesville University, 1859–1860. *Wisconsin Magazine of History* 73 (4): 274–86.

Bound, J., and S. Turner. 2002. Going to war and going to college: Did World War II and the G.I. Bill increase educational attainment for returning veterans? *Journal of Labor Economics* 20 (4): 784–815.

Bower, K. P. 2004. "A favored child of the state": Federal student aid at Ohio colleges and universities, 1934–1943. *History of Education Quarterly* 44 (3): 364–87.

Braman, S., and H. Cleveland. 1984. *The costs and benefits of openness: Sunshine laws and higher education.* Washington, DC: Association of Governing Boards of Universities and Colleges.

Brubacher, J. S., and W. Rudy. 1958. *Higher education in transition: An American history, 1636–1956.* New York: Harper and Brothers.

Bush, V. 1945. *The endless frontier: A report to the president.* Washington, DC: U.S. Government Printing Office.

Capen, S. P. 1931. The principles which should govern standards and accrediting practices. *Bulletin of the American Association of University Professors* 17 (7): 550–52.

————. 1939. Seven devils in exchange for one. In *Coordination of accrediting activities: A summary of proceedings of a conference on accrediting attended by representatives of accrediting associations and others, held in Washington, D.C., April 7 and 8, 1939*, edited by E. J. McGrath, 5–17. Washington, DC: American Council on Education.

Cattell, J. M. 1906. A statistical study of American men of science. *Science* 24 (623): 732–42.

Cattell, J. M., ed. 1910. *American men of science*. 2nd ed. New York: Science Press.

College of William and Mary. n.d. *History and traditions*. Accessed May 31, 2016 from http://www.wm.edu/about/history.

Conway, M. M. 1979. The commissioner's authority to list accrediting agencies and associations: Necessity for an eligibility issue. *Journal of Higher Education* 50 (2): 158–70.

Curti, M., and R. Nash. 1965. *Philanthropy in the shaping of American higher education*. New Brunswick, NJ: Rutgers University Press.

Davis, C. O. 1945. *A history of the North Central Association of Colleges and Secondary Schools*. Ann Arbor, MI: North Central Association of Colleges and Secondary Schools.

DeParle, J. 2009, January 6. A plan to turn the lowly bureaucrat into a cherished public servant. *New York Times*. http://www.nytimes.com/2009/01/07/us/07academy.html.

Douglass, J. A. 2000. *The California idea and American higher education*. Stanford, CA: Stanford University Press.

Duryea, E. D. 2000. *The academic corporation: A history of college and university governing boards*. New York: Falmer Press.

Emrey-Arras, M. 2014. *State funding trends and policies on affordability*. Washington, DC: U.S. Government Accountability Office Report GAO-15-151.

Finkin, M. W. 1973. Federal reliance on voluntary accreditation: The power to recognize as the power to regulate. *Journal of Law and Education* 2 (3): 339–76.

Flemming, A. S. 1960. The philosophy and objectives of the National Defense Education Act. *Annals of the American Academy of Political and Social Science* 327: 132–38.

Flexner, A. 1910. *Medical education in the United States and Canada*. New York: Carnegie Foundation for the Advancement of Teaching.

Floden, R. E. 1980. Flexner, accreditation, and evaluation. *Educational Evaluation and Policy Analysis* 2 (2): 35–46.

Foster, L. 1936. *The functions of a graduate school in a democratic society*. New York: Huxley House.

Fraser, J. W. 2007. *Preparing America's teachers: A history*. New York: Teachers College Press.

Fryar, A. H. 2015. The comprehensive university: How it came to be and what it is now. In *The university next door: What is a comprehensive university, who does it educate, and can it survive?*, edited by M. Schneider and K. Deane, 19–42. New York: Teachers College Press.

Geiger, R. 2000. The era of multipurpose colleges in American higher education, 1850–1890. In *The American college in the nineteenth century*, edited by R. Geiger, 127–52. Nashville: Vanderbilt University Press.

Gelber, S. M. 2011. *The university and the people: Envisioning American higher education in an era of populist protest.* Madison: University of Wisconsin Press.

Gilbert, C. K., and D. E. Heller. 2013. Access, equity, and community colleges: The Truman Commission and federal higher education policy from 1947 to 2011. *Journal of Higher Education* 84 (3): 417–43.

Greenleaf, W. J. 1935. Federal aid to college students. *Journal of Higher Education* 6 (2): 94–97.

Harcleroad, F. F. 1980. *Accreditation: History, processes, and problems.* Washington, DC: American Association for Higher Education.

Hawkins, H. 1992. *Banding together: The rise of national associations in American higher education, 1887–1950.* Baltimore: Johns Hopkins University Press.

Herbst, J. 1982. *From crisis to crisis: American college government, 1636–1819.* Cambridge, MA: Harvard University Press.

Herfurth, T. 1949. *Sifting and winnowing: A chapter in the history of academic freedom at the University of Wisconsin.* Madison: University of Wisconsin Press.

Hirsch, M. D. 1945. More light on Boss Tweed. *Political Science Quarterly* 60 (2): 267–78.

Hofstadter, R., and W. Smith, eds. 1961. *American higher education: A documentary history.* Chicago: University of Chicago Press.

Hohner, R. A. 1987. Southern education in transition: William Waugh Smith, the Carnegie Foundation, and the Methodist Church. *History of Education Quarterly* 27 (2): 181–203.

Hollis, E. V. 1945. Forces that have shaped doctoral work. *Bulletin of the American Association of University Professors* 31 (3): 357–82.

Hughes, R. M. 1925. *A study of the graduate schools in America.* Oxford, OH: Miami University Press.

———. 1934. Report of the committee on graduate instruction. *Educational Record* 15 (2): 192–234.

———. 1946. *A study of American graduate schools conferring the doctorate from 1937–38 to 1941–42.* Ames: Iowa State College Press.

Hutt, E. 2014. The GED and the rise of contextless accountability. *Teachers College Record* 116 (9): 1–20.

———. 2016. *A brief history of the student record.* New York: Ithaka S+R.

Investigation of GI Schools. 1951. *Hearings before the House select committee to investigate educational and training program under GI Bill.* Washington, DC: U.S. Government Printing Office.

Kelly, F. J., and J. H. McNeely. 1933. *The state and higher education: Phases of their relationship.* New York: The Carnegie Foundation for the Advancement of Teaching.

———. 1935. *Federal student aid program.* Washington, DC: U.S. Office of Education.

Keniston, H. 1959. *Graduate study and research in the arts and sciences at the University of Pennsylvania.* Philadelphia: University of Pennsylvania Press.

Key, S. 1996. Economics or education: The establishment of American land-grant universities. *Journal of Higher Education* 67 (2): 196–220.

Kimball, B. A. 2014. The first campaign and the paradoxical transformation of fundraising in American higher education, 1915–1925. *Teachers College Record* 116 (9): 1–44.

Lagemann, E. C. 1983. *Private power for the public good: A history of the Carnegie Foundation for the Advancement of Teaching.* Middletown, CT: Wesleyan University Press.

Laitinen, A. 2012. *Cracking the credit hour.* Washington, DC: New America Foundation.

Lawrence, I. M., G. W. Rigol, T. Van Essen, and C. A. Jackson. 2003. *A historical perspective on the content of the SAT.* New York: College Board Publications.

Loss, C. P. 2012. *Between citizens and the state: The politics of American higher education in the 20th century.* Princeton, NJ: Princeton University Press.

Lucas, C. J. 2006. *American higher education: A history.* 2nd ed. New York: Palgrave Macmillan.

Ludlum, R. P. 1950. Academic freedom and tenure: A history. *Antioch Review* 10 (1): 3–34.

Lykes, R. W. 1975. *Higher education and the United States office of education (1867–1953).* Washington, DC: Bureau of Postsecondary Education, U.S. Office of Education.

Madsen, D. 1966. *The national university: Enduring dream of the USA.* Detroit: Wayne State University Press.

McAnear, B. 1952. The raising of funds by the colonial colleges. *Mississippi Valley Historical Review* 38 (4): 591–612.

McCaul, R. L. 1960. Whitefield's Bethesda College and other major attempts to found colonial colleges. *Georgia Historical Quarterly* 44 (4): 381–98.

McGrath, E. J. 1945. The education of the veteran. *Annals of the American Academy of Political and Social Science* 238: 77–88.

McGuinness, A. 2016. *State policy leadership for the future: History of state coordination and governance and alternatives for the future.* Boulder: Education Commission of the States.

McLendon, M. K. 2003. State governance reform of higher education: Patterns, trends, and theories of the public policy process. In *Higher education: Handbook of theory and research*, vol. 18, edited by J. C. Smart, 57–144. London: Kluwer Academic.

National Defense Education Act. 1958. Public Law 85-864.

Ogren, C. A. 2005. *The American state normal school*. New York: Palgrave Macmillan.

Olson, K. W. 1973. The G.I. Bill and higher education: Success and surprise. *American Quarterly* 25 (5): 596–610.

Pfnister, A. O. 1971. Regional accrediting agencies at the crossroads. *Journal of Higher Education* 42 (7): 558–73.

President's Commission on Higher Education. 1947. *Higher education for democracy: A report of the president's commission on higher education*. Vol. 1, *Establishing the goals*. New York: Harper and Brothers.

Pritchett, H. S. 1908. The relations of Christian denominations to colleges. Address to the Conference on Education of the Methodist Episcopal Church, South, Atlanta.

———. 1915. Should the Carnegie Foundation be suppressed? *North American Review* 201 (713): 554–66.

Proffitt, J. R. 1979. The federal connection for accreditation. *Journal of Higher Education* 50 (2): 145–57.

Riccards, M. P. 2010. *The College Board and American higher education*. Madison, NJ: Fairleigh Dickinson University Press.

Riordon, W. L. 1948. *Plunkitt of Tammany Hall: A series of very plain talks on very practical politics*. New York: Alfred A. Knopf.

Robson, D. W. 1985. *Educating republicans: The college in the era of the American Revolution, 1750–1800*. Westport, CT: Greenwood Press.

Rudolph, F. 1990. *The American college and university: A history*. Athens: University of Georgia Press.

Rutgers University. n.d. History. Accessed May 31, 2016 from http://www.rutgers.edu/about/history.

Sanders, J. B. 1969. Evolution of accreditation. In *Accreditation in higher education*, edited by L. E. Blauch, 9–14. New York: Greenwood Press.

Schmidtlein, F. O., and R. O. Berdahl. 2005. Autonomy and accountability: Who controls academe? In *American higher education in the twenty-first century*, 2nd ed., edited by P. G. Altbach, R. O. Berdahl, and P. J. Gumport, 71–90. Baltimore: Johns Hopkins University Press.

Selden, W. K. 1960. *Accreditation: A struggle over standards in higher education*. New York: Harper and Brothers.

Seligman, E. R. A., C. E. Bennett, J. Q. Dealey, R. T. Ely, H. W. Farnam, F. A. Fetter, et al. 1915. General report of the committee on academic freedom and academic tenure. *Bulletin of the American Association of University Professors* 1 (1): 15–43.

Servicemen's Readjustment Act. 1944. Public Law 78-346.

Sharpless, I. 1915. *The American college*. Garden City, NY: Doubleday, Page.

Shedd, J. M. 2003. The history of the student credit hour. *New Directions for Higher Education* 122: 5–12.

Snyder, T. D., ed. 1993. *120 years of American education: A statistical portrait*. Washington, DC: National Center for Education Statistics.

Speicher, A. L. n.d. *The Association of American Universities: A century of service to higher education*. Accessed June 19, 2017. https://www.aau.edu/association -american-universities-century-service-higher-education-1900-2000.

Stout, D. 1996, June 28. Trenton State gets new name and a battle. *New York Times*. http://www.nytimes.com/1996/06/28/nyregion/trenton-state-gets-new-name -and-a-battle.html.

Tewksbury, D. G. 1932. *The founding of American colleges and universities before the Civil War, with particular reference to the religious influences bearing upon the college movement*. New York: Teachers College, Columbia University.

Thelen, D. P. 1972. *The new citizenship: Origins of progressivism in Wisconsin, 1885–1900*. Columbia: University of Missouri Press.

Thelin, J. R. 2011. *A history of American higher education*. 2nd ed. Baltimore: Johns Hopkins University Press.

———. 2015. Why did college cost so little? Affordability and higher education a century ago. *Society* 52: 585–89.

Tolbert, P. S., and L. G. Zucker. 1983. Institutional sources of change in the formal structure of organizations: The diffusion of civil service reform, 1880–1935. *Administrative Science Quarterly* 28 (1): 22–39.

Trow, M. 2003. In praise of weakness: Chartering, the University of the United States, and Dartmouth College. *Higher Education Policy* 16 (1): 9–26.

U.S. Bureau of Education. 1888. *Report of the commissioner of education for the year 1886–87*. Vol. 2. Washington, DC: U.S. Government Printing Office.

Valentine, J. A. 1987. *The College Board and the school curriculum: A history of the College Board's influence on the substance and standards of American education, 1900–1980*. New York: College Board Publications.

VanOverbeke, M. A. 2008. *The standardization of American schooling: Linking secondary and higher education, 1870–1910*. New York: Palgrave Macmillan.

Veysey, L. R. 1965. *The emergence of the American university*. Chicago: University of Chicago Press.

Webster, D. S. 1984. The Bureau of Education's suppressed rating of colleges, 1911–1912. *History of Education Quarterly* 24 (4): 499–511.

———. 1986. *Academic quality rankings of American colleges and universities*. Springfield, IL: Charles C. Thomas.

Wesley, E. B. 1936. *Proposed: The University of the United States*. Minneapolis: University of Minnesota Press.

Wheeler, K. H. 2011. Cultivating regionalism: Higher education and the making of the Midwest. DeKalb: Northern Illinois University Press.

Whitehead, J. S., and J. Herbst. 1986. How to think about the Dartmouth College case. *History of Education Quarterly* 26 (3): 333–49.

Wiley, M. G., and M. N. Zald. 1968. The growth and transformation of educational accrediting agencies: An explanatory study in social control of institutions. *Sociology of Education* 41 (1): 36–56.

Zook, G. F., and M. E. Haggerty. 1936. *The evaluation of higher institutions.* Chicago: University of Chicago Press.

Chapter Three: Federal Accountability Policies

Alexander, L. 2015, May 20. Alexander: If colleges share in the risk of student loan defaults, they can help reduce overborrowing—and the cost of college. http://www.help.senate.gov/chair/newsroom/press/alexander-if-colleges-share-in-the-risk-of-student-loan-defaults-they-can-help-reduce-overborrowingand-the-cost-of-college.

Anthony, A. M., L. C. Page, and A. Seldin. 2015. In the right ballpark? Assessing the accuracy of net price calculators. Accessed July 8, 2015. http://papers.ssrn.com/sol3/papers.cfm?abstract_id=2555051.

APSCU (Association of Private Sector Colleges and Universities). 2014, November 6. APSCU files suit against anti-student gainful employment regulation. http://www.career.org/news/apscu-files-suit-against-anti-student-gainful-employment-regulation.

Art and Science Group. 2013. A majority of students look at a college's sticker price without Taking financial aid into consideration. Accessed July 8, 2015. http://www.artsci.com/studentpoll/v1on1/index.aspx.

———. 2015. Student perceptions on price, aid, and debt provide an extraordinary opportunity for colleges and universities. Accessed July 8, 2015. http://www.artsci.com/studentpoll/2015/june/index.aspx.

Baum, S., J. Ma, M. Pender, and M. Welch. 2016. *Trends in student aid.* Washington, DC: College Board.

Blumenstyk, G. 2009, June 9. More than 100 colleges fail education department's test of financial strength. *Chronicle of Higher Education.* http://chronicle.com/article/More-Than-100-Colleges-Fail/47492.

———. 2010. Business is up in keeping default rates down. *Chronicle of Higher Education.* http://chronicle.com/article/Business-Is-Up-in-Keeping/66226.

———. 2013, 1 July. Education Dept. faces renewed criticism over colleges' financial-health scores. *The Chronicle of Higher Education.* http://chronicle.com/article/Education-Dept-Faces-Renewed/140085.

———. 2014, July 8. Education Department didn't set out to shut down Corinthian. *Chronicle of Higher Education.* http://chronicle.com/article/Education-Department-Didn-t/147533.

Broad, M. C. 2014, January 31. Postsecondary institution ratings system RFI. http://www.acenet.edu/news-room/Documents/Higher-Ed-Assoc-PIRS-Comments.pdf.

Carey, K., and A. P. Kelly. 2011. *The truth behind higher education disclosure laws.* Washington, DC: Education Sector.

Carnevale, D. 2000. Web site provides detailed information on U.S. colleges. *Chronicle of Higher Education.* Accessed July 8, 2015. http://chronicle.com /article/Web-Site-Provides-Detailed/105123.

Castleman, B. L. 2015. Prompts, personalization, and pay-offs: Strategies to improve the design and delivery of college and financial aid information. In *Decision making for student success: Behavioral insights to improve college access and persistence,* edited by S. Baum, and B. L. Castleman, 79–101. New York: Routledge.

Cellini, S. R., and C. Goldin. 2014. Does federal student aid raise tuition? New evidence on for-profit colleges. *American Economic Journal: Economic Policy* 6 (4): 174–206.

Cheng, D. 2012. *Adding it all up 2012: Are college net price calculators easy to find, use, and compare?* Oakland, CA: Institute for College Access and Success.

Ciaramella, A. 2015, September 15. Today on the bus tour. *Politico.* http://www .politico.com/tipsheets/morning-education/2015/09/today-on-the-bus-tour -college-scorecard-makes-a-splash-reverse-transfer-gets-results-210207.

Cochrane, D., and L. Szabo-Kubitz. 2016. *States of denial: Where community college students lack access to federal student loans.* Oakland, CA: Institute for College Access and Success.

Collins, H., S. M. Jenkins, and N. Strzelecka. 2014. *Ranking and rewarding access: An alternative college scorecard.* Philadelphia: Penn Center for Minority Serving Institutions.

Cooney, M. K. 2012. *US private college and university meidans underscore revenue challenge and mixed outlook for sector.* New York: Moody's Investor Service.

Cooper, P., and J. Delisle. 2017. *Measuring quality or subsidy? How state appropriations rig the federal gainful employment test.* Washington, DC: American Enterprise Institute.

Council of Economic Advisers. 2015. *Using federal data to measure and improve the performance of U.S. institutions of higher education.* Washington, DC: Executive Office of the President of the United States.

Cunningham, A. F., and D. A. Santiago. 2008. *Student aversion to borrowing: Who borrows and who doesn't .* Washington, DC: Institute for Higher Education Policy and Excelencia in Education.

DeLoughry, T. J. 1990a, April 18. Loan-default rate is dipping slightly, Education Dept. says. *Chronicle of Higher Education.* http://chronicle.com/article/Loan -Default-Rate-Is-Dipping/67295.

———. 1990b, February 14. U.S. told to study colleges' financial health *Chronicle of Higher Education.* http://chronicle.com/article/US-Told-to-Study-Colleges /69531.

Draeger, J., K. McCarthy, and M. McClean. 2013. *Reimagining financial aid to improve student access and outcomes.* Washington, DC: National Association of Student Financial Aid Administrators.

Dunn, A. 2015, May 13. For-profit Brookstone College of Business closing down. *Charlotte Observer.* http://www.charlotteobserver.com/news/local/education/article20818347.html.

Fain, P. 2015, June 25. Ratings without . . . rating. *Inside Higher Ed.* https://www.insidehighered.com/news/2015/06/25/education-department-says-rating-system-will-be-consumer-tool-rather-comparison.

———. 2016, June 7. For-profit college association changes its name. *Inside Higher Ed.* https://www.insidehighered.com/quicktakes/2016/06/07/profit-college-association-changes-name.

Fallon, M. A. 2011. Enrollment management's sleeping giant: The net price calculator mandate. *Journal of College Admission* 211: 6–13.

Field, K. 2013. Maker of net-price calculators updates its language barring aggregators. *Chronicle of Higher Education.* Accessed July 8, 2015. http://chronicle.com/article/Maker-of-Net-Price-Calculators/142707.

———. 2014a, September 25. As default rates drop, so does confidence in how the Education Dept. counts them. *Chronicle of Higher Education.* http://chronicle.com/article/As-Default-Rates-Drop-So-Does/148997.

———. 2014b, February 6. Skepticism abounds at Education Dept.'s college-ratings symposium. *Chronicle of Higher Education.* http://chronicle.com/blogs/ticker/live-blog-the-education-dept-s-technical-symposium-on-college-ratings/72377.

———. 2015, March 16. Education Dept. considers creating not 1 but 2 college-ratings systems. *Chronicle of Higher Education.* http://chronicle.com/article/Education-Dept-Considers/228531.

Field, K., and J. Newman. 2014. Have U.S. "shame lists" helped lower tuition? Probably not. *Chronicle of Higher Education.* Accessed July 9, 2015. http://chronicle.com/article/Have-US-Shame-Lists-/144909.

Friedrich, A. 2013, July 5. Why Bethel University is fighting the U.S. Department of Education. http://blogs.mprnews.org/oncampus/2013/07/why-bethel-university-is-fighting-the-u-s-department-of-education.

Fuller, A. 2017, January 18. Student debt payback far worse than believed. *Wall Street Journal.* https://www.wsj.com/articles/student-debt-payback-far-worse-than-believed-1484777880.

Fuller, C., and C. Salerno. 2009. *Information required to be disclosed under the Higher Education Act of 1965: Suggestions for dissemination.* Updated. Washington, DC: National Postsecondary Education Cooperative.

Gay, M. 2017, January 17. Harvard's ART Institute suspends admissions. *Boston Globe.* https://www.bostonglobe.com/arts/theater/dance/2017/01/17/harvard-art-institute-suspends-admissions-after-failing-student-debt-grade/28mvKiBLFCBYtZBCgnuvRP/story.html.

Gelobter, L. 2015, September 12. Under the hood: Building a new College Scorecard with students. White House. https://www.whitehouse.gov/blog/2015/09/12/under-hood-building-new-college-scorecard-students.

Ginder, S. A., J. E. Kelly-Reid, and F. B. Mann. 2014. *2013–14 Integrated Post-secondary Education Data System (IPEDS) methodology report.* Washington, DC: National Center for Education Statistics.

Gladieux, L. E. 1996. Federal student aid policy: A history and an assesment. In *Financing postsecondary education: The federal role. Proceedings of the National Conference on the Best Ways for the Federal Government to Help Students and Families Finance Postsecondary Education,* 43–56. Washington, DC: U.S. Government Printing Office.

Gladieux, L. E., and T. R. Wolanin. 1976. *Congress and the colleges: The national politics of higher education.* Lexington, MA: Lexington Books.

Goldrick-Rab, S., and R. Kelchen. 2015. Making sense of loan aversion: Evidence from Wisconsin. In *Student loans and the dynamics of debt,* edited by K. M. Hollenbeck, and B. J. Hershbein, 307–71. Kalamazoo, MI: W. E. Upjohn Institute for Employment Research.

Goldrick-Rab, S., L. Schudde, and J. Stampen. 2014. Creating cultures of affordability: Can institutional incentives improve the effectiveness of financial aid? In *Reinventing financial aid: Charting a new course to college affordability,* edited by A. P. Kelly, 191–206. Cambridge, MA: Harvard Education Press.

Gonzalez, J. 2010, April 13. Proposed rules on measuring "gainful employment" of graduates please for-profit colleges. *Chronicle of Higher Education.* http://chronicle.com/article/Proposed-Rules-on-Measuring/65048.

Grasgreen, A. 2014, October 30. Obama retreats on college crackdown. *Politico.* http://www.politico.com/story/2014/10/obama-for-profit-colleges-crackdown-112340.html

Gross, J. P., O. Cekic, D. Hossler, and W. N. Hillman. 2009. What matters in student loan default: A review of the literature. *Journal on Student Financial Aid* 39 (1): 19–29.

Hershbein, B. J., and K. Hollenbeck. 2014. *College costs: Students can't afford not to know.* Kalamazoo, MI: W. E. Upjohn Institute for Employment Research.

Higher Education Amendments. 1992. Public Law 102-325.

Hillman, N. W. 2014. College on credit: A multilevel analysis of student loan default. *Review of Higher Education* 37 (2): 169–95.

———. 2015. Cohort default rates: Predicting the probability of federal sanctions. *Educational Policy* 29 (4): 559–82.

Hillman, N. W., and O. Jaquette. 2014. *Opting out of federal student loan programs: Examining the community college sector.* Paper presented at the Association for Education Finance and Policy annual conference, San Antonio.

Hoxby, C., and S. Turner. 2013. Expanding college opportunities for high-achieving, low-income students. Stanford, CA: Stanford Institute for Economic Policy Research Discussion Paper No. 12-014.

Huckabee, C. 2012, July 2. Judge strikes down several provisions of "gainful employment" rule. *Chronicle of Higher Education.* http://chronicle.com/blogs/ticker/judge-strikes-down-several-provisions-of-gainful-employment-rule/45125.

Hurwitz, M., and J. Smith. 2016. Student responsiveness to earnings data in the College Scorecard. Working paper.

Jackson, B. A., and J. R. Reynolds. 2013. The price of opportunity: Race, student loan debt, and college achievement. *Sociological Inquiry* 83 (3): 335–68.

Jaschik, S. 2013, December 16. Dubious of Obama plan. *Inside Higher Ed*. https://www.insidehighered.com/news/2013/12/16/most-presidents-doubt-obamas-plan-promote-affordable-higher-education.

Jaschik, S., and D. Lederman. 2017. 2017 survey of college and university presidents. *Inside Higher Ed* and Gallup. Accessed June 20, 2017. https://www.insidehighered.com/booklet/2017-inside-higher-ed-survey-college-and-university-presidents.

Kelchen, R. 2015, April 9. Where 3 accountability measures meet, a hazardous intersection. *Chronicle of Higher Education*. http://chronicle.com/article/Where-3-Accountability/229195.

———. 2016. Do financial responsibility scores affect institutional behaviors? Working paper.

———. 2017a. How do colleges respond to accountability pressures? Examining the relationship between cohort default rates and college pricing. Working paper.

———. 2017b, January 11. How much do for-profit colleges rely on federal funds. *Brown Center Chalkboard*, Brookings Institution. https://www.brookings.edu/blog/brown-center-chalkboard/2017/01/11/how-much-do-for-profit-colleges-rely-on-federal-funds/.

Kelchen, R., S. Goldrick-Rab, and B. J. Hosch. 2017. The costs of college attendance: Examining variation and consistency in institutional living cost allowances. *Journal of Higher Education* 88(6): 947–71.

Kelchen, R., and A. Li. 2017. Institutional accountability: A comparison of the predictors of student loan repayment and default rates. *ANNALS of the American Academy of Political and Social Science* 671: 202–23.

Kelly, A. P. 2014, March 31. The thorny politics of higher education reform. *Forbes*. http://www.forbes.com/sites/akelly/2014/03/31/the-thorny-politics-of-higher-education-reform.

Kelly-Reid, J. 2016. Report and suggestions from College Scorecard technical review panel 1: Consumer information. *RTI International*. Accessed December 7, 2016. https://edsurveys.rti.org/IPEDS_TRP_DOCS/prod/documents/CS1_Summary.pdf.

Kreighbaum, A. 2017, June 15. Reset of rules aimed at for-profits begins. *Inside Higher Ed*. https://www.insidehighered.com/news/2017/06/15/education-department-hit-pause-two-primary-obama-regulations-aimed-profits.

Lederman, D. 2015, June 24. Senate plan portends budget battles. *Inside Higher Ed*. https://www.insidehighered.com/news/2015/06/24/senate-spending-plan-college-programs-sets-likely-budget-fights.

Leichter, M. 2015, July 17. What if the gainful employment rule were applied to all law schools? *Law School Tuition Bubble*. https://lawschooltuitionbubble. wordpress.com/2015/06/29/what-if-the-gainful-employment-rule-were -applied-to-all-law-schools.

Mahaffie, L. 2017, January 13. Updated data for College Scorecard and Financial Aid Shopping Sheet. *Federal Student Aid*. https://ifap.ed.gov/eannouncements /011317UpdatedDataForCollegeScorecardFinaidShopSheet.html.

Marcus, J. 2014, September 8. College-rating proposal shines spotlight on power- ful lobby. *Hechinger Report*. http://hechingerreport.org/college-rating-proposal -shines-spotlight-powerful-lobby.

Massimino, J. 2011, April 8. 90/10 rule: A 'Catch-22' for Corinthian Colleges. *Chronicle of Higher Education*. http://chronicle.com/article/90-10-Rule-a-Catch -22-for/127072.

McCann, C., and A. Laitinen. 2014. *College blackout: How the higher education lobby fought to keep students in the dark*. Washington, DC: New America.

Miller, B. 2013. No one's watching the watch list. *New America Higher Ed Watch*. Accessed July 9, 2015. https://web.archive.org/web/20130914111010/http:// higheredwatch.newamerica.net/blogposts/2013/the_failed_tuition_watch _lists-86916.

———. 2014, October 30. *The final gainful rule: What will holding firm on debt- to-earnings mean for dropouts?* New America EdCentral. http://www.edcentral .org/finalgainfulopinion/.

NAICU (National Association of Independent Colleges and Universities). 2012. Re- port of the NAICU financial responsibility task force. Washington, DC: Author.

Natow, R. S. 2015. From Capitol Hill to Dupont Circle and beyond: The influence of policy actors in the federal higher education rulemaking process. *Journal of Higher Education* 86 (3): 360–86.

NCES (National Center for Education Statistics). 2013. *Integrated Postsecondary Education Data System (IPEDS) 2014–2016 and 2013 carry over—supporting statement part A: OMB Paperwork Reduction Act submission*. Washington, DC: Office of Management and Budget.

———. 2015a. Changes to the 2014–15 and 2015–16 IPEDS data collections. Accessed July 7, 2015. https://surveys.nces.ed.gov/ipeds_py/VisChangesFor NextYear.aspx.

———. 2015b. *College Navigator*. Accessed July 9 2015. https://nces.ed.gov/col legenavigator.

Nelson, L. 2014, May 21. Yet another update on rating system timing. *Vox*. http:// www.vox.com/2014/5/21/5738958/yet-another-update-on-rating-system -timing.

Obama, B. 2013, August 22. Remarks by the president on college affordability— Buffalo, NY. White House. https://www.whitehouse.gov/the-press-office/2013 /08/22/remarks-president-college-affordability-buffalo-ny.

Office of Federal Student Aid. 2014. 2014–2015 Federal Student Aid handbook. Washington, DC: U.S. Department of Education.

———. 2016a. Three-year official cohort default rates for schools. Accessed December 2, 2016. http://www2.ed.gov/offices/OSFAP/defaultmanagement/cdr.html.

———. 2016b. Proprietary school 90/10 revenue percentages. Accessed April 1, 2017. https://studentaid.ed.gov/sa/about/data-center/school/proprietary.

———. 2017, March 6. Gainful employment electronic announcement #105. https://ifap.ed.gov/eannouncements/030617GEAnnounce105AddtlSubTimeAEAandGEDisReq.html.

———. n.d.-a. Financial responsibility composite scores. Accessed June 20, 2017. https://studentaid.ed.gov/sa/about/data-center/school/composite-scores.

———. n.d.-b. Participation rate index appeal: Low program participation. Accessed July 14, 2015. http://www.ifap.ed.gov/DefaultManagement/guide/attachments/CDRGuideCh4Pt8PRI.pdf.

Office of Inspector General. 2003. *Audit to determine if cohort default rates provide sufficient information on defaults in the Title IV loan programs: Final audit report.* Philadelphia: U.S. Department of Education.

Office of Postsecondary Education, U.S. Department of Education. 2010. Program integrity: Gainful employment. *Federal Register* 75 (142): 43616–708.

Office of Postsecondary Education, U.S. Department of Education. 2014. Program integrity: Gainful employment. *Federal Register* 79 (211): 64890–65103.

Omnibus Budget Reconciliation Act. 1990. Public Law 101-508.

Reback, R., J. Rockoff, and H. L. Schwartz. 2014. Under pressure: Job security, resource allocation, and productivity in schools under No Child Left Behind. *American Economic Journal: Economic Policy* 6 (3): 207–41.

Scott, A. 2015, June 30. University of Phoenix to shrink enrollment. *Marketplace.* http://www.marketplace.org/topics/education/university-phoenix-shrink-enrollment.

Secretary of Education's Commission on the Future of Higher Education. 2006. *A test of leadership: Charting the future of U.S. higher education.* Washington, DC: U.S. Department of Education.

Shear, M. D. 2014, May 25. Colleges rattled as Obama seeks rating system. *New York Times.* http://www.nytimes.com/2014/05/26/us/colleges-rattled-as-obama-presses-rating-system.html.

Skinner, R. R. 2007. *Institutional eligibility and the Higher Education Act: Legislative history of the 90/10 rule and its current status.* Washington, DC: Congressional Research Service.

Smith, A. A. 2016, September 20. DeVry adopts reform favored by for-profit critics. *Inside Higher Ed.* https://www.insidehighered.com/news/2016/09/20/devry-university-plans-adopt-financial-reform-favored-profit-critics.

Stratford, M. 2014a, September 24. Reprieve on default rates. *Inside Higher Ed.* https://www.insidehighered.com/news/2014/09/24/education-dept-tweaks-default-rate-calculation-help-colleges-avoid-penalties.

———. 2014b, June 11. Obama defends college ratings. *Inside Higher Ed.* https://

www.insidehighered.com/news/2014/06/11/obama-defends-college-ratings
-system-amid-growing-backlash-capitol-hill.

———. 2015a, March 31. Cash monitoring list unveiled. *Inside Higher Ed.*
https://www.insidehighered.com/news/2015/03/31/education-department
-names-most-colleges-facing-heightened-scrutiny-federal.

———. 2015b, May 21. Risk sharing, yes. But how? *Inside Higher Ed.* https://
www.insidehighered.com/news/2015/05/21/bipartisan-agreement-risk
-sharing-concept-only.

Thomason, A. 2015, June 23. Gainful-employment rule survives for-profit group's
court challenge. *Chronicle of Higher Education.* http://chronicle.com/blogs
/ticker/gainful-employment-rule-survives-for-profit-groups-court-challenge
/101079.

U.S. Department of Education. 2014a. A new system of college ratings—invitation
to comment. Washington, DC: Author.

———. 2014b. College affordability and transparency explanation form: Summary guide to college costs for the 2014 collection year. Washington, DC:
Author.

———. 2016, December 21. New analysis finds many for-profits skirt federal
funding limits. https://www.ed.gov/news/press-releases/new-analysis-finds-many
-profits-skirt-federal-funding-limits.

———. n.d. College affordability and transparency center. Accessed July 9, 2015.
http://collegecost.ed.gov/catc/Default.aspx.

U.S. General Accounting Office. 1989. Guaranteed student loans: Analysis of student default rates at 7,800 postsecondary schools. Washington, DC: Author.

———. 1997. Proprietary schools: Poorer student outcomes at schools that rely
more on Federal Student Aid. Washington, DC: Author.

U.S. Government Accountability Office. 2010. Higher education: Institutions' reported data collection burden is higher than estimated but can be reduced
through increased coordination. Washington, DC: Author.

U.S. Senate Committee on Health, Education, Labor and Pensions. 2015. Risk-
sharing/Skin-in-the-game concepts and proposals. Washington, DC: Author.

Washington Post Editoral Board. 2015, September 16. Which school is the better
investment? The College Scorecard can help you decide. *Washington Post.*
https://www.washingtonpost.com/opinions/which-school-is-the-better-invest
ment/2015/09/16/c07e1590-5ca0-11e5-8e9e-dce8a2a2a679_story.html.

White House. 2012. Fact Sheet: President Obama's blueprint for keeping college
affordable and within reach for all Americans. Accessed July 9, 2015. https://
www.whitehouse.gov/the-press-office/2012/01/27/fact-sheet-president-obama
-s-blueprint-keeping-college-affordable-and-wi.

Wiederspan, M. 2016. Denying loan access: The student-level consequences when
community colleges opt out of the Stafford loan program. *Economics of Education Review* 51: 79–96.

Zook, J., and S. Burd. 1994, September 28. Victory for trade schools. *Chronicle of Higher Education.* http://chronicle.com/article/Victory-for-Trade-Schools /84218.

Chapter Four: State Accountability Policies

Allen, R. 2016, November 9. After tuition autonomy vote fails in Louisiana, here's what happens next. *Advocate.* http://www.theadvocate.com/baton_rouge/news /education/article_8d756df8-a6bc-11e6-975b-3ba99761ac8a.html.

Andrews, R., and K. Stange. 2016. Price regulation, price discrimination, and equality of opportunity in higher education: Evidence from Texas. Cambridge, MA: National Bureau of Economic Research Working Paper 22901.

Armstrong, J., and C. Whitfield. 2016. *The state of state postsecondary data systems: Strong foundations 2016.* Boulder, CO: State Higher Education Executive Officers Association.

Banta, T. W., L. B. Rudolph, J. Van Dyke, and H. S. Fisher. 1996. Performance funding comes of age in Tennessee. *Journal of Higher Education* 67 (1): 23–45.

Belson, K. 2011, November 11. Penn State has exemption from disclosure law. *New York Times.* http://www.nytimes.com/2011/11/12/sports/ncaafootball/penn -state-has-exemption-from-disclosure-law.html.

Bill and Melinda Gates Foundation. 2015, March. Postsecondary success advocacy priorities. Accessed August 3, 2016. http://postsecondary.gatesfoundation .org/wp-content/uploads/2015/03/PS-ADV-Priorities-V1.pdf.

Boatright, K. J. 1995. University of Wisconsin's system accountability. *New Directions for Higher Education* 91: 51–64.

Bowerman, B. 2015. *Tuition restraint: FY 2011–12 through 2015–16.* Lansing: Michigan Senate Fiscal Agency.

Brackett, A. 2016. Public college lobbying and institutional appropriations: The role of lobbying in state higher education budgets. Doctoral dissertation, Seton Hall University.

Braman, S., and H. Cleveland. 1984. *The costs and benefits of openness: Sunshine laws and higher education.* Minneapolis: Hubert H. Humphrey Institute of Public Affairs, University of Minnesota.

Burke, J. C., and H. Minassians. 2002. *Performance reporting: The preferred "no cost" accountability program: The sixth annual report.* Albany, NY: Nelson A. Rockefeller Institute of Government.

———. 2003. *Performance reporting: "Real" accountability or accountability "lite:" Seventh annual survey 2003.* Albany, NY: Nelson A. Rockefeller Institute of Government.

Calhoun, J., and D. R. Kamerschen. 2010. The impact of governing structure on the pricing behavior and market structure of public institutions of higher education in the U.S. *International Review of Economics* 57 (3): 317–33.

Capeloto, A. 2015. A case for placing public-university foundations under the existing oversight regime of freedom of information laws. *Communication Law and Policy* 20 (4): 311–42.

Carlson, A. 2013. *State tuition, fees, and financial assistance policies for public colleges and universities.* Boulder: State Higher Education Executive Officers Association.

Chatterji, A. K., J. Kim, and R. C. McDevitt. 2016. School spirit: Legislator school ties and state funding for higher education. Working paper. Accessed June 20, 2017. https://faculty.fuqua.duke.edu/~rcm26/ckm_schoolties_sept_2016.pdf.

Cheslock, J. J., and R. P. Hughes. 2011. Differences across states in higher education finance policy. *Journal of Education Finance* 36 (4): 369–93.

College Opportunity Fund. n.d. *College Opportunity Fund.* Accessed August 1, 2016. https://cof.college-assist.org.

Columbus, R. 2016. *Report and disclose: State oversight of institutional performance in higher education.* Washington, DC: American Enterprise Institute.

Cook, M. 2007, August 11. MU tuition, funding increases both exceed tuition rate. *Columbia Business Times.* http://columbiabusinesstimes.com/2007/08/11/mu-tuition-funding-increases-both-exceed-inflation-rate.

Cornwell, C., and D. B. Mustard. 2007. Merit-based college scholarships and car sales. *Education Finance and Policy* 2 (2): 133–51.

Cowan, B. W., and D. R. White. 2015. The effects of merit-based financial aid on drinking in college. *Journal of Health Economics* 44: 137–49.

Dar, L., and D. Lee. 2014. Partisanship, political polarization, and state higher education budget outcomes. *Journal of Higher Education* 85 (4): 469–98.

Delaney, J. A., and T. D. Kearney. 2015a. Guaranteed tuition policies and state general appropriations for higher education: A difference-in-difference analysis. *Journal of Education Finance* 40 (4): 359–90.

———. 2015b. The impact of guaranteed tuition policies on postsecondary tuition levels: A difference-in-difference approach. *Economics of Education Review* 47: 80–99.

———. 2016. Alternative student-based revenue streams for higher education institutions: A difference-in-difference analysis using guaranteed tuition policies. *Journal of Higher Education* 87 (5): 731–69.

Dougherty, K. J., S. M. Jones, H. Lahr, R. S. Natow, L. Pheatt, and V. Reddy. 2014. Performance funding for higher education: Forms, origins, impacts, and futures. *ANNALS of the American Academy of Political and Social Science* 655: 163–84.

———. 2016a. *Performance funding for higher education.* Baltimore: Johns Hopkins University Press.

———. 2016b. Looking inside the black box of performance funding for higher education: Policy instruments, organizational obstacles, and intended and unintended impacts. *RSF: The Russell Sage Foundation Journal of the Social Sciences* 2 (1): 147–73.

Dougherty, K. J., and R. S. Natow. 2015. *The politics of performance funding for higher education: Origins, discontinuations, and transformations.* Baltimore: Johns Hopkins University Press.

Dougherty, K. J., R. S. Natow, and B. E. Vega. 2012. Popular but unstable: Explaining why state performance funding systems in the United States often do not persist. *Teachers College Record* 114 (1): 1–41.

Dougherty, K. J., and V. Reddy. 2011. The impacts of state performance funding systems of higher education institutions: Research literature review and policy implications. New York: Community College Research Center Working Paper No. 37.

Doyle, W. R. 2010. Does merit-based aid "crowd-out" need-based aid? *Research in Higher Education* 51 (5): 397–415.

———. 2012. The politics of public college tuition and state financial aid. *Journal of Higher Education* 83 (5): 617–47.

Eisenhower, M. S. 1959. *The efficiency of freedom: Report of the committee on government and higher education.* Baltimore: Johns Hopkins Press.

Esack, S. 2015, April 9. Pennsylvania higher education board reluctantly approves Gov. Tom Wolf's tuition freeze "ultimatum." *Morning Call.* http://www.mcall.com/news/nationworld/pennsylvania/mc-pa-wolf-budget-higher-education-20150409-story.html.

Finney, J. E., C. Riso, K. Orosz, and W. C. Boland. 2014. *From master plan to mediocrity: Higher education performance and policy in California.* Philadelphia: Institute for Research on Higher Education.

Fisher, J. 2016, June 16. FOIA bill targets UD, DSU committees. *News Journal.* http://www.delawareonline.com/story/news/local/2016/06/15/foia-bill-targets-ud-dsu-committees/85939666.

Flores, S. M., and J. C. Shepherd. 2014. Pricing out the disadvantaged? The effect of tuition deregulation in Texas public four-year institutions. *ANNALS of the American Academy of Political and Social Science* 655: 99–122.

Fryar, A. H. 2011. *The disparate impacts of accountability—searching for causal mechanisms.* Paper presented at the Public Management Research Conference, Syracuse, New York, June 2–4, 2011.

Ginder, S. A., J. E. Kelly-Reid, and F. B. Mann. 2015. *Enrollment and employees in postsecondary institutions, Fall 2014; and financial statistics and academic libraries, fiscal year 2014.* Washington, DC: Institute of Education Sciences, National Center for Education Statistics.

Goldrick-Rab, S., and T. Kolbe. 2015, September 28. Rethinking state support for higher ed. *Inside Higher Ed.* https://www.insidehighered.com/views/2015/09/28/essay-need-consider-which-institutions-should-bear-brunt-state-cuts-public-higher.

Heller, D. E. 2002. The policy shift in state financial aid programs. Pp. In *Higher Education: Handbook of theory and research,* vol. XVII, edited by J. C. Smart, 221–62. New York: Agathon.

Hillman, N. W. 2016. *Why performance-based college funding doesn't work.* New York: The Century Foundation.

Hillman, N. W., D. A. Tandberg, and A. H. Fryar. 2015. Evaluating the impacts of "new" performance funding in higher education. *Educational Evaluation and Policy Analysis* 37 (4): 501–19.

Hillman, N. W., D. A. Tandberg, and J. P. K. Gross. 2014a. Market-based higher education: Does Colorado's voucher model improve higher education access and efficiency? *Research in Higher Education* 55 (6): 601–25.

———. 2014b. Performance funding in higher education: Do financial incentives impact college completions? *Journal of Higher Education* 85 (6): 826–57.

Indiana Commission for Higher Education. n.d. Performance-based funding for public colleges and universities: Frequently asked questions. Accessed April 4, 2017. https://www.in.gov/che/files/Performance_Funding_FAQ_FINAL.pdf.

Jones, D. 2013. *Outcomes-based funding: The wave of implementation.* Boulder: National Center for Higher Education Management Systems.

Jones, T. 2014. *Performance funding at MSIs: Considerations and possible measures for public minority-serving institutions.* Atlanta: Southern Education Foundation.

Kelchen, R. 2016. An analysis of student fees: The roles of states and institutions. *Review of Higher Education* 39 (4): 597–619.

———. 2017. Do performance-based funding policies affect underrepresented student enrollment? Working paper.

Kelchen, R., and L. J. Stedrak. 2016. Does performance-based funding affect colleges' fiscal priorities? *Journal of Education Finance* 41 (3): 302–21.

Kelly, A. P., K. J. James, and R. Columbus. 2015. *Inputs, outcomes, quality assurance: A closer look at state oversight of higher education.* Washington, DC: American Enterprise Institute.

Kim, J., and K. Stange. 2016. Pricing and university autonomy: Tuition deregulation in Texas. *RSF: The Russell Sage Foundation Journal of the Social Sciences* 2 (1): 112–46.

Kim, M. M., and J. Ko. 2015. The impacts of state control policies on college tuition increase. *Educational Policy* 29 (5): 815–38.

Knott, J. H., and A. A. Payne. 2004. The impact of state governance structures on management and performance of public organizations: A study of higher education institutions. *Journal of Policy Analysis and Management* 23 (1): 13–30.

Koshal, R. K., and M. Koshal. 2000. State appropriation and higher education tuition: What is the relationship? *Education Economics* 8 (1): 81–89.

Lane, J. E., K. Kinser, and D. Knox. 2013. Regulating cross-border higher education: A case study of the United States. *Higher Education Policy* 26: 147–72.

Layzell D. T., and J. W. Lyddon. 1990. Budgeting for higher education at the state level: Enigma, paradox, and ritual. Washington, DC: ASHE-ERIC Higher Education Report 4.

Li, A. Y. 2016. The renaissance of performance funding for higher education: Policy adoption, implementation, and impacts. Doctoral dissertation, University of Washington.

———. 2017a. Dramatic declines in higher education appropriations: State conditions for budget punctuations. *Research in Higher Education* 58 (4): 395–429.

———. 2017b. The point of the point: Washington's student achievement initiative through the looking glass of a community college. *Community College Journal of Research and Practice* 41 (3): 183–202.

Li, A. Y., and W. Zumeta. 2016. *Performance funding on the ground: Campus responses and perspectives in two states.* New York: TIAA Institute.

Louisiana Board of Regents. n.d. *Granting resources and autonomies for diplomas.* Accessed August 1, 2016. http://www.regents.la.gov/page/grad-act.

Lowry, R. C. 2001a. Governmental structure, trustee selection, and public university prices and spending: Multiple means to similar ends. *American Journal of Political Science* 45 (4): 845–61.

———. 2001b. The effects of state political interests and campus outputs on public university revenues. *Economics of Education Review* 20: 105–19.

———. 2016. Subsidizing institutions vs. outputs vs. individuals: States' choices for financing postsecondary education. *Journal of Public Administration Research and Theory* 26 (2): 197–210.

Lumina Foundation. n.d. Frequently asked questions: Outcomes-based funding. Accessed August 3, 2016. https://www.luminafoundation.org/outcomes-based-funding-faq.

McGuinness, A. 1995. *Restructuring state roles in higher education: A case study of the 1994 New Jersey Higher Education Restructuring Act.* Boulder: Education Commission of the States.

———. 2016. *State policy leadership for the future: History of state coordination and governance and alternatives for the future.* Boulder: Education Commission of the States.

McKeown, M. P. 1993. State funding formulas for higher education: Trends and issues. *Journal of Education Finance* 19 (3): 319–46.

———. 1996. *State funding formulas for public four-year institutions.* Denver: State Higher Education Executive Officers Association.

McKinney, L., and L. S. Hagedorn. 2017. Performance-based funding for community colleges in Texas: Are colleges disadvantaged for serving the most disadvantaged students? *Journal of Higher Education* 88 (2): 159–82.

McLendon, M. K. 2003a. State governance reform of higher education: Patterns, trends, and theories of the public policy process. In *Higher education: Handbook of theory and practice*, vol. 18, edited by J. C. Smart, 57–144. London: Kluwer Academic.

———. 2003b. Setting the governmental agenda for state decentralization of higher education. *Journal of Higher Education* 74 (5): 479–515.

McLendon, M. K., S. B. Deaton, and J. C. Hearn. 2007. The enactment of reforms in state governance of higher education: Testing the political instability hypothesis. *Journal of Higher Education* 78 (6): 645–75.

McLendon, M. K., and J. C. Hearn. 2006a. Mandated openness and higher-education governance: Policy, theoretical, and analytic perspectives. In *Higher education: Handbook of theory and research*, vol. 21, edited by J. C. Smart, 39–97. Dordrecht, Netherlands: Springer.

———. 2006b. Mandated openness in public higher education: A field study of state sunshine laws and institutional governance. *Journal of Higher Education* 77 (4): 645–83.

McLendon, M. K., J. C. Hearn, and R. Deaton. 2006. Called to account: Analyzing the origins and spread of state performance-accountability policies for higher education. *Educational Evaluation and Policy Analysis* 28 (1): 1–24.

McLendon, M. K., J. C. Hearn, and C. G. Mokher. 2009. Partisans, professionals, and power: The role of political factors in state higher education funding. *Journal of Higher Education* 80 (6): 686–713.

McLendon, M. K., D. E. Heller, and S. P. Young. 2005. State postsecondary policy innovation: Politics, competition, and the interstate migration of policy ideas. *Journal of Higher Education* 76 (4): 364–400.

McLendon, M. K., D. A. Tandberg, and N. W. Hillman. 2014. Financing college opportunity: Factors influencing state spending on student financial aid and campus appropriations, 1990 through 2010. *ANNALS of the American Academy of Political and Social Science* 655: 143–62.

Minckler, T. V. 2016. Improving higher education results through performance-based funding: An analysis of initial outcomes and leader perceptions of the 2012 Ohio 100 percent performance-based funding policy. Doctoral dissertation, University of Pennsylvania.

Moos, M., and F. E. Rourke. 1959. *The campus and the state*. Baltimore: Johns Hopkins Press.

Morrison, G. M. 2010. *Perspectives on program duplication*. Columbia: South Carolina Commission on Higher Education.

Moss, C. E., and G. H. Gaither. 1976. Formula budgeting: Requiem or renaissance? *Journal of Higher Education* 47 (5): 543–63.

Moynihan, D. P. 2006. Managing for results in state government: Evaluating a decade of reform. *Public Administration Review* 66 (1): 77–89.

Murphy, E. 2011, October 11. Closing time in California. *Inside Higher Ed*. https://www.insidehighered.com/news/2011/10/11/california_postsecondary _education_commission_closes.

National Association of State Student Grant and Aid Programs. 2015. 45th annual survey report on state-sponsored student financial aid. Washington, DC: Author.

National Center for Education Statistics. n.d. Statewide longitudinal data systems grant program. Accessed August 2, 2016. https://nces.ed.gov/Programs/SLDS /stateinfo.asp.

National Conference of State Legislatures. 2015, July 31. Performance-based funding for higher education. http://www.ncsl.org/research/education/performance -funding.aspx.

———. 2016, April 20. State partisan composition. http://www.ncsl.org/research /about-state-legislatures/partisan-composition.aspx.

National Consumer Law Center. 2014. Government investigations and lawsuits involving for-profit schools (2004–May 2014). Boston: Author.

NC-SARA (National Council for State Authorization Reciprocity Agreements). 2016, June 16. SARA states and institutions. http://nc-sara.org/sara-states -institutions.

Ness, E. C., and D. A. Tandberg. 2013. The determinants of state spending on higher education: How capital project funding differs from general fund appropriations. *Journal of Higher Education* 84 (3): 329–62.

New Jersey Higher Education Task Force. 2010. The report of the governor's task force on higher education. Trenton, NJ: Author.

Office of Missouri State Auditor. 2016. Public higher education funding and affordability. Jefferson City, MO: Author.

Opoczynski, R. 2016. The creation of performance funding in Michigan: Partnerships, promotions, and points. *Education Policy Analysis Archives* 24 (122): 1–25.

Palochko, J. 2015, July 10. Despite Wolf's plea for freeze, tuition going up at Pennsylvania's state-owned universities. *Morning Call.* http://www.mcall.com /news/local/pa--state-universities-tuition-20150709-story.html.

Payne, A. A., and J. Roberts. 2010. Government oversight of public universities: Are centralized performance schemes related to increased quantity or quality? *Review of Economics and Statistics* 92 (1): 207–12.

Pew Charitable Trusts. 2015. Federal and state funding of higher education: A changing landscape. Philadelphia: Author.

Poulin, R., and M. Boeke. n.d. History of state authorization. *Western Interstate Cooperative for Higher Education.* Accessed June 20, 2017. http://wcet.wiche .edu/focus-areas/policy-and-regulation/state-authorization/history.

Rabovsky, T. M. 2012. Accountability in higher education: Exploring impacts on state budgets and institutional spending patterns. *Journal of Public Administration Research and Theory* 22: 675–700.

———. 2014. Support for performance-based funding: The role of political ideology, performance, and dysfunctional information environments. *Public Administration Review* 74 (6): 761–74.

Ruppert, S. S. 1995. Roots and realities of state-level performance indicator systems. *New Directions for Higher Education* 91: 11–23.

Rutherford, A., and T. Rabovsky. 2014. Evaluating impacts of performance funding policies on student outcomes in higher education. *ANNALS of the American Academy of Political and Social Science* 655: 185–208.

Sanford, T., and J. M. Hunter. 2011. Impact of performance-funding on retention and graduation rates. *Education Policy Analysis Archives* 19 (33). doi: 10.14507 /epaa.v19n33.2011

Schmidtlein, F. A. 1999. Assumptions underlying performance-based budgeting. *Tertiary Education and Management* 5 (2): 157–74.

SHEEO (State Higher Education Executive Officers Association). n.d. SHEEO state authorization surveys. Accessed July 25, 2016. http://sheeo.org/sheeo_surveys.

———. 2015. SHEF: FY 2014 state higher education finance. Boulder: Author.

———. 2016. SHEF: FY 2015 state higher education finance. Boulder: Author.

Shin, J. C. 2010. Impacts of performance-based accountability on institutional performance in the U.S. *Higher Education* 60 (1): 47–68.

Shin, J., and S. Milton. 2004. The effects of performance budgeting and funding programs on graduation rate in public four-year colleges and universities. *Education Policy Analysis Archives* 12 (22). doi: 10.14507/epaa.v12n22.2004

Shulock, N., and M. Snyder. 2013, December 5. Don't dismiss performance funding. *Inside Higher Ed.* https://www.insidehighered.com/views/2013/12/05/performance-funding-isnt-perfect-recent-study-shortchanges-it-essay.

Sjoquist, D. L., and J. V. Winters. 2015. State merit-based financial aid programs and college attainment. *Journal of Regional Science* 55 (3): 364–90.

Snyder, M. 2016, April 18. Jumping to conclusions. *Inside Higher Ed.* https://www.insidehighered.com/views/2016/04/18/essay-challenging-academic-studies-states-performance-funding-formulas.

Snyder, M., and B. Fox. 2016. *Driving better outcomes: Fiscal year 2016 state status and typology update.* Washington, DC: HCM Strategists.

SRI International. 2012. States' methods of funding higher education. Princeton, NJ: Author.

State Council of Higher Education for Virginia. n.d. Student outcomes: Reports and resources. Accessed August 2, 2016. http://research.schev.edu.

State of New Jersey. 2011, June 29. A plan for the abolition of the New Jersey Commission on Higher Education and providing for the transfer of the functions, powers, and duties of the commission to the Secretary of Higher Education. http://www.state.nj.us/highereducation/documents/005-2011.pdf.

Tandberg, D. A. 2010a. Interest groups and governmental institutions: The politics of state funding of public higher education. *Educational Policy* 24 (5): 735–78.

———. 2010b. Politics, interest groups, and state funding of public higher education. *Research in Higher Education* 51: 416–50.

———. 2013. The conditioning role of state higher education governance structures. *Journal of Higher Education* 84 (4): 506–43.

Tandberg, D. A., and N. W. Hillman. 2014. State higher education performance funding: Data, outcomes, and policy implications. *Journal of Education Finance* 39 (3): 222–43.

Tandberg, D. A., N. W. Hillman, and M. Barakat. 2014. State higher education performance funding for community colleges: Diverse effects and policy implications. *Teachers College Record* 116 (12): 1–31.

Tandberg, D. A., and E. C. Ness. 2011. State capital expenditures for higher education: "Where the real politics happens." *Journal of Education Finance* 36 (4): 394–423.

Toutkoushian, R. K., and N. W. Hillman. 2012. The impact of state appropriations and grants on access to higher education and outmigration. *Review of Higher Education* 36 (1): 51–90.

Toutkoushian, R. K., and M. N. Shafiq. 2010. A conceptual analysis of state support for higher education: Appropriations versus need-based financial aid. *Research in Higher Education* 51 (1): 40–64.

Umbricht, M. R., F. Fernandez, and J. C. Ortagus. 2017. An examination of the (un)intended consequences of performance funding in higher education. *Educational Policy.* 31 (5): 643–73

University of Wisconsin–Madison. 2008, November 7. Local paper posting Madison salaries from UW System Redbook. http://news.wisc.edu/local-paper -posting-madison-salaries-from-uw-system-redbook.

University of Wisconsin System. 2014. Legislated accountability report 2014. Madison, WI: Author.

U.S. Department of Education. 2016, June 16. *Notice of proposed rulemaking.* http://www2.ed.gov/policy/highered/reg/hearulemaking/2016/bd-unofficial -nprm-061316.pdf.

Waldman, A. 2016, April 11. Attorneys general come down on accreditor of for-profit colleges. *ProPublica.* https://www.propublica.org/article/attorneys-general -come-down-on-accreditor-of-for-profit-colleges.

Weerts, D. J., and J. M. Ronca. 2012. Understanding differences in state support for higher education across states, sectors, and institutions: A longitudinal study. *Journal of Higher Education* 83 (2): 155–85.

Western Interstate Commission for Higher Education. 2009. An evaluation of Colorado's college opportunity fund and related policies. Boulder: Author.

Zhang, L., and E. C. Ness. 2010. Does state merit-based aid stem brain drain? *Educational Evaluation and Policy Analysis* 32 (2): 143–65.

Zumeta, W. 2001. Public policy and accountability in higher education: Lessons from the past and present for the new millennium. In *The states and public higher education policy: Affordability, access, and accountability*, edited by D. E. Heller, 155–97. Baltimore: Johns Hopkins University Press.

Zumeta, W., and A. Y. Li. 2016. *Assessing the underpinnings of performance funding 2.0: Will this dog hunt?* New York: TIAA Institute.

Chapter Five: Accreditation and Accountability

AACSB (Association to Advance Collegiate Schools of Business). n.d. Accredited school listings. Accessed September 27, 2016. http://www.aacsb.edu/accredita tion/accredited-members.

AALE (American Academy for Liberal Education). 2016. Members. Accessed September 27, 2016. http://www.aale.org/index.php/top-blocks/item/46-members.

ABA Task Force on the Future of Legal Education. 2014. Report and recommendations. Accessed October 1, 2016. http://www.americanbar.org/content/dam /aba/administrative/professional_responsibility/report_and_recommendations _of_aba_task_force.authcheckdam.pdf.

ABET (Accrediting Board for Engineering and Technology). n.d. About ABET. Accessed September 27, 2016. http://www.abet.org/about-abet.

ACBSP (Accreditation Council for Business Schools and Programs). 2015. Search accredited programs. Accessed September 27 2016. http://www.acbsp.org/?page =search_accredited.

ACCJC (Accrediting Commission for Community and Junior Colleges). 2014. *Accreditation standards.* Novato, CA: Author.

Accrediting Commission of Career Schools and Colleges. 2016. *Standards of accreditation.* Arlington, VA: Author.

ACE National Task Force on Institutional Accreditation. 2012. *Assuring academic quality in the 21st century: Self-regulation in a new era.* Washington, DC: American Council on Education.

Association of Specialized and Professional Accreditors. 2016. Our members. Accessed October 2, 2016. http://www.aspa-usa.org/our-members.

Barba, M. 2016, July 13. CCSF special trustee contract extension suggested by state. *San Francisco Examiner.* http://www.sfexaminer.com/ccsf-special-trustee -contract-extension-suggested-state.

———. 2017, January 13. CCSF keeps accreditation, ending years of uncertainty. *San Francisco Examiner.* http://www.sfexaminer.com/ccsfs-accreditation-reaf firmed-7-years.

Basken, P. 2008, September 3. Education Department acknowledges that its accreditation panel won't meet again. *Chronicle of Higher Education.* http:// www.chronicle.com/article/Time-Runs-Out-for-Federal/1125.

Belkin, D., and A. Fuller. 2015, June 26. College accreditors weigh aggressive steps. *Wall Street Journal.* http://www.wsj.com/articles/college-accreditors-weigh -aggressive-steps-1435346210.

Bollag, B. 2007, March 9. Education Department relents on measuring achievement. *Chronicle of Higher Education.* http://www.chronicle.com/article/Edu cation-Department-Relents/28222.

Brittingham, B. 2009. Accreditation in the United States: How did we get to where we are? *New Directions for Higher Education* 145: 7–27.

Broad, M. C., P. McPherson, and H. Rawlings. 2015, December 4. Association letter urges Education Secretary to implement differential accreditation. https://www.aau.edu/key-issues/association-letter-urges-education-secretary -implement-differential-accreditation.

Brown, H. 2013. *Protecting students and taxpayers: The federal government's failed regulatory approach and steps for reform.* Washington, DC: American Enterprise Institute.

CHEA (Council for Higher Education Accreditation). 2015. *The condition of accreditation: U.S. accreditation in 2013.* Washington, DC: CHEA Institute for Research and Study of Accreditation and Quality Assurance.

———. 2017a. 2016–2017 directory of CHEA-recognized organizations. Washington, DC: Author.

————. 2017b, May 17. CHEA almanac online. http://www.chea.org/4DCGI /cms/review.html?Action=CMS_Document&DocID=29&MenuKey=almanac.

Cochran-Smith, M., R. Stern, J. G. Sanchez, A. Miller, E. S. Keefe, M. B. Fernandez, et al. 2016. *Holding teacher preparation accountable: A review of claims and evidence.* Boulder: National Education Policy Center.

Conway, M. M. 1979. The commissioner's authority to list accrediting agencies and associations: Necessity for an eligibility issue. *Journal of Higher Education* 50 (2): 158–70.

Cooper, P. 2016. *Not impartial: Examining accreditation commissioners' conflicts of interest.* New York: Manhattan Institute for Policy Research.

Council for the Accreditation of Educator Preparation. 2016. *CAEP accreditation handbook.* Washington, DC: Author.

Crow, S. 2009. Musings on the future of accreditation. *New Directions for Higher Education* 145: 87–97.

Davenport, C. A. 2000. Recognition chronology. Accessed October 2, 2016. http:// www.aspa-usa.org/wp-content/uploads/2015/02/Davenport.pdf.

Dickeson, R. C. 2006. *The need for accreditation reform.* Washington, DC: Secretary of Education's Commission on the Future of Higher Education.

Distance Education Accrediting Commission. n.d. Frequently asked questions for institutions seeking accreditation. Accessed September 29, 2016. http://www .deac.org/Discover-DEAC/FAQ-for-Institutions.aspx.

Donahoo, S., and W. Y. Lee. 2008a. Serving two masters: Quality and conflict in the accreditation of religious institutions. *Christian Higher Education* 7 (4): 319–38.

————. 2008b. The adversity of diversity: Regional associations and the accreditation of minority-serving institutions. In *Understanding minority-serving institutions*, edited by M. Gasman, B. Baez, and C. S. V. Turner, 292–310. Albany: State University of New York Press.

Eaton, J. S. 2009. Accreditation in the United States. *New Directions for Higher Education* 145: 79–86.

————. 2015. Accreditation: What it does and what it should do. *Change* 47 (1): 24–26.

————. 2016, June 24. A statement from Judith Eaton. *Council for Higher Education Accreditation.* http://www.chea.org/4DCGI/cms/review.html?Action=CMS _Document&DocID=489.

Edwards, H. S. 2013. America's worst community colleges. *Washington Monthly* (September/October). Accessed August 22, 2016. http://washingtonmonthly .com/magazine/septoct-2013/americas-worst-community-colleges.

Ewell, P. 2010. Twenty years of quality assurance in higher education: What's happened and what's different? *Quality in Higher Education* 16 (2): 173–75.

Fain, P. 2012, July 6. Something has to give. *Inside Higher Ed.* https://www.inside highered.com/news/2012/07/06/accreditation-crisis-hits-city-college-san -francisco.

———. 2013, August 5. Setting limits for outsourcing online. *Inside Higher Ed.* https://www.insidehighered.com/news/2013/08/05/tiffin-u-drops-ivy-bridge -college-partnership-altius-over-accreditors-concerns.

———. 2016a, May 4. Watchdog barks—and gets slapped down. *Inside Higher Ed.* https://www.insidehighered.com/news/2016/05/04/controversial-accreditor -acics-tried-shut-down-profit-was-blocked-judge.

———. 2016b, June 21. Scorecard for accreditors. *Inside Higher Ed.* https://www .insidehighered.com/news/2016/06/21/education-department-release-data -reports-accreditors-based-measures-student.

———. 2016c, June 24. Accreditor on life support. *Inside Higher Ed.* https:// www.insidehighered.com/news/2016/06/24/federal-panel-votes-terminate -acics-and-tightens-screws-other-accreditors.

Finkin, M. W. 1973. Federal reliance on voluntary accreditation: The power to recognize as the power to regulate. *Journal of Law and Education* 2 (3): 339– 76.

Flores, A. 2015, December 14. Hooked on accreditation: A historical perspective. https://www.americanprogress.org/issues/higher-education/report/2015/12 /14/127200/hooked-on-accreditation-a-historical-perspective.

———. 2016. *Watching the watchdogs: A look at what happens when accreditors sanction colleges.* Washington, DC: Center for American Progress.

———. 2017. *Getting what we pay for on quality assurance.* Washington, DC: Center for American Progress.

Fuller, A., and D. Belkin. 2015a, June 17. The watchdogs of college education rarely bite. *Wall Street Journal.* http://www.wsj.com/articles/the-watchdogs-of -college-education-rarely-bite-1434594602.

———. 2015b, July 6. How ailing colleges stay accredited. *Wall Street Journal.* http://www.wsj.com/articles/colleges-seek-workarounds-to-keep-their-seal -of-approval-1436206962.

Gaston, P. L. 2014a. Accreditation's alchemy hour: Riding the wave of innovation. *Liberal Education* 100 (2): 12–17.

———. 2014b. *Higher education accreditation: How it's changing, why it must.* Sterling, VA: Stylus.

Gillen, A., D. L. Bennett, and R. Vedder. 2010. *The inmates running the asylum? An analysis of higher education accreditation.* Washington, DC: Center for College Affordability and Productivity.

Glidden, R. 1996. Accreditation at a crossroads. *Educational Record* 77 (4): 22–24.

Goldrick-Rab, S., R. Kelchen, and J. Houle. 2014. *The color of student debt: Implications of federal loan program reforms for black students and historically black colleges and universities.* Madison: Wisconsin HOPE Lab.

Hacker, H. K. 2012, January 26. Accrediting decision means good news for Paul Quinn College. *Dallas Morning News.* http://www.dallasnews.com/news/edu cation/2012/01/26/accrediting-decision-means-good-news-for-paul-quinn -college.

Harcleroad, F. F. 1980. *Accreditation: History, processes, and problems.* Washington, DC: American Association for Higher Education.

Hawkins, D. B. 2013, May 31. After 125 years of service, St. Paul's College shutting down June 30. *Diverse Issues in Higher Education.* http://diverseeducation.com/article/53664.

Hebel, S. 2010, December 2. Accreditor decides not to seek continued recognition from Education Dept. *Chronicle of Higher Education.* http://www.chronicle.com/blogs/ticker/accreditor-decides-not-to-seek-continued-recognition-from-education-dept/28841.

Higher Learning Commission. 2016. *Policy book.* Chicago: Author.

Honan, W. H. 1995, August 6. A new group will accredit some colleges. *New York Times.* http://www.nytimes.com/1995/08/06/us/a-new-group-will-accredit-some-colleges.html.

———. 1998, November 11. Some say college accreditation is out of control. *New York Times.* http://www.nytimes.com/1998/11/11/us/some-say-college-accreditation-is-out-of-control.html.

Kelderman, E. 2015, November 6. U.S. to put new requirements on accreditors. *Chronicle of Higher Education.* http://www.chronicle.com/article/US-to-Put-New-Requirements/234082.

———. 2016a, January 29. Accreditors feel the heat, but are torn over calls for change. http://www.chronicle.com/article/Accreditors-Feel-the-Heat-but/235103.

———. 2016b, September 22. In San Francisco, the fates of a college and its accreditor are on the line. *Chronicle of Higher Education.* http://www.chronicle.com/article/In-San-Francisco-the-Fates-of/237870.

———. 2016c, September 30. Accreditors rarely lose lawsuits, but they keep getting sued. Here's why. *Chronicle of Higher Education.* http://www.chronicle.com/article/Accreditors-Rarely-Lose/237944.

Kezar, A. 2014, April 11. Innovator or protector of status quo? *Inside Higher Ed.* https://www.insidehighered.com/views/2014/04/11/accreditation-pushes-colleges-innovate-not-stagnate-essay.

Kreighbaum, A. 2016a, September 21. Tougher scrutiny for colleges with low graduation rates. *Inside Higher Ed.* https://www.insidehighered.com/news/2016/09/21/regional-accreditors-refocus-institutions-low-grad-rates.

———. 2016b, September 23. Warren, other Democrats take aim at accreditors. *Inside Higher Ed.* https://www.insidehighered.com/quicktakes/2016/09/23/warren-other-democrats-take-aim-accreditors.

Lederman, D. 2007, January 17. Another front on accreditation. *Inside Higher Ed.* https://www.insidehighered.com/news/2007/01/17/accredit.

———. 2008, July 23. A break from purgatory, barely. *Inside Higher Ed.* https://www.insidehighered.com/news/2008/07/23/aale.

———. 2010, November 29. Accreditor under the gun again. *Inside Higher Ed.* https://www.insidehighered.com/news/2010/11/29/naciqi.

———. 2015, May 29. CAEPed crusader ousted. *Inside Higher Ed.* https://www

.insidehighered.com/news/2015/05/29/teacher-education-accreditor-dumps
-its-founding-leader.

Liaison Committee on Medical Education. 2016. Functions and structure of a
medical school: Standards for accreditation of medical education programs
leading to the MD degree. Washington, DC: Author.

Marklein, M. B. 2010, September 29. For-profit colleges under fire over value,
accreditation. *USA Today.* http://usatoday30.usatoday.com/news/education/2010
-09-29-1Aforprofit29_CV_N.htm.

Marvin, C. H. 1952. The problems of accreditation. *Phi Delta Kappan* 34 (1):
4–5, 8.

Middle States Commission on Higher Education. 2011. Characteristics of excellence in higher education: Requirements of affiliation and standards for accreditation. Philadelphia: Author.

Miller, B. 2014, July 10. Improving accreditation part III: Innovation through
alternatives. *New America.* https://www.newamerica.org/education-policy/ed
central/improving-accreditation-iii.

———. 2016. *ACICS must go.* Washington, DC: Center for American Progress.

Mori, R. 2009. Accreditation systems in Japan and the United States: A comparative perspective on governmental involvement. *New Directions for Higher
Education* 145: 69–78.

Moser, E., and C. J. Guback, eds. 2016. *Comprehensive guide to bar admission
requirements 2016.* Madison, WI: National Conference of Bar Examiners and
the American Bar Association.

NACIQI (National Advisory Committee on Institutional Quality and Integrity).
2016, June 22. *Recognized institutional accreditors: Federal postsecondary
education and student aid data.* http://www2.ed.gov/admins/finaid/accred/ac
creditor-dashboards.pdf.

Nelson, L. A. 2013, June 14. No love for accreditation. *Inside Higher Ed.* https://
www.insidehighered.com/news/2013/06/14/congressional-panel-hears-criticism
-broken-accreditation-system.

Office of Postsecondary Education. 2017. Download accreditation data files.
Accessed April 13, 2017. http://ope.ed.gov/accreditation/GetDownLoadFile
.aspx.

Office of Senator Elizabeth Warren. 2016, June 10. Rubber stamps: ACICS and
the troubled oversight of college accreditors. http://www.warren.senate.gov/files
/documents/2016-6-10_ACICS_Report.pdf

Pfnister, A. O. 1971. Regional accrediting agencies at the crossroads. *Journal of
Higher Education* 42 (7): 558–73.

Quinn, C. 2016, September 21. Historically black college wins reprieve from accreditation loss. *Atlanta Journal-Constitution.* http://www.ajc.com/news/local
-education/historically-black-college-wins-reprieve-from-accreditation-loss
/g2SjgWXcZ6WARWFBRvm9SN.

Rogers, J. 2012, October 29. A business school's drive for accreditation sidelines some professors. *Chronicle of Higher Education.* http://www.chronicle.com /article/Drive-for-Accreditation-Pushes/135408.

Sawchuk, S. 2016, August 23. Teacher-prep accreditation group seeks to regain traction. *Education Week.* http://www.edweek.org/ew/articles/2016/08/24/tea cher-prep-accreditation-group-seeks-to-regain-traction.html.

Schmidt, P. 2013a, April 1. A faculty refuge becomes an accreditor's target. *Chronicle of Higher Education.* http://chronicle.com/article/A-Faculty-Refuge-Becomes -an/138195.

———. 2013b, July 3. City College of San Francisco is told it will lose accreditation in 2014. *Chronicle of Higher Education.* http://chronicle.com/article/City -College-of-San-Francisco/140133.

Schray, V. 2006. Assuring quality in higher education: Recommendations for improving accreditation. Washington, DC: Secretary of Education's Commission on the Future of Higher Education.

Semrow, J. J., J. A. Barney, M. Fredericks, J. Fredericks, P. Robinson, and A. O. Pfnister. 1992. *In search of quality: The development, status and forecast of standards in postsecondary education.* New York: Peter Lang.

Senate Committee on Health, Education, Labor and Pensions. 2015. Higher education accreditation: Concepts and proposals. Washington, DC: Author.

Shah, M., S. Nair, and M. Wilson. 2011. Quality assurance in Australian higher education: Historical and future development. *Asia Pacific Education Review* 12: 475–83.

Sibolski, E. H. 2012. What's an accrediting agency supposed to do? Institutional quality and improvement vs. regulatory compliance. *Planning for Higher Education* 40 (3): 22–28.

———. 2014, April 9. Regional accreditors announce efforts to improve public understanding of commission actions. *Council of Regional Accrediting Commissions.* http://www.msche.org/documents/CRACCommonTermsRelease.pdf.

Song, J., V. Kim, and S. Poindexter. 2015, July 25. Nearly 9 in 10 students drop out of unaccredited law schools in California. *Los Angeles Times.* http://www .latimes.com/local/education/la-me-law-schools-20150726-story,amp.html.

Stancill, J. 2016, June 16. UNC removed from probation by accrediting agency. *News and Observer.* http://www.newsobserver.com/news/local/education/arti cle84158937.html.

Suskie, L. 2015. *Five dimensions of quality: A common sense guide to accreditation and accountability.* San Francisco: Jossey-Bass.

Thomason, A. 2015a, October 30. Judge throws out suit against accreditor that shut down for-profit venture. *Chronicle of Higher Education.* http://www .chronicle.com/blogs/ticker/judge-throws-out-suit-against-accreditor-that -shut-down-for-profit-venture.

———. 2015b, December 2. Academic leader urges colleges to "take the lead" on accreditation. *Chronicle of Higher Education.* http://www.chronicle.com/blogs /ticker/academic-leader-urges-colleges-to-take-the-lead-on-accreditation/107085.

————. 2016, September 22. Education Dept. revokes recognition of embattled accreditor of for-profit colleges. *Chronicle of Higher Education.* http://www.chronicle.com/blogs/ticker/education-dept-revokes-recognition-of-embattled-accreditor-of-for-profit-colleges/114592.

TRACS (Transnational Association of Christian Colleges and Schools). 2015. *Accreditation manual.* Forest, VA: Author.

Trivett, D. A. 1976. *Accreditation and institutional eligibility.* Washington, DC: American Association for Higher Education.

UNT Dallas College of Law. 2015, September 11. Financial aid and loans. https://lawschool.untsystem.edu/financial-aid/financial-aid-and-loans.

U.S. Department of Education. 2006. *A test of leadership: Charting the future of U.S. higher education.* Washington, DC: Author.

————. 2016. Staff report to the senior departmental official on recognition compliance issues. Washington, DC: Author.

————. 2017, June 12. Accrediting agencies recognized for Title IV purposes. http://www2.ed.gov/admins/finaid/accred/accreditation_pg9.html.

U.S. Government Accountability Office. 2010. Undercover testing finds colleges encouraged fraud and engaged in deceptive and questionable marketing practices. Washington, DC: Author.

————. 2014. Higher education: Education should strengthen oversight of schools and accreditors. Washington, DC: Author.

Vanderbilt University. 2015. The cost of federal regulatory compliance in higher education: A multi-institutional study. Nashville: Author.

Volkwein, J. F., L. R. Lattuca, B. J. Harper, and R. J. Domingo. 2007. Measuring the impact of professional accreditation on student experiences and learning outcomes. *Research in Higher Education* 48 (2): 251–82.

Watkins, M. 2016, August 23. How UNT-Dallas' grand law school experiment could be overruled. *Texas Tribune.* https://www.texastribune.org/2016/08/23/unt-dallas-wants-fix-law-school-it-may-not-get-cha.

Wood, P. 2015, August 28. Sojourner-Douglass College loses bid to restore accreditation. *Baltimore Sun.* http://www.baltimoresun.com/news/maryland/education/bs-md-sojourner-ruling-20150828-story.html.

Woolston, P. J. 2012. The costs of institutional accreditation: A study of direct and indirect costs. Doctoral dissertation, University of Southern California.

Young, K. E. 1979. New pressures on accreditation. *Journal of Higher Education* 50 (2): 132–44.

Chapter Six: Private-Sector Accountability

Altbach, P. G. 2015. The Carnegie classification of American higher education: More—and less—than meets the eye. *International Higher Education* 80: 21–23.

Alter, M., and R. Reback. 2014. True for your school? How changing reputations alter demand for selective U.S. colleges. *Educational Evaluation and Policy Analysis* 36 (3): 346–70.

Ambrose, S., and D. Tarrant. 2016, May 26. Baylor regents strip Ken Starr of president's title, apologize for mishandling sex assault cases. *Dallas Morning News*. http://www.dallasnews.com/news/news/2016/05/26/baylor-football-coach -briles-out-starr-no-longer-president-as-baylor-releases-sexual-assault-report.

Anderson, M. L. 2012. The benefits of college athletic success: An application of the propensity score design with instrumental variables. Cambridge, MA: National Bureau of Economic Research Working Paper 18196.

Anderson, N. 2014, February 2. U-Md.'s unusual admissions approach: One out of every five freshmen starts in spring term. *Washington Post*. https://www .washingtonpost.com/local/education/u-mds-unusual-admissions-approach -one-out-of-every-five-freshmen-start-in-spring-term/2014/01/31/21d99a64 -8794-11e3-916e-e01534b1e132_story.html.

———. 2016, February 4. In new sorting of colleges, Dartmouth falls out of an exclusive group. *Washington Post*. https://www.washingtonpost.com/news/grade -point/wp/2016/02/04/in-new-sorting-of-colleges-dartmouth-falls-out-of-an -exclusive-group.

Archibald, R. B., and D. H. Feldman. 2008. Graduation rates and accountability: Regressions versus production frontiers. *Research in Higher Education* 49 (1): 80–100.

Art and Science Group, LLC. 2013, October. *Influence of the rankings on college choice*. Accessed October 13, 2016. http://www.artsci.com/studentpoll/october /index.aspx.

Askin, N., and M. S. Bothner. 2016. Status-aspirational pricing: The "Chivas Regal" strategy in U.S. higher education, 2006–2012. *Administrative Science Quarterly* 61 (2): 217–53.

Avery, C. N., M. E. Glickman, C. M. Hoxby, and A. Metrick. 2013. A revealed preference ranking of U.S. colleges and universities. *Quarterly Journal of Economics* 128 (1): 425–67.

Baker, A., and N. Schweber. 2010, September 25. Seton Hall student is fatally shot at a party. *New York Times*. http://www.nytimes.com/2010/09/26/nyregion/26 seton.html.

Barron's Educational Series. 2016. *Barron's profiles of American colleges 2017*. Hauppauge, NY: Author.

Bastedo, M. N., and N. A. Bowman. 2010. *U.S. News and World Report* college rankings: Modeling institutional effects on organizational reputation. *American Journal of Education* 116 (2): 163–83.

———. 2011. College rankings as an interorganizational dependency: Establishing the foundation for strategic and institutional accounts. *Research in Higher Education* 52: 3–23.

Beale, C. L. 2013. *Fact book 2012–13*. South Orange, NJ: Seton Hall University.

Beaton, A. 2016, September 14. Atlantic Coast Conference to move championships from North Carolina, citing bathroom law. *Wall Street Journal*. http://

www.wsj.com/articles/atlantic-coast-conference-to-move-championships
-from-north-carolina-citing-bathroom-law-1473878119.

Bowman, N. A., and M. N. Bastedo. 2009. Getting on the front page: Organizational reputation, status signals, and the impact of *U.S. News and World Report* on student decisions. *Research in Higher Education* 50 (5): 415–36.

———. 2011. Anchoring effects in world university rankings: Exploring biases in reputation scores. *Higher Education* 61 (4): 431–44.

Brint, S., M. Riddle, and R. A. Hanneman. 2006. Reference sets, identities, and aspirations in a complex organizational field: The case of American four-year colleges and universities. *Sociology of Education* 79 (3): 229–52.

Brown, S., K. Mangan, and B. McMurtrie. 2016, May 24. At the end of a watershed year, can student activists sustain momentum? *Chronicle of Higher Education*. http://www.chronicle.com/article/At-the-End-of-a-Watershed/236577.

Cabrera, A. F., and S. M. La Nasa. 2000. Understanding the college choice process. *New Directions for Institutional Research* 107: 5–22.

Carnegie Classification of Institutions of Higher Education. 2016. 2015 update: Facts and figures. Bloomington: Center for Postsecondary Research, Indiana University School of Education.

Clark, A. 2015, June 12. Last women's college in N.J. going co-ed. *Star-Ledger*. http://www.nj.com/education/2015/06/njs_last_all-womens_college_to_admit_men.html.

Clarke, M. 2002. News or noise? An analysis of *U.S. News and World Report*'s ranking scores. *Educational Measurement: Issues and Practice* 21 (4): 39–48.

Crabbe, N. 2009, June 16. On survey, Machen rates UF with Harvard, other Fla. Schools low. *Gainesville Sun*. http://www.gainesville.com/news/20090616/on-survey-machen-rates-uf-with-harvard-other-fla-schools-low.

Cunha, J. M., and T. Miller. 2014. Measuring value-added in higher education: Possibilities and limitations in the use of administrative data. *Economics of Education Review* 42: 64–77.

Dennis, C., S. Papagiannidis, E. Alamanos, and M. Bourlakis. 2016. The role of brand attachment strength in higher education. *Journal of Business Research* 69: 3049–57.

Dichev, I. 2001. News or noise: Estimating the noise in the *U.S. News* university rankings. *Research in Higher Education* 42 (3): 237–66.

Dosh, K. 2013, April 29. Why are colleges at odds with adidas? *ESPN*. http://www.espn.com/blog/playbook/dollars/post/_/id/3390/why-are-colleges-at-odds-with-adidas.

Eagan, K., E. B. Stolzenberg, A. K. Bates, M. C. Aragon, M. R. Suchard, and C. Rios-Aguilar. 2016. *The American freshman: National norms for fall 2015*. Los Angeles: Cooperative Institutional Research Program, University of California, Los Angeles.

Eckles, J. E. 2010. Evaluating the efficiency of top liberal arts colleges. *Research in Higher Education* 51 (3): 266–93.

Education Conservancy, The. 2007. Letter to presidents. Accessed October 14, 2016. http://www.educationconservancy.org/presidents_letter.html.

Eff, E. A., C. C. Klein, and R. Kyle. 2012. Identifying the best buys in U.S. higher education. *Research in Higher Education* 53 (8): 860–87.

Ellis, L. 2016, December 13. Baylor sexual assault scandal could cost the college $220 million. *Houston Chronicle.* http://www.houstonchronicle.com/news /houston-texas/article/Costs-of-Baylor-scandal-may-reach-more-than-200 -10793488.php.

Espeland, W. N., and M. Sauder. 2007. Rankings and reactivity: How public measures recreate social worlds. *American Journal of Sociology* 113 (1): 1–40.

Espinosa, L. L., J. R. Crandall, and M. Tukibayeva. 2014. *Rankings, institutional behavior, and college and university choice: Framing the national dialogue on Obama's ratings plan.* Washington, DC: American Council on Education.

Fowles, J., H. G. Frederickson, and J. G. S. Koppell. 2016. University rankings: Evidence and a conceptual framework. *Public Administration Review* 76 (5): 790–803.

Freeland, R. E., K. I. Spenner, and G. McCalmon. 2015. I gave at the campus: Exploring student giving and its link to young alumni donations after graduation. *Nonprofit and Voluntary Sector Quarterly* 44 (4): 755–74.

Friedrich, A. 2011, September 13. College administrators: Rankings can be problematic. *Minnesota Public Radio.* http://blogs.mprnews.org/oncampus/2011 /09/college-administrators-rankings-can-be-problematic.

Gallup. 2016. *Gallup college and university presidents survey: 2016 survey findings.* Washington, DC: Gallup Education.

Global Credit Research. 2015, July 20. Moody's: US higher education outlook revised to stable as revenues stabilize. *Moody's Investors Service.* https://www .moodys.com/research/Moodys-US-higher-education-outlook-revised-to -stable-as-revenues--PR_330530.

Gnolek, S. L., V. T. Falciano, and R. Kuncl. 2014. Modeling change and variation in the *U.S. News and World Report* college rankings: What would it really take to be in the top 20? *Research in Higher Education* 55 (8): 761–79.

Grewal, R., J. A. Dearden, and G. L. Lilien. 2008. The university rankings game: Modeling the competition among universities for ranking. *American Statistician* 62 (3): 232–37.

Griffith, A., and K. Rask. 2007. The influence of the *US News and World Report* collegiate rankings on the matriculation decision of high-ability students, 1995–2004. *Economics of Education Review* 26: 244–55.

Harris, A. 2017, April 3. Media attention at Morehouse College will trigger investigation by accreditor. *Chronicle of Higher Education.* http://www.chronicle .com/blogs/ticker/media-attention-at-morehouse-college-will-trigger-investi gation-by-accreditor/117587.

Hazelkorn, E., ed. 2017. *Global rankings and the geopolitics of higher education.* New York: Routledge.

Hess, F. M., and T. Hochleitner. 2012. *College rankings inflation: Are you over-paying for prestige?* Washington, DC: American Enterprise Institute.

Hillman, N. W. 2016. Geography of college opportunity: The case of education deserts. *American Educational Research Journal* 53 (4): 987–1021.

Hillman, N. W., and T. Weichman. 2016. *Education deserts: The continued significance of "place" in the twenty-first century.* Washington, DC: American Council on Education.

Holmes, J. 2009. Prestige, charitable deductions, and other determinants of alumni giving: Evidence from a highly selective liberal arts college. *Economics of Education Review* 28: 18–28.

Hossler, D., J. Schmit, and N. Vesper. 1999. *Going to college: How social, economic, and educational factors influence the decisions students make.* Baltimore: Johns Hopkins University Press.

Hurwitz, M., and J. Smith. 2016. Student responsiveness to earnings data in the College Scorecard. Working paper.

Hutchinson, M., D. A. Rascher, and K. Jennings. 2016. A smaller window to the university: The impact of athletic de-escalation on status and reputation. *Journal of Intercollegiate Sport* 9: 73–89.

Iglesias, K. W. 2014. The price of prestige: A study of the impact of striving behavior on the expenditure patterns of American colleges and universities. Doctoral dissertation, Seton Hall University.

Jack Kent Cooke Foundation. 2015. List of selective colleges. Accessed October 27, 2016. http://www.jkcf.org/assets/1/7/The_Transfer_Process-2015_list_of _selective_colleges.pdf.

Jacob, B., B. McCall, and K. Stange. 2013. College as country club: Do colleges cater to students' preferences for consumption? Cambridge, MA: National Bureau of Economic Research Working Paper 18745.

Jaquette, O., and B. R. Curs. 2015. Creating the out-of-state university: Do public universities increase nonresident freshman enrollment in response to declining state appropriations? *Research in Higher Education* 56 (6): 535–65.

Jaquette, O., B. R. Curs, and J. R. Posselt. 2016. Tuition rich, mission poor: Nonresident enrollment growth and the socioeconomic and racial composition of public research universities. *Journal of Higher Education* 87 (5): 635–73.

Jaschik, S. 2007, March 19. Should *U.S. News* make presidents rich? *Inside Higher Ed.* https://www.insidehighered.com/news/2007/03/19/usnews.

———. 2012, July 27. Whose survey on "U.S. News"? *Inside Higher Ed.* https:// www.insidehighered.com/news/2012/07/27/questions-about-how-presidents -rank-institutions-are-raising-eyebrows.

———. 2013, January 28. How much admission misreporting? *Inside Higher Ed.* https://www.insidehighered.com/news/2013/01/28/bucknells-admission-raises -questions-about-how-many-colleges-are-reporting-false.

———. 2015, September 9. "U.S. News" adjusts survey calculations. *Inside Higher*

Ed. https://www.insidehighered.com/quicktakes/2015/09/09/us-news-adjusts
-survey-calculations.

Jaschik, S., and D. Lederman. 2014. *The 2014 Inside Higher Ed survey of college and university admissions directors.* Washington, DC: Gallup and Inside Higher Ed.

Jones, M. 2016, August 29. BYU celebrates 19th "stone-cold sober" designation with special-edition chocolate milk. *Deseret News.* http://www.deseretnews .com/article/865661282/BYU-celebrates-19th-Stone-Cold-Sober-designation -with-special-edition-chocolate-milk.html.

Kelchen, R., and D. N. Harris. 2012. *Can "value added" methods improve the measurement of college performance? Empirical analyses and policy implications.* Washington, DC: HCM Strategists.

Kim, J. 2015. The cost of rankings? The influence of college rankings on institutional management. Doctoral dissertation, University of Michigan.

Kingkade, T. 2016, August 29. UW-Madison is ranked the top party school for 2017 by *Princeton Review. Huffington Post.* http://www.huffingtonpost.com /entry/uw-madison-top-party-school_us_57c09881e4b04193420f1b9c.

Kurlaender, M., S. Carrell, and J. Jackson. 2016. The promises and pitfalls of measuring community college quality. *RSF: The Russell Sage Foundation Journal of the Social Sciences* 2 (1): 174–90.

Kutner, M. (2014, September). How to game the college rankings. *Boston Magazine.* http://www.bostonmagazine.com/news/article/2014/08/26/how-northeast ern-gamed-the-college-rankings.

Lane, J. E. 2007. The spider web of oversight: An analysis of external oversight of higher education. *Journal of Higher Education* 78 (6): 615–44.

Lederman, D. 2009, June 3. "Manipulating," er, influencing "U.S. News." *Inside Higher Ed.* https://www.insidehighered.com/news/2009/06/03/rankings.

Lee, S. 2009, August 19. Reputation without rigor. *Inside Higher Ed.* https://www .insidehighered.com/news/2009/08/19/rankings.

Leonhardt, D. 2013, April 4. What makes a college "selective"—and why it matters. *New York Times.* http://economix.blogs.nytimes.com/2013/04/04/what -makes-a-college-selective-and-why-it-matters.

Long, K. 2016, June 16. Green River College president resigns. *Seattle Times.* http://www.seattletimes.com/seattle-news/education/green-river-college-presi dent-resigns.

Longden, B. 2011. Ranking indicators and weights. In *University rankings: Theoretical basis, methodology, and impacts on global higher education,* edited by J. C. Shin, R. K. Toutkoushian, and U. Teichler, 73–104. Dordrecht, Netherlands: Springer.

Luca, M., P. Rooney, and J. Smith. 2016. The impact of campus scandals on college applications. Harvard Business School Working Paper 16–137.

Luca, M., and J. Smith. 2013. Salience in quality disclosure: Evidence from the

U.S. *News* college rankings. *Journal of Economics and Management Strategy* 22 (1): 58–77.

———. 2015. Strategic disclosure: The case of business school rankings. *Journal of Economic Behavior and Organizations* 112: 17–25.

Lydgate, C. 2015, September 29. Reed and the rankings game. *Reed College.* https://www.reed.edu/apply/college-rankings.html.

Lynch, M., and K. Alexander. 2015, September 13. All 128 Division I colleges ranked by everything other than sports (also, sports). *Thrillist.* https://www.thrillist.com/lifestyle/nation/every-bcs-division-i-school-ranked.

Marshall, M. 2016, January 13. President weighs in on "strategic plan." *Setonian.* http://www.thesetonian.com/2016/01/13/president-weighs-in-on-strategic-plan.

Martin, A. 2013, January 16. Moody's gives colleges a negative grade. *New York Times.* http://www.nytimes.com/2013/01/17/business/moodys-outlook-on-higher-education-turns-negative.html.

Martinez, J. M., J. L. Stinson, M. Kang, and C. B. Jubenville. 2010. Intercollegiate athletics and institutional fundraising: A meta-analysis. *Sport Marketing Quarterly* 19: 36–47.

McMurtrie, B. 2014, December 15. American Studies Association. *Chronicle of Higher Education.* http://www.chronicle.com/article/Boycotters-American-Studies/150845.

Merchant, A., G. M. Rose, G. Moody, and L. Mathews. 2015. Effect of university heritage and reputation on attitudes of prospective students. *International Journal of Nonprofit and Voluntary Sector Marketing* 20: 25–37.

Meredith, M. 2004. Why do universities compete in the ratings game? An empirical analysis of the effects of the *U.S. News and World Report* college rankings. *Research in Higher Education* 45 (5): 443–61.

Meyer, R 2013, October 29. Ranking the college ranking rankings. *Atlantic.* http://www.theatlantic.com/education/archive/2013/10/ranking-the-college-ranking-rankings/280965.

Monks, J., and R. G. Ehrenberg. 1999. The impact of *U.S. News and World Report* college rankings on admissions outcomes and pricing policies at selective private institutions. Cambridge, MA: National Bureau of Economic Research Working Paper 7227.

Moody's Investors Service. 2015, January 5. The financial and strategic outlook for private colleges. New York: Author.

Morphew, C. C. 2000. Institutional diversity, program acquisition, and faculty members: Examining academic drift at a new level. *Higher Education Policy* 13: 55–77.

Morphew, C. C., and B. D. Baker. 2004. The cost of prestige: Do new research I universities incur higher administrative costs? *Review of Higher Education* 27 (3): 365–84.

Morphew, C. C., and C. Swanson. 2011. On the efficacy of raising your university's rankings. In *University rankings: Theoretical basis, methodology, and impacts on global higher education*, edited by J. C. Shin, R. K. Toutkoushian, and U. Teichler, 185–99. Dordrecht, Netherlands: Springer.

Mytelka, A. 2016, May 27. Spellings says UNC system won't try to enforce controversial bathroom law. *Chronicle of Higher Education.* http://www.chronicle.com/blogs/ticker/spellings-says-unc-system-wont-try-to-enforce-controversial-bathroom-law/111714.

National Association for College Admission Counseling. 2011. A view of the U.S. News and World Report rankings of undergraduate institutions from the college admission counseling perspective. Arlington, VA: Author.

National Center for Education Statistics. 2016. *Digest of education statistics.* Washington, DC: Institute of Education Sciences, United States Department of Education.

New, J. 2016, October 25. The have and have-not gap *Inside Higher Ed.* https://www.insidehighered.com/news/2016/10/25/knight-commission-meeting-worries-over-spending-and-stability-football-bowl.

New Jersey Educational Facilities Authority. 2016. *2016 financings.* http://www.njefa.com/njefa/activity/recent/2016.

Nichols, A. 2015. *The Pell Partnership: Ensuring a shared responsibility for low-income student success.* Washington, DC: Education Trust.

Nichols, A., and J. L. Santos. 2016. *A glimpse inside the coffers: Endowment spending at wealthy colleges and universities.* Washington, DC: Education Trust.

North, A. 2013, April 30. The sexiest, smartest colleges in the country. *BuzzFeed.* https://www.buzzfeed.com/annanorth/the-sexiest-smartest-colleges-in-the-country.

Office of the President. 2007. 2011 goals. *Clemson University.* Accessed October 11, 2016. https://web.archive.org/web/20071110185207/http://www.clemson.edu/president/goals.html.

Ortagus, J. C. 2016. Pursing prestige in higher education: Stratification, status, and the influence of college rankings. *College and University* 91 (2): 11–19.

Peralta, E. 2016, September 13. N.C. GOP says NCAA should focus concern on the women "raped at Baylor." *National Public Radio.* http://www.npr.org/sections/thetwo-way/2016/09/13/493774034/n-c-gop-says-ncaa-should-focus-concern-on-the-women-raped-at-baylor.

Pike, G. R. 2004. Measuring quality: A comparison of *U.S. News* rankings and NSSE benchmarks. *Research in Higher Education* 45 (2): 193–208.

Playboy. 2015, September 14. *Playboy's* top party schools 2015. http://www.playboy.com/articles/playboys-top-party-schools-2015.

Pope, D. G., and J. C. Pope. 2009. The impact of college sports success on the quantity and quality of student applications. *Southern Economic Journal* 75 (3): 750–80.

Pryor, J. H., S. Hurtado, V. B. Saenz, J. A. Lindholm, W. S. Korn, and K. M. Mahoney.

2006. *The American freshman: National norms for fall 2005*. Los Angeles: Cooperative Institutional Research Program, University of California, Los Angeles.

Rivard, R. 2014, January 6. About-face on rankings. *Inside Higher Ed*. https://www.insidehighered.com/news/2014/01/06/syracuse-after-refusing-play-rankings-game-may-care-again.

Rothwell, J., and S. Kulkarni. 2015. *Beyond college rankings: A value-added approach to assessing two- and four-year schools*. Washington, DC: Brookings Institution Metropolitan Policy Program.

Saichaie, K., and C. C. Morphew. 2014. What college and university websites reveal about the purposes of higher education. *Journal of Higher Education* 85 (4): 499–530.

Sauder, M., and W. N. Espeland. 2009. The discipline of rankings: Tight coupling and organizational change. *American Sociological Review* 74 (1): 63–82.

Sax, L. J., A. W. Astin, W. S. Korn, and K. M. Mahoney. 1996. *The American freshman: National norms for fall 1995*. Los Angeles: Cooperative Institutional Research Program, University of California, Los Angeles.

Scarborough, A. 2015, July 21. UAB to reinstate football for 2017 season. *ESPN*. http://www.espn.com/college-football/story/_/id/13295966/uab-blazers-bring-back-football-program-2017.

Schisler, B., and R. Golden. 2016, January 19. Mount president's attempt to improve retention rates included seeking dismissal of 20–25 first-year students. *Mountain Echo*. http://msmecho.com/2016/01/19/mount-presidents-attempt-to-improve-retention-rate-included-seeking-dismissal-of-20-25-first-year-students.

Schlabach, M. 2015, May 28. Fired coaches who are still on the payroll. *ESPN*. http://www.espn.com/college-football/story/_/id/12963172/notre-dame-auburn-nebraska-pay-fired-coaches-huge-buyouts.

Scolforo, M. 2017, January 7. Penn State abuse scandal costs approach a quarter-billion. Associated Press. http://collegefootball.ap.org/article/penn-state-abuse-scandal-costs-approach-quarter-billion.

Segal, D. 2011, July 16. Law school economics: Ka-ching! *New York Times*. http://www.nytimes.com/2011/07/17/business/law-school-economics-job-market-weakens-tuition-rises.html.

Seton Hall University. 2016. *Rankings*. Accessed October 18, 2016. http://www.shu.edu/rankings.cfm.

Stevens, M. L. 2009. *Creating a class: College admissions and the education of elites*. Cambridge, MA: Harvard University Press.

Svrluga, S. 2016a, January 14. Ithaca College president resigns after protests over race issues. *Washington Post*. https://www.washingtonpost.com/news/grade-point/wp/2016/01/14/ithaca-college-president-resigns-after-protests-over-race-issues.

———. 2016b, February 29. Mount St. Mary's University president resigns. *The Washington Post*. Accessed October 25, 2016 from https://www.washington

post.com/news/grade-point/wp/2016/02/29/mount-st-marys-future-direction
-on-the-table-as-leaders-meet-today.

Teacher.org. 2016. Educational leadership degree. Accessed October 22, 2016.
http://www.teacher.org/degree/educational-administration/#college-rankings.

Thompson, N. 2003, August 3. The best, the top, the most. *New York Times.*
http://www.nytimes.com/2003/08/03/education/the-best-the-top-the-most
.html.

Tracy, M. 2017, April 4. N.C.A.A. ends boycott of North Carolina after so-called
bathroom bill is repealed. *New York Times.* https://www.nytimes.com/2017
/04/04/sports/ncaa-hb2-north-carolina-boycott-bathroom-bill.html.

van Raan, T., T. van Leeuwen, and M. Visser. 2011. Non-English papers decrease
rankings. *Nature* 469: 34.

Van Thiel, S., and F. L. Leeuw. 2002. The performance paradox in the public sector. *Public Performance and Management Review* 25 (3): 267–81.

Volkwein, J. F., and K. V. Sweitzer. 2006. Institutional prestige and reputation
among research universities and liberal arts colleges. *Research in Higher Education* 47 (2): 129–48.

Watt, C. 2009. Strategic planning: Project management and lessons in moving
up the US News ranks. Presentation given at the Association for Institutional
Research annual conference, Atlanta.

White, L., J. Harvey, and T. Ludwig. 2014, June. Bond ratings begin to part ways.
Business Officer. http://www.nacubo.org/Business_Officer_Magazine/Magazine
_Archives/June_2014/Bond_Ratings_Begin_to_Part_Ways.html.

Winston, G. C. 1999. Subsidies, hierarchy and peers: The awkward economics of
higher education. *Journal of Economic Perspectives* 13 (1): 13–36.

Wolverton, B., and D. Bauman. 2016, October 9. As sports spending soars, programs scramble to keep up. *Chronicle of Higher Education.* http://www.chron
icle.com/article/As-Sports-Spending-Soars/238017.

Woodhouse, K. 2015, September 28. Closures to triple. *Inside Higher Ed.* https://
www.insidehighered.com/news/2015/09/28/moodys-predicts-college-closures
-triple-2017.

Chapter Seven: Institutional Accountability Policies and Practices

AAUP (American Association of University Professors). n.d. Statement on government on colleges and universities. Accessed August 16, 2016. https://www
.aaup.org/report/statement-government-colleges-and-universities.

———. 1940. 1940 statement of principles on academic freedom and tenure.
Washington, DC: Author.

———. 2015, June 13. AAUP censures four, removes censure from one. https://
www.aaup.org/media-release/aaup-censures-four-removes-censure-one.

ACE (American Council on Education). 2012. *The American college president:
2012 edition.* Washington, DC: Author.

ACTA (American Council of Trustees and Alumni). 2015. Temperate radicals: Celebrating two decades of hard-charging higher education reform. Washington, DC: Author.

———. 2016, July 6. ACTA statement: Association of Governing Boards shows true colors.https://www.goacta.org/news/acta_statement_association_of_gov erning_boards_shows_true_colors.

Adair, D., and K. Shattuck. 2015. Quality Matters: An educational input in an ongoing design-based research project. *American Journal of Distance Education* 29 (3): 159–65.

AGB (Association of Governing Boards of Universities and Colleges). 2010. Statement on board responsibility for institutional governance. Washington, DC: Author.

AGB Editor. 2016, May 12. Board demographics [infographic]. *Association of Governing Boards of Universities and Colleges*. http://agb.org/blog/2016/05/12 /board-demographics-infographic.

APLU (Association of Public and Land-Grant Universities). n.d. Voluntary system of accountability (VSA). Accessed August 19, 2016. http://www.aplu.org /projects-and-initiatives/accountability-and-transparency/voluntary-system-of -accountability.

Bastedo, M. N. 2005. The making of an activist governing board. *Review of Higher Education* 28 (4): 551–70.

———. 2009a. Convergent institutional logics in public higher education: State policymaking and governing board activism. *Review of Higher Education* 32 (2): 209–34.

———. 2009b. Conflicts, commitments, and cliques in the university: Moral seduction as a threat to trustee independence. *American Educational Research Journal* 46 (2): 354–86.

Baylor University. n.d. About the board of regents. Accessed September 6, 2016. http://www.baylor.edu/president/index.php?id=1457.

Benjamin, R. 2007. Recreating the faculty role in university governance. In *Fixing the fragmented university*, edited by J. C. Burke, 70–98. Bolton, MA: Anker.

Berry, J., and M. Savarese. 2012. *Directory of U.S. faculty contracts and bargaining agents in institutions of higher education*. New York: National Center for the Study of Collective Bargaining in Higher Education and the Professions.

Bettinger, E. P., and B. T. Long. 2010. Does cheaper mean better? The impact of using adjunct instructors on student outcomes. *Review of Economics and Statistics* 92 (3): 598–613.

Bok, D. 2013. The trouble with shared governance. *Trusteeship* 21 (5): 18–23.

Braga, M., M. Paccagnella, and M. Pellizzari. 2014. Evaluating students' evaluations of professors. *Economics of Education Review* 41: 71–88.

Brint, S., M. Riddle, and R. A. Hanneman. 2006. Reference sets, identities, and aspirations in a complex organizational field: The case of American four-year colleges and universities. *Sociology of Education* 79 (3): 229–52.

Brown, W. O., Jr. 2013. University board composition: Causes and consequences. *Managerial and Decision Economics* 35: 318–36.

Bucklew, N., J. D. Houghton, and C. N. Ellison. 2013. Faculty union and faculty senate co-existence: A review of the impact of academic collective bargaining on traditional academic governance. *Labor Studies Journal* 37 (4): 373–90.

Carrell, S. E., and J. E. West. 2010. Does professor quality matter? Evidence from random assignment of students to professors. *Journal of Political Economy* 118 (3): 409–32.

Cassell, M., and O. Halaseh. 2014. The impact of unionization on university performance. *Journal of Collective Bargaining in the Academy* 6, article 3.

Charis-Carlson, J. 2016, June 19. University of Iowa sanctioned by national professor group. *Des Moines Register.* http://www.desmoinesregister.com/story/news/education/2016/06/18/national-professor-group-sanctions-university-iowa/86085620.

Clemson University. 2015. Board of trustees home. Accessed August 16, 2016. http://www.clemson.edu/administration/bot.

Cohen, J. S. 2015, November 12. University of Illinois OKs $875,000 settlement to end Steven Salaita dispute. *Chicago Tribune.* http://www.chicagotribune.com/news/local/breaking/ct-steven-salaita-settlement-met-20151112-story.html.

Cohen, J. S., S. St. Clair, and T. Malone. 2009a, May 29. Clout goes to college. *Chicago Tribune.* http://www.chicagotribune.com/news/chi-uofi-clout-story.html.

———. 2009b, September 24. University of Illinois president B. Joseph White resigns. *Chicago Tribune.* http://www.chicagotribune.com/news/chi-u-of-i-white-resign-24-sep24-story.html.

Corrigan, M. E. 2002. *The American college president: 2002 edition.* Washington, DC: American Council on Education Center for Policy Analysis.

Eagan, M. K., Jr., and A. J. Jaeger. 2009. Effects of exposure to part-time faculty on community college transfer. *Research in Higher Education* 50 (2): 168–88.

Ehrenberg, R. G., R. Patterson, and A. Key. 2012. Faculty members on boards of trustees: The 2012 Cornell higher education research institute survey of faculty trustees. Ithaca, NY: Cornell University School of Industrial and Labor Relations Working Paper 149.

Ehrenberg, R. G., and L. Zhang. 2005. Do tenured and tenure-track faculty matter? *Journal of Human Resources* 40 (3): 647–59.

Fairweather, J. S. 2005. Beyond the rhetoric: Trends in the relative value of teaching and research in faculty salaries. *Journal of Higher Education* 76 (4): 401–22.

Field, K., and P. Fain. 2011, February 13. For-profit college boards tap leaders from government and nonprofit higher education. *Chronicle of Higher Education.* http://chronicle.com/article/on-for-profit-college-boards/126338.

Figlio, D. N., M. O. Schapiro, and K. B. Soter. 2015. Are tenure track professors better teachers? *Review of Economics and Statistics* 97 (4): 715–24.

Finkelstein, M. J., V. M. Conley, and J. H. Schuster. 2016. *The faculty factor: Reassessing the American academy in a turbulent era.* Baltimore: Johns Hopkins University Press.

Finkin, M. W., and M. Decesare. 2016. College and university governance: The University of Iowa governing board's selection of a president. *Academe* 102: 52–68.

Flaherty, C. 2013, November 18. Adjunct connections. *Inside Higher Ed.* https://www.insidehighered.com/news/2013/11/18/union-conference-marks-growth-adjunct-organizing-strategy.

———. 2016, September 1. Going hungry for tenure. *Inside Higher Ed.* https://www.insidehighered.com/news/2016/09/01/lafayette-professor-goes-hunger-strike-protest-presidents-veto-his-tenure-bid.

Gagliardi, J. S., L. L. Espinosa, J. M. Turk, and M. Taylor. 2017. *American college president study 2017.* Washington, DC: American Council on Education.

Gardner, L. 2016, June 19. Turmoil raises specter of faculty exodus from public colleges. *Chronicle of Higher Education.* http://chronicle.com/article/Turmoil-Raises-Specter-of/236854.

Gerber, L. G. 2014. *The rise and decline of faculty governance: Professionalization and the modern American university.* Baltimore: Johns Hopkins University Press.

Ginsberg, B. 2011. *The fall of the faculty: The rise of the all-administrative university and why it matters.* New York: Oxford University Press.

Glauber, B. 2016, May 24. Appeals court judge orders Wisconsin's right to work law reinstated. *Milwaukee Journal Sentinel.* http://archive.jsonline.com/news/statepolitics/appeals-court-judge-orders-wisconsins-right-to-work-law-reinstated-b99731959z1-380738391.html.

Gonzales, L. D. 2013. Faculty sensemaking and mission creep: Interrogating institutionalized ways of knowing and doing legitimacy. *Review of Higher Education* 36 (2): 179–209.

Hedrick, D. W., S. E. Henson, J. M. Krieg, and C. S. Wassell Jr. 2011. Is there really a faculty union salary premium? *Industrial and Labor Relations Review* 64 (3): 558–75.

Helfing, K. 2015, July 12. Walker erodes college professor tenure. *Politico.* http://www.politico.com/story/2015/07/scott-walker-college-professor-tenure-120009.

Hermalin, B. E. 2004. Higher education boards of trustees. In *Governing academia: Who is in charge at the modern university?*, edited by R. Ehrenberg, 28–48. Ithaca, NY: Cornell University Press.

Herzog, K. 2016, December 8. Nonresident tuition at UW schools going up. *Inside Higher Ed.* http://www.jsonline.com/story/news/education/2016/12/08/nonresident-tuition-uw-schools-going-up/95145354.

Hodge-Clark, K. 2014. *The 2014 AGB survey of higher education governance.* Washington, DC: Association of Governing Boards of Universities and Colleges.

Iglesias, K. W. 2014. The price of prestige: A study of the impact of striving behavior on the expenditure patterns of American colleges and universities. Doctoral dissertation, Seton Hall University.

Inside Higher Ed. 2013, April 18. Groups retract paper that criticized faculty workloads. *Inside Higher Ed.* https://www.insidehighered.com/quicktakes/2013/04/18/groups-retract-paper-criticized-faculty-workloads.

———. 2016, September 2. Moody's: Grad student unionization "credit negative." https://www.insidehighered.com/quicktakes/2016/09/02/moodys-grad-student-unionization-credit-negative.

Jaeger, A. J., and M. K. Eagan Jr. 2009. Unintended consequences: Examining the effect of part-time faculty members on associate's degree completion. *Community College Review* 36 (3): 167–94.

Jaschik, S. 2007, September 10. Dartmouth approves controversial board changes. *Inside Higher Ed.* https://www.insidehighered.com/news/2007/09/10/Dartmouth.

———. 2015a, January 2. Big union win. *Inside Higher Ed.* https://www.insidehighered.com/news/2015/01/02/nlrb-ruling-shifts-legal-ground-faculty-unions-private-colleges.

———. 2015b, March 4. Shocking decision at Sweet Briar. *Inside Higher Ed.* https://www.insidehighered.com/news/2015/03/04/sweet-briar-college-will-shut-down.

———. 2016. Is tenure essential? *Inside Higher Ed.* https://www.insidehighered.com/news/2016/01/06/private-college-presidents-draft-list-essential-qualities-institutions-leaves-tenure.

Jaschik, S., and D. Lederman. 2014. *The 2014 Inside Higher Ed survey of college and university chief academic officers.* Washington, DC: Gallup.

———. 2015. *The 2015 Inside Higher Ed survey of college and university chief academic officers.* Washington, DC: Gallup.

———. 2016. *The 2016 Inside Higher Ed survey of college and university chief academic officers.* Washington, DC: Gallup.

Jung, Y. 2017, April 7. Arizona Board of Regents approves nearly $1M contract for new UA president. *Arizona Daily Star.* http://tucson.com/news/local/education/arizona-board-of-regents-approves-nearly-m-contract-for-new/article_9d2a3446-3cf1-5b94-b545-ef8c852ace97.html.

Kaplan, G. E. 2004. Do governance structures matter? *New Directions for Higher Education* 127: 23–34.

Kapsidelis, K. 2015, June 20. Agreement reached to keep Sweet Briar open. *Richmond Times-Dispatch.* http://www.richmond.com/news/virginia/article_4b2fo3d8-a089-5f8c-9c39-6faa19da07ce.html.

Katsinas, S. G., J. A. Ogun, and N. J. Bray. 2016. Monetary compensation of full-time faculty at American public regional universities: The impact of geography and the existence of collective bargaining. Paper presented at the National Conference of the National Center for the Study of Collective Bargaining in Higher Education and the Professions, New York.

Kelderman, E. 2015, November 30. Upheaval in Missouri highlights football players' power. *Chronicle of Higher Education.* http://www.chronicle.com/article /Upheaval-in-Missouri/234130.

Keller, R. 2015, November 29. Legislative questions about faculty teaching loads add to University of Missouri woes. *Columbia Daily Tribune.* http://www.co lumbiatribune.com/news/politics/legislative-questions-about-faculty-teaching -loads-add-to-university-of/article_005504f7-1ce0-516a-bd94-9e75ae94d5cb .html.

———. 2016, August 27. Other Missouri universities gain enrollment as MU numbers drop. *Columbia Daily Tribune.* http://www.chronicle.com/article/Inside -How-Missouri-s/236208.

Kremer, R. 2016, May 30. UW-Eau Claire faculty approves no-confidence vote on UW System leadership. *Wisconsin Public Radio.* http://www.wpr.org/uw-eau -claire-faculty-approves-no-confidence-vote-uw-system-leadership.

Kuta, S. 2016, January 30. In purple Colorado, at-large CU regents seat anyone's to win. *Boulder Daily Camera.* http://www.dailycamera.com/cu-news/ci _29451918/purple-colorado-at-large-cu-regents-seat-anyones.

Legon, R. 2014, August 21. Board accountability, not board activism. *Association of Governing Boards of Universities and Colleges.* http://agb.org/blog/2014/08 /21/board-accountability-not-board-activism.

Legon, R., and J. Runyon. 2007. *Research on the impact of the Quality Matters course review process.* Paper presented at the 23rd Annual Conference on Distance Teaching and Learning, Madison, WI.

Lewin, T. 2007, September 8. Battle over board structures at Dartmouth raises passions of alumni. *New York Times.* http://www.nytimes.com/2007/09/08/us /08dartmouth.html.

Longanecker, D. A. 2006. The "new" new challenge of governance by governing boards. In *Governance and the public good,* edited by W. G. Tierney, 95–116. Albany, NY: State University of New York Press.

Lounder, A. 2016. *Shared governance: Is OK good enough?* Washington, DC: Association of Governing Boards of Universities and Colleges.

Mackey, R. 2014, September 12. Professor's angry tweets on Gaza cost him a job. *New York Times.* https://www.nytimes.com/2014/09/13/world/middleeast/pro fessors-angry-tweets-on-gaza-cost-him-a-job.html.

MacNell, L., A. Driscoll, and A. N. Hunt. 2014. What's in a name: Exposing gender bias in student ratings of teaching. *Innovative Higher Education* 40: 291–303.

Malone, T., S. St. Clair, and J. S. Cohen. 2009, August 19. University of Illinois: 4 more trustees offer to quit. *Chicago Tribune.* http://www.chicagotribune.com /news/chi-u-of-i-clout-19-aug19-story.html.

McClure, K. R. 2016. Building the innovative and entrepreneurial university: An institutional case study of administrative academic capitalism. *Journal of Higher Education* 87 (4): 516–43.

McCrea, E., and M. Deyrup. 2016. The devil is in the details: A review of merit pay in higher education. Paper presented at the Eastern Academy of Management annual conference, New Haven, CT.

McNair, J. 2015, August 6. Democrat heavy college boards run counter to Kentucky law. *Kentucky Center for Investigative Reporting*. http://kycir.org/2015/08/06/democrat-heavy-college-boards-run-counter-to-kentucky-law.

Middleton, C. R. 2010. The virtues of student and faculty trustees. *Trusteeship* 18 (4): 24–27.

Minor, J. T. 2008. The relationship between selection processes of public trustees and state higher education performance. *Educational Policy* 22 (6): 830–53.

Morphew, C. C. 2000. Institutional diversity, program acquisition, and faculty members: Examining academic drift at a new level. *Higher Education Policy* 13: 55–77.

Morphew, C. C., and B. D. Baker. 2004. The cost of prestige: Do new research I universities incur higher administrative costs? *Review of Higher Education* 27 (3): 365–84.

NAICU (National Association of Independent Colleges and Universities. 2014). The university and college accountability network. Accessed August 19, 2016. https://www.naicu.edu/special%5Finitiatives/accountability/publications.

National Conference of State Legislatures. 2016. Right-to-work resources. Accessed September 13, 2016. http://www.ncsl.org/research/labor-and-employment/right-to-work-laws-and-bills.aspx.

Porter, S. R. 2013. The causal effect of faculty unions on institutional decision-making. *Industrial and Labor Relations Review* 66 (5): 1192–1211.

Pounds, J. 2016, August 17. Sweet Briar profs gear up for semester: year of rebuilding, reassessment ahead. *News and Advance*. http://www.newsadvance.com/news/local/sweet-briar-profs-gear-up-for-semester-year-of-rebuilding/article_c41a8037-ba37-51cb-8339-c56dc7eca82a.html.

Premeaux, S. R. 2008. Administrative versus faculty perspectives regarding academic tenure. *Journal of Academic Administration in Higher Education* 4 (1): 47–55.

Pusser, B., S. Slaughter, and S. L. Thomas. 2006. Playing the board game: An empirical analysis of university trustee and corporate board interlocks. *Journal of Higher Education* 77 (5): 747–75.

Quality Matters. 2016. 2016 QM-recognized courses—all programs. https://www.qmprogram.org/qmresources/courses/index.cfm?year=2016andprogram=0.

Reid, L. D. 2010. The role of perceived race and gender in the evaluation of college teaching on ratemyprofessors.com. *Journal of Diversity in Higher Education* 3 (3): 137–52.

Rivard, R. 2013, September 4. Limited confidence in boards. *Inside Higher Ed.* https://www.insidehighered.com/news/2013/09/04/college-presidents-harbor-doubts-about-governing-boards.

Rogers, S. E., A. E. Eaton, and P. B. Voos. 2013. Effects of unionization on graduate student employees: Faculty-student relations, academic freedom, and pay. *Industrial and Labor Relations Review* 66 (2): 487–510.

Rothgeb, J. M., Jr. 2014. When tenure protects the incompetent: Results from a survey of department chairs. *PS: Political Science and Politics* 47 (1): 182–87.

Rutgers, the State University of New Jersey. 2016. Governing boards of the university. Accessed August 24, 2016. http://governingboards.rutgers.edu.

Savidge, N. 2016, May 10. Scott Walker blasts professors as UW-Milwaukee faculty vote "no confidence" in leaders. *Wisconsin State Journal*. http://host.mad ison.com/wsj/news/local/education/university/scott-walker-blasts-professors -as-uw-milwaukee-faculty-vote-no/article_2ab47aeb-3344-50c2-a026-8693 86f1144c.html.

Schmidt, P. 2015, June 4. Wisconsin's fight over faculty rights: What's at stake, and what's next. *Chronicle of Higher Education*. http://chronicle.com/article /Wisconsin-s-Fight-Over/230663.

———. 2016, March 10. Wisconsin regents approve new layoff and tenure policies over faculty objections. *Chronicle of Higher Education*. http://chronicle .com/blogs/ticker/wisconsin-regents-approve-new-layoff-and-tenure -policies-over-faculty-objections/109380.

Schneider, P. 2016, May 23. Robin Vos: UW faculty no-confidence votes "a big mistake." *Capital Times*. http://host.madison.com/ct/news/local/education/uni versity/robin-vos-uw-faculty-no-confidence-votes-a-big-mistake/article_aefea 4c4-66c3-5e2b-bba5-b3f867176f3d.html.

Schultz, D. 2015. The rise and coming demise of the corporate university. *Academe* 101 (5): 21–23.

Schwartz, M. P. 2010a. *Policies, practices, and composition of governing boards of public colleges, universities, and systems.* Washington, DC: Association of Governing Boards of Universities and Colleges.

———. 2010b. *Policies, practices, and composition of governing boards of independent colleges and universities.* Washington, DC: Association of Governing Boards of Universities and Colleges.

Schwartz, M. P., R. Skinner, and Z. Bowen. 2009. *Faculty, governing boards, and institutional governance.* Washington, DC: Association of Governing Boards of Universities and Colleges.

Seton Hall University. 2016, August 4. University by-laws. https://www13.shu .edu/offices/board-affairs/upload/University-By-Laws.pdf.

Slaughter, S., and G. Rhoades. 2004. *Academic capitalism and the new economy.* Baltimore: Johns Hopkins University Press.

Slaughter, S., S. L. Thomas, D. R. Johnson, and S. N. Barringer. 2014. Institutional conflict of interest: The role of interlocking directorates in the scientific relationships between universities and the corporate sector. *Journal of Higher Education* 85 (1): 1–35.

Spencer Stuart. 2015. 2015 Spencer Stuart board index. Chicago: Author.

State of Illinois Admissions Review Commission. 2009. Report and recommendations. Springfield, IL: Author.

Stolberg, S. G. 2015, June 23. Sweet Briar College is saved but not in the clear.

New York Times. http://www.nytimes.com/2015/06/24/us/sweet-briar-college
is-saved-but-not-in-the-clear.html.

Stripling, J. 2011, February 15. With unions under threat, academics join huge
rally in Wisconsin. *Chronicle of Higher Education.* http://www.chronicle.com
/article/with-unions-under-threat/126379.

Student Achievement Measure. 2013. Participants. Accessed June 23, 2017. http://
www.studentachievementmeasure.org/participants.

Suntrup, E. L. 1981. *NLRB v. Yeshiva University* and unionization in higher education. *Berkeley Journal of Employment and Labor Law* 4 (2): 287–307.

Svrluga, S. 2015, June 9. Va. Supreme Court says lower court erred in Sweet Briar
case, sends it back, as advocates cheer. *Washington Post.* https://www.washing
tonpost.com/news/grade-point/wp/2015/06/09/va-supreme-court-says-lower
-court-erred-in-sweet-briar-case-sends-it-back-as-advocates-cheer.

Thomas, R. S., and R. L. Van Horn. 2016. Are college presidents like football
coaches? Evidence from their employment contracts. Nashville, TN: Vanderbilt University Law School Law and Economics Working Paper Number 16-4.

Thomason, A. 2016, August 23. In victory for union efforts, NLRB rules Columbia U. grad students are employees. *Chronicle of Higher Education.* http://
chronicle.com/blogs/ticker/in-victory-for-union-efforts-nlrb-rules-columbia
-u-grad-students-are-employees/113679.

Thornton, S., and J. W. Curtis. 2012. A very slow recovery: The annual report on
the economic status of the profession, 2011–12. *Academe* 98 (2): 4–15.

Todd, L. 2014, September 27. Party makeup of University of Wyoming trustees
violates state rules. *Casper Star-Tribune.* http://trib.com/news/local/education
/party-makeup-of-university-of-wyoming-trustees-violates-state-rules/article
_d5b0c6d0-1e0a-53af-ad75-b15f1202b22f.html.

Trustees of Princeton University. 2012, September 11. Composition, responsibilities and committees. https://www.princeton.edu/vpsec/trustees/composition.

Umbach, P. D. 2007. How effective are they? Exploring the impact of contingent faculty on undergraduate education. *Review of Higher Education* 30 (2): 91–118.

University of Missouri System. 2016, August 23. Board of curators. https://www
.umsystem.edu/curators.

University of Rochester. 2015, May 14. Board of trustees: Bylaws of the University of Rochester. https://www.rochester.edu/aboutus/bylaws.pdf.

University of Vermont. 2015. Board of trustees. Accessed August 16, 2016. http://
www.uvm.edu/trustees.

Wexler, E. 2016, April 13. Dual loyalties. *Inside Higher Ed.* https://www.inside
highered.com/news/2016/04/13/presidents-public-universities-criticized-joining
-boards-profit-university.

Wilkins, W. K. 2012. On NOT aspiring to the presidency. *Presidency* 15 (2): 8–10.

Will, M. 2015, April 23. Iowa legislator wants to give students the chance to fire
underwhelming faculty. *Chronicle of Higher Education.* http://www.chronicle
.com/article/Iowa-Legislator-Wants-to-Give/229589.

Wisconsin State Legislature. 2016, August 19. Chapter 36: University of Wisconsin system. Accessed August 19, 2016. http://docs.legis.wisconsin.gov/statutes/statutes/36/09.

Youn, T. I. K., and T. M. Price. 2009. Learning from the experience of others: The evolution of faculty tenure and promotion rules in comprehensive institutions. *Journal of Higher Education* 80 (2): 204–37.

Zumeta, W. 2001. Public policy and accountability in higher education: Lessons from the past and present for the new millennium. In *The states and public higher education policy: Affordability, access, and accountability*, edited by D. E. Heller, 155–97. Baltimore: Johns Hopkins University Press.

Chapter Eight: Ten Lessons Learned from Accountability Policies

Alter, M., and R. Reback. 2014. True for your school? How changing reputations alter demand for selective U.S. colleges. *Educational Evaluation and Policy Analysis* 36 (3): 346–70.

Anderson, N. 2014, February 2. U-Md.'s unusual admissions approach: One out of every five freshmen starts in spring term. *Washington Post.* https://www.washingtonpost.com/local/education/u-mds-unusual-admissions-approach-one-out-of-every-five-freshmen-start-in-spring-term/2014/01/31/21d99a64-8794-11e3-916e-e01534b1e132_story.html.

Armstrong, J., and K. Zaback. 2016. *Assessing and improving state postsecondary data systems.* Washington, DC: Institute for Higher Education Policy.

Bailey, T., and D. Xu. 2012. *Input-adjusted graduation rates and college accountability: What is known from twenty years of research?* Washington, DC: HCM Strategists.

Bastedo, M. N., and N. A. Bowman. 2011. College rankings as an interorganizational dependency: Establishing the foundation for strategic and institutional accounts. *Research in Higher Education* 52: 3–23.

Baty, P. 2016, September 5. THE university world rankings 2016–2017 passes independent audit. https://www.timeshighereducation.com/news/world-university-rankings-2016-2017-passes-independent-audit.

Blumenstyk, G., and A. Richards. 2011, March 13. Many for-profits are "managing" defaults to mask problems, analysis indicates. *Chronicle of Higher Education.* http://www.chronicle.com/article/Many-For-Profits-Are/126689.

Booher-Jennings, J. 2005. Below the bubble: "Educational triage" and the Texas accountability system. *American Educational Research Journal* 42 (2): 231–68.

Campbell, D. T. 1979. Assessing the impact of planned social change. *Evaluation and Program Planning* 2 (1): 67–90.

Chakrabarti, R. 2013. Accountability with voucher threats, responses, and the test-taking population: Regression discontinuity evidence from Florida. *Education Finance and Policy* 8 (2): 121–67.

Cochrane, D., and L. Szabo-Kubitz. 2016. *States of denial: Where community* college students lack access to federal student loans. Oakland, CA: Institute for College Access and Success.

Council of Economic Advisers. 2015. *Using federal data to measure and improve the performance of U.S. institutions of higher education*. Washington, DC: Executive Office of the President of the United States.

Darling-Hammond, L. 2010. Teacher education and the American future. *Journal of Teacher Education* 61 (1/2): 35–47.

Dougherty, K. J., and R. S. Natow. 2015. *The politics of performance funding for higher education: Origins, discontinuations, and transformations*. Baltimore: Johns Hopkins University Press.

Eagan, K., E. B. Stolzenberg, A. K. Bates, M. C. Aragon, M. R. Suchard, and C. Rios-Aguilar. 2016. *The American freshman: National norms for fall 2015*. Los Angeles: Cooperative Institutional Research Program, University of California, Los Angeles.

Federal Student Aid. n.d. What do I do if I'm told I've been selected for verification? Accessed November 5, 2016. https://studentaid.ed.gov/sa/fafsa/next-steps #verification.

———. 2016a, June 17. 2014–2015 federal Pell Grant program end-of-year report. http://www2.ed.gov/finaid/prof/resources/data/pell-2014-15/pell-eoy-2014 -15.html.

———. 2016b, September 25. eCDR appeals system. https://ecdrappeals.ed.gov /ecdra/index.html.

Figlio, D. N. 2006. Testing, crime and punishment. *Journal of Public Economics* 90 (4/5): 837–51.

Gallup. 2015. *Great jobs, great lives: The relationship between student debt, experiences and perceptions of college worth*. Washington, DC: Author.

Hillman, N. W. 2016. *Why performance-based college funding doesn't work*. Washington, DC: Century Foundation.

Holmes, J. 2009. Prestige, charitable deductions, and other determinants of alumni giving: Evidence from a highly selective liberal arts college. *Economics of Education Review* 28: 18–28.

Horn, A. S., and G. Lee. 2016. The reliability and validity of using regression residuals to measure institutional effectiveness in promoting degree completion. *Research in Higher Education* 57 (4): 469–96.

Internal Revenue Service. 2016. *2015 Internal Revenue Service data book*. Washington, DC: Author.

Kelchen, R. 2016. A note on methodology: 4-year colleges and universities. *Washington Monthly*. Accessed November 5, 2016. http://washingtonmonthly.com /magazine/septemberoctober-2016/a-note-on-methodology-4-year-colleges -and-universities-7.

Kelchen, R., and A. Li. 2017. Institutional accountability: A comparison of the predictors of student loan repayment and default rates. *The ANNALS of the American Academy of Political and Social Science* 671: 202–23.

Kelchen, R., and L. J. Stedrak. 2016. Does performance-based funding affect colleges' fiscal priorities? *Journal of Education Finance* 41 (3): 302–21.

Koedel, C., K. Mihaly, and J. E. Rockoff. 2015. Value-added modeling: A review. *Economics of Education Review* 47: 180–95.

Koning, P., and C. Heinrich. 2013. Cream-skimming, parking, and other intended and unintended effects of high-powered, performance-based contracts. *Journal of Policy Analysis and Management* 32 (3): 461–83.

Kreighbaum, A. 2016, September 21. Tougher scrutiny for colleges with low graduation rates. *Inside Higher Ed.* https://www.insidehighered.com/news/2016/09/21/regional-accreditors-refocus-institutions-low-grad-rates.

Laitinen, A., and C. McCann. 2014. *College blackout: How the higher education lobby fought to keep students in the dark.* Washington, DC: New America.

Massy, W. F. 2016. *Course-level activity-based costing as an academic and financial tool.* New York: TIAA Institute and NACUBO.

McGuire, P. 2007, May 14. Rank this, *US News. Los Angeles Times.* http://www.latimes.com/la-oe-mcguire14may14-story.html.

Minaya, V., and J. Scott-Clayton. 2016. Labor market outcomes and postsecondary accountability: Are imperfect metrics better than none? Cambridge, MA: National Bureau of Economic Research Working Paper 22880.

Morse, R. 2013, May 14. Updates to 2 schools' 2013 best colleges ranks. *U.S. News and World Report.* http://www.usnews.com/education/blogs/college-rankings-blog/2013/05/14/updates-to-2-schools-2013-best-colleges-ranks.

National Conference of State Legislatures. 2015, July 31. *Performance-based funding for higher education.* http://www.ncsl.org/research/education/performance-funding.aspx.

NCES (National Center for Education Statistics). n.d. Survey design. Accessed November 5, 2016. https://nces.ed.gov/statprog/handbook/ipeds_surveydesign.asp.
———. 2016. IPEDS 2015–16 prior year data revision system. Accessed November 5, 2016. https://surveys.nces.ed.gov/ipeds_py.

Neal, D., and D. W. Schanzenbach. 2010. Left behind by design: Proficiency counts and test-based accountability. *Review of Economics and Statistics* 92 (2): 263–83.

Schisler, B., and R. Golden. 2016, January 19. Mount president's attempt to improve retention rates included seeking dismissal of 20–25 first-year students. *Mountain Echo.* http://msmecho.com/2016/01/19/mount-presidents-attempt-to-improve-retention-rate-included-seeking-dismissal-of-20-25-first-year-students.

Selingo, J. J., and M. Van Der Werf. 2016. *Linking appropriations for the Texas State Technical College system to student employment outcomes.* Indianapolis: Lumina Foundation.

Seltzer, R. 2016, November 1. Law schools flagged for job data. *Inside Higher Ed.* https://www.insidehighered.com/news/2016/11/01/initial-audit-finds-flaws-some-law-school-employment-reporting-practices.

Snyder, M., and B. Fox. 2016. *Driving better outcomes: Fiscal year 2016 state status and typology update.* Washington, DC: HCM Strategists.

Sparks, D., and N. Malkus. 2013. First-year undergraduate remedial counseling: 1999–2000, 2003–04, 2007–08. Washington, DC: National Center for Education Statistics Report 2013–013.

State Council of Higher Education for Virginia. n.d. Four-year bachelor's degree, all graduates at this degree level, graduates from 2007–08 to 2011–12 (five-year rollups), wage outcomes. Accessed November 1, 2016. http://research .schev.edu/eom/opportunity_4yrbachelors_report.asp.

Umbricht, M. R., F. Fernandez, and J. C. Ortagus. 2017. An examination of the (un)intended consequences of performance funding in higher education. *Educational Policy* 31 (5): 643–73.

Van Thiel, S., and F. L. Leeuw. 2002. The performance paradox in the public sector. *Public Performance and Management Review* 25 (3): 267–81.

Wiederspan, M. 2016. Denying loan access: The student-level consequences when community colleges opt out of the Stafford loan program. *Economics of Education Review* 51: 79–96.

Chapter Nine: The Future of Higher Education Accountability

Belkin, D. 2017, March 27. Some colleges step up to ease students' debt burden. *Wall Street Journal.* https://www.wsj.com/articles/some-colleges-step-up-to-ease -students-debt-burden-1490653047.

Belkin, D., and A. Fuller. 2015, June 17. Princeton and other elite colleges critical of accreditation process. *Wall Street Journal.* http://www.wsj.com/articles/prince ton-and-other-elite-colleges-critical-of-accreditation-process-1434594604.

Blagg, K., and M. M. Chingos. 2016. *Choice deserts: How geography limits the potential impact of earnings data on higher education.* Washington, DC: Urban Institute.

Blumenstyk, G. 2015, June 25. Education Department now plans a college-rating system minus the ratings. *Chronicle of Higher Education.* http://www.chronicle .com/article/Education-Department-Now-Plans/231137.

Broad, M. C., P. McPherson, and H. Rawlings. 2015, December 4. Association letter urges Education Secretary to implement differential accreditation. https:// www.aau.edu/key-issues/association-letter-urges-education-secretary-implement -differential-accreditation.

Brown, R. 2016. College closures since 2009. *College History Garden.* Accessed November 18, 2016. http://tinyurl.com/ClosuresSince2009.

Camera, L. 2016, September 22. Education Department strips authority of largest for-profit accreditor. *U.S. News and World Report.* http://www.usnews.com /news/articles/2016-09-22/education-department-strips-authority-of-acics-the -largest-for-profit-college-accreditor.

Conger, S. B., A. Bell, and J. Stanley. 2010. *Four-state cost study.* Boulder: State Higher Education Executive Officers Association.

Crow, S. 2009. Musings on the future of accreditation. *New Directions for Higher Education* 145: 87–97.

Dougherty, K. J., and R. S. Natow. 2015. *The politics of performance funding for higher education: Origins, discontinuations, and transformations.* Baltimore: Johns Hopkins University Press.

Dudnick, L. 2014, September 18. Governor approves bill increasing transparency for California community college accreditation. *San Francisco Examiner.* http://archives.sfexaminer.com/sanfrancisco/governor-approves-bill-increasing-transparency-for-california-community-college-accreditation/Content?oid=2903135.

Dynarski, S. 2016, November 18. With Trump, investors see profits again in for-profit colleges. *New York Times.* http://www.nytimes.com/2016/11/19/upshot/with-trump-investors-see-profits-again-in-for-profit-colleges.html.

Education Trust, The. 2014. *Tough love: Bottom-line quality standards for colleges.* Washington, DC: Author.

Federal Student Aid 2016, August 6. Comparison of FY 2013 official national cohort default rates to prior two cohort default rates. http://www2.ed.gov/offices/OSFAP/defaultmanagement/schooltyperates.pdf.

Field, K. 2014, September 24. In 11th-hour move, Education Dept. spares the rod on loan defaults. *Chronicle of Higher Education.* http://www.chronicle.com/article/In-11th-Hour-Move-Education/148971.

Foster, L. 1936. *The functions of a graduate school in a democratic society.* New York: Huxley House.

Fuller, A., and D. Belkin. 2015, June 17. The watchdogs of college accreditation rarely bite. *Wall Street Journal.* http://www.wsj.com/articles/the-watchdogs-of-college-education-rarely-bite-1434594602.

Goldrick-Rab, S., R. Kelchen, and J. Houle. 2014. *The color of student debt: Implications of federal loan program reforms for black students and historically black colleges and universities.* Madison: Wisconsin HOPE Lab.

Hammill, D. 2014, May 27. Pelosi, Speier, Eshoo condemn continued ACCJC failure of leadership in CCSF matter. Congresswoman Nancy Pelosi. https://pelosi.house.gov/news/press-releases/pelosi-speier-eshoo-condemn-continued-accjc-failure-of-leadership-in-ccsf-matter.

Hearn, J. C., D. R. Lewis, L. Kallsen, J. M. Holdsworth, and L. M. Jones. 2006. "Incentives for managed growth": A case study of incentives-based planning and budgeting in a large public research university. *Journal of Higher Education* 77 (2): 286–316.

Hensley-Clancy, M. 2016, September 23. The industry that was crushed by the Obama administration. *BuzzFeed News.* https://www.buzzfeed.com/mollyhensleyclancy/the-industry-that-was-crushed-by-the-obama-administration.

Hiler, T., and L. E. Hatalsky. 2016, August 11. What free won't fix: Too many public colleges are dropout factories. *Third Way.* http://www.thirdway.org/report/what-free-wont-fix-too-many-public-colleges-are-dropout-factories.

Hillman, N. W. 2016. Geography of college opportunity: The case of education deserts. *American Educational Research Journal* 53 (4): 987–1021.

Hillman, N. W., and T. Weichman. 2016. *Education deserts: The continued significance of "place" in the twenty-first century.* Washington, DC: American Council on Education.

Huelsman, M., and A. F. Cunningham. 2013. *Making sense of the system: Financial aid reform for the 21st century student.* Washington, DC: Institute for Higher Education Policy.

Hughes, R. M. 1925. *A study of the graduate schools in America.* Oxford, OH: Miami University Press.

Jaschik, S. 2015, November 9. Merging an HBCU. *Inside Higher Ed.* https://www .insidehighered.com/news/2015/11/09/georgia-chancellor-wants-merge-his torically-black-albany-state-darton-state.

Jenkins, D., and J. Fink. 2016. *Tracking transfer: New measures of institutional and state effectiveness in helping community college students attain bachelor's degrees.* New York: Community College Research Center.

Kelchen, R. 2015. *Proposing a federal risk-sharing policy.* Indianapolis: Lumina Foundation.

———. 2017. Campus-based financial aid programs: Trends and alternative allocation strategies. *Educational Policy* 31 (4): 448–80.

Kelly, A. P. 2016, September 7. Share the risk on student loans. *American Enterprise Institute.* https://www.aei.org/publication/share-the-risk-on-student-loans.

Kelly, A. P., K. J. James, and R. Columbus. 2015. *Inputs, outcomes, quality assurance: A closer look at state oversight of higher education.* Washington, DC: American Enterprise Institute.

Kiley, K. 2013, January 30. Another liberal arts critic. https://www.insidehigh ered.com/news/2013/01/30/north-carolina-governor-joins-chorus-republicans -critical-liberal-arts.

Klein, A. 2016, September 16. ESSA guidance issued on "evidence based" school improvement. *Education Week.* http://blogs.edweek.org/edweek/campaign-k -12/2016/09/essa_ed_dept_releases_guidance.html.

Kosten, L. A. 2016. *Outcomes-based funding and responsibility center management: Combining the best of state and institutional budget models to achieve shared goals.* Indianapolis: Lumina Foundation.

Kreighbaum, A. 2016, September 21. Tougher scrutiny for colleges with low graduation rates. https://www.insidehighered.com/news/2016/09/21/regional-accred itors-refocus-institutions-low-grad-rates.

———. 2017, June 15. Reset of rules aimed at for-profits begins. *Inside Higher Ed.* https://www.insidehighered.com/news/2017/06/15/education-department -hit-pause-two-primary-obama-regulations-aimed-profits.

McClure, P. 2005. *School improvement under No Child Left Behind.* Washington, DC: Center for American Progress.

NASFAA (National Association of Student Financial Aid Administrators). 2013a. Report of the NASFAA task force on student loan indebtedness. Washington, DC: Author.

———. 2013b. Reimagining financial aid to improve student access and outcomes. Washington, DC: Author.

NAICU (National Association of Independent Colleges and Universities). 2012. Report of the NAICU financial responsibility task force. Washington, DC: Author.

National Conference of State Legislatures. 2015, July 31. Performance-based funding for higher education. http://www.ncsl.org/research/education/performance-funding.aspx.

National Consumer Law Center. 2014. Government investigations and lawsuits involving for-profit schools (2004-May 2014). Boston: Author.

Nelson, L. A. 2012, January 30. "Gainful" comes to the nonprofits. *Inside Higher Ed.* https://www.insidehighered.com/news/2012/01/30/obama-higher-education-plan-signals-policy-shift.

Peters, J. W. 2015, July 7. Marco Rubio calls for overhaul of the "cartel" of colleges. *New York Times.* http://www.nytimes.com/politics/first-draft/2015/07/07/marco-rubio-attacks-higher-education-cartel-and-jabs-rivals.

Rivard, R. 2013, November 6. Merging into controversy. *Inside Higher Ed.* https://www.insidehighered.com/news/2013/11/06/secret-merger-now-public-meets-opposition-georgia.

Russell, L. 2016. Short-term effects of college consolidations: Evidence from the University System of Georgia. Working paper.

Schneider, M., and J. Klor de Alva. 2014, September 22. Real cost of Obama's war against for-profit colleges. *The Hill.* http://thehill.com/blogs/congress-blog/education/218374-real-cost-of-obamas-war-against-for-profit-colleges.

Seltzer, R. 2016a, May 5. Sweet Briar's incomplete recovery. *Inside Higher Ed.* https://www.insidehighered.com/news/2016/05/05/sweet-briar-falls-short-initial-enrollment-target-leaders-remain-optimistic.

———. 2016b, November 11. The future of the tiny liberal arts college. *Inside Higher Ed.* https://www.insidehighered.com/news/2016/11/11/leaders-consider-future-tiny-liberal-arts-colleges.

Smith, A. A. 2016, August 30. Consolidating for success. *Inside Higher Ed.* https://www.insidehighered.com/news/2016/08/30/completion-rates-are-key-georgia-state-us-merger-georgia-perimeter-college.

———. 2017, April 3. A step ahead of for-profits. *Inside Higher Ed.* https://www.insidehighered.com/news/2017/04/03/milwaukee-passes-ordinance-aimed-blocking-low-quality-profit-colleges.

Snyder, M. 2015. *Driving better outcomes: Typology and principles to inform outcomes-based funding models.* Washington, DC: HCM Strategists.

Snyder, M., and B. Fox. 2016. *Driving better outcomes: Fiscal year 2016 state status and typology update.* Washington, DC: HCM Strategists.

Stevens, M., and M. Kirst. 2015. *Remaking college: The changing ecology of higher education.* Palo Alto, CA: Stanford University Press.

Stratford, M. 2015a, July 21. Debt protests target aid officers. *Inside Higher Ed.*

https://www.insidehighered.com/news/2015/07/21/student-debt-protesters
-crash-annual-gathering-college-financial-aid-officers.

———. 2015b, October 1. Default rates drop. *Inside Higher Ed*. https://www.in
sidehighered.com/news/2015/10/01/student-loan-defaults-drop-obama
-admin-again-tweaks-rates.

Strauss, J. C., and J. R. Curry. 2002. *Responsibility center management: Lessons
from 25 years of decentralized management*. Washington, DC: National Association of College and University Business Officers.

Student Achievement Measure. 2013. Accessed March 28, 2017. http://www.stu
dentachievementmeasure.org.

U.S. Department of Justice. 2015, November 16. For-profit college company to
pay $95.5 million to settle claims of illegal recruiting, consumer fraud and
other violations. https://www.justice.gov/opa/pr/profit-college-company-pay-955
-million-settle-claims-illegal-recruiting-consumer-fraud-and.

U.S. Senate Committee on Health, Education, Labor and Pensions. 2015a. Risk-
sharing/Skin-in-the-game concepts and proposals. Washington, DC : Author.

———. 2015b. Higher education accreditation concepts and proposals. Washington, DC: Author.

Vedder, R. 2016, September 7. ITT Technical Institute's closing leaves for-profit
college industry struggling to survive. *Forbes*. http://www.forbes.com/sites/ccap
/2016/09/07/the-obama-administrations-war-against-the-poor-and-capitalism.

Voluntary System of Accountability. n.d. *The college portrait*. Accessed March 28,
2017, http://www.voluntarysystem.org.

Webber, D. 2015, June 8. Colleges should share the risk for student-loan defaults.
Chronicle of Higher Education. http://www.chronicle.com/article/Colleges-Should
-Share-the-Risk/230717.

Woodhouse, K. 2015, September 28. Closures to triple. *Inside Higher Ed*. https://
www.insidehighered.com/news/2015/09/28/moodys-predicts-college-closures
-triple-2017.

Yes We Must Coalition. 2016. About. Accessed November 18, 2016. https://yeswe
mustcoalition.org/about.html.

governing boards: alumni trustees, 138–140; elected boards, 31, 135; faculty trustees, 137–138; at for-profit colleges, 140–141; history, 28–29; multiple boards, 135, 139; politically appointed members, 135–137; and presidential relationships, 141–142; at private nonprofit colleges, 138–140; at public colleges, 134–138; selection process, 136–137; self-perpetuating trustees, 135, 138–139; staff trustees, 138; student trustees, 138, 148; and tenure, 147–148

grade inflation, 19

graduate student unionization, 149–150

graduation rates, 98, 120, 121, 127, 154, 162, 168

Grand Canyon University, 97

Granting Resources and Autonomies for Diplomas (GRAD) Act, 76

Great Depression, 41–42

Great Recession, 1–2, 57, 85–86, 118

Green River Community College (WA), 115

gross domestic product, 5

group- and individual-level incentives, 19

Guaranteed Student Loan program. *See* federal student loans

Hamilton College (NY), 118

Harper, William Rainey, 33

Harreld, Bruce, 142

Hart, Ann Weaver, 141

Harvard University, 27–29, 41, 65, 98, 121

Hatch Act, 33

Haverford College, 36

HCM Strategists, 86

heightened cash monitoring (HCM), 57, 60–61, 178n6

Higher Education Act (HEA), 43, 45–50, 52, 57, 61–62, 105–106, 154, 163, 181n2

Higher Learning Commission, 38, 97, 101

historically black colleges and universities (HBCUs), 33, 100, 108, 168–169

Hosch, Braden, 56

income-driven repayment, 55, 182n3

Inside Higher Ed, 60, 130

institutional reputations, 113–116

Integrated Postsecondary Education Data System (IPEDS), 46, 156, 177n5

intercollegiate athletics, 114–115, 180n2

international students, 5

Ithaca College, 115

ITT Technical Institute, 109, 171

Ivy Bridge College (Tiffin University), 101

Ivy League, 27, 118

job placement rates, 156

Job Training Partnership Act (JTPA), 23

Johns Hopkins University, 65

Joint Commission on Accrediting, 105

Jordan, David Starr, 35

Kaplan University, 141

Katehi, Linda, 141

Kerr, Clark, 116

King of the Hill, 23

Kiplinger's college rankings, 120–121

Komissarova, Olga, 117, 179n10

Korean War, 43

Lafayette College, 147

land grants, 32. *See also* Morrill Act

Laws, Samuel, 35

law schools, 66, 104

Li, Amy, 55, 158

Liaison Committee on Medical Education, 103

liberal arts colleges. *See* private nonprofit colleges

Lincoln, Abraham, 32

lobbying, 20–21, 26, 68–70, 73, 77, 172

Los Angeles Times, 153

loss aversion, 17

low-income students, 10

Loyola Marymount University, 139

Lumina Foundation, 1, 86, 91

Machen, Bernie, 130

Madison, James, 31

Marshall, John, 30

Mason, Sally, 142

Massa, Tod, 181n1

Truman Commission on Higher Education, 43
Trump, Donald, 21, 150, 163–164, 171
trustees (governance). *See* governing boards
Trustees of Dartmouth College v. Woodward, 30–31

University and College Accountability (U-CAN) system, 150–151
University at Buffalo, 38
University of Arizona, 37, 141
University of California, Berkeley, 33, 116
University of California, Davis, 141
University of California, Los Angeles, 6
University of Chicago, 33
University of Colorado, 135
University of Delaware, 82
University of Florida, 130
University of Illinois, 137, 147
University of Iowa, 142
University of Kentucky, 124
University of Maryland–College Park, 24, 129
University of Michigan–Ann Arbor, 31, 50
University of Minnesota–Twin Cities, 118
University of Missouri–Columbia, 35, 115, 135, 145, 148–149
University of North Carolina–Chapel Hill, 102, 131, 142
University of Northern Colorado, 55, 158
University of North Texas, 104, 180n6
University of Pennsylvania, 28
University of Phoenix, 66, 97, 141
University of Rochester, 139
University of Southern California, 65
University of Vermont, 135
University of Wisconsin–Madison, 18, 35, 36, 123, 130, 148. *See also* Wisconsin Idea
University of Wisconsin System, 83, 147–148
U.S. Congress, 31–32, 43, 45, 49, 51, 61–62, 68–69, 107, 169, 172, 181n2

U.S. Department of Education, 49, 115; and accreditation, 93–94, 96, 102, 106–107, 109–110, 165; and borrower defense to repayment, 91, 164; and cohort default rate, 21, 51, 54; and College Scorecard, 2, 54, 121; and financial responsibility scores, 59; and gainful employment, 64, 164; and heightened cash monitoring, 60; history of, 36–37; and negotiated rulemaking, 21; and Postsecondary Education Ratings System, 67–69
U.S. Department of Justice, 131
U.S. Military Academy (West Point), 32
U.S. News & World Report college rankings, 7, 11, 22, 24, 114, 117, 119–130, 153, 156, 177n4
U.S. Supreme Court, 30, 146

value-added estimates, 121, 127, 159, 168
value of higher education, 2
Vanderbilt University, 104
veterans' benefits, 63
Veterans Readjustment Assistance Act, 43, 93
Villanova University, 117
Virginia Commonwealth University, 124
Virginia Polytechnic Institute and State University (Virginia Tech), 147
Viterbo College, 127
voluntary associations, 150–151
Voluntary System of Accountability, 151, 174

Walker, Scott, 147–148
Wall Street Journal, 94, 172
Wall Street Journal/Times Higher Education college rankings, 120–121, 128
warning (accreditation), 95, 98, 100
Warren, David, 68
Warren, Elizabeth, 110
Washington, George, 31
Washington Higher Education Secretariat, 21
Washington Monthly college rankings, 9, 117, 119–121, 124, 126, 159, 177n4, 181n6, 181n9
Watt, Catherine, 129–130

Western Association of Schools and
  Colleges, 97, 178n4
Williams College, 29
Wilson, Woodrow, 37
Wisconsin Idea, 35

Woodward, William H., 178n3
World War II, 42–43

Yale University, 28–29, 33, 121
Yes We Must Coalition, 174